DATE DUE

AUG 1 5 2006	

THE ADOLESCENT
DILEMMA

THE ADOLESCENT DILEMMA
International Perspectives on the Family Planning Rights of Minors

edited by

Hyman Rodman and Jan Trost

PRAEGER

PRAEGER SPECIAL STUDIES • PRAEGER SCIENTIFIC

New York • Westport, Connecticut • London

363.96
A239

Library of Congress Cataloging-in-Publication Data
Main entry under title:

The adolescent dilemma.

    Includes index.
    1. Birth control--Cross-cultural studies.
2. Children's rights--Cross-cultural studies. 3. Birth
control--Law and legislation--Cross-cultural studies.
4. Children--Legal status, Laws, etc. Cross-cultural studies. I. Hyman, Rodman. II. Trost, Jan,
1935-
HQ766.A33 1986   363.9'6'088055   86-608
ISBN 0-275-92080-1 (alk paper)

Library of Congress Catalog Card Number: 86-608
ISBN: 0-275-92080-1

First published in 1986

Praeger Publishers, 521 Fifth Avenue, New York, NY 10175
A division of Greenwood Press, Inc.

Printed in the United States of America

The paper used in this book complies with the Permanent
Paper Standard issued by the National Information Standards
Organization (Z39.48-1984)

10 9 8 7 6 5 4 3 2 1

CONTENTS

PREFACE

This book is a distinctive collection of information on the family planning rights of minors in eleven societies. Each chapter has been prepared especially for this book, and each contributor gives a summary statement of the situation in one country. A wide geographical area is covered, including Western Europe, Eastern Europe, Scandinavia, and North America. One chapter, based on a World Health Organization (WHO) study, discusses many societies in WHO's European Region.

The editors provided each contributor with organizational guidelines. As a result, all chapters focus on the rights of minors to birth control and abortion services. In addition, depending on what is relevant in the society, information is included on such topics as sex education, sexual behavior, and the nature and extent of contraceptive practices.

The introduction presents a framework for the topic of minors' family planning rights, and the concluding chapter draws on the information in the various chapters for a brief comparative look at the topic. There is enough detail in each chapter to provide readers with both a reference source on family planning in the country and a data source for their own comparative interests.

Family planning for minors is a controversial topic in most national states, becoming part of the political debate and creating groups of opposing partisans. It is controversial for several reasons. In some instances, as in countries with a strong Catholic influence, the topic has a strong moral undertone. In other instances, differences of opinion about optimal population size are at issue: Is population control needed to restrain the demand on the country's resources, or is population growth needed to maintain the country's political and economic strength?

Family planning policies and practices change with changing political, social, moral, and economic climates. Such changes are discussed in this book. Moreover, the basic facts about minors' family planning rights given herein, as well as the contributors' general interpretations, should help in understanding changes that will occur in the future.

The Editors

ACKNOWLEDGEMENTS

The University of North Carolina at Greensboro provided one year of research leave to Rodman, as well as support and encouragement in his position as Excellence Foundation Professor in Child Development and Family Relations and as Director of the Family Research Center. Trost served as Distinguished Visiting Professor in the Department of Child Development and Family Relations and as Faculty Associate in the Family Research Center in 1983-1984. This University support is gratefully acknowledged, with thanks especially to Garrett Lange, William E. Moran, Jacqueline H. Voss, J. Allen Watson, and Elisabeth A. Zinser.

The book was started while Rodman spent a year as Guest Scholar at the Brookings Institution in Washington, D.C. A companion volume, focused on the United States (The Sexual Rights of Adolescents: Competence, Vulnerability, and Parental Control, New York, Columbia University Press, 1984) was in large part written at Brookings. We are grateful to the Brookings Institution.

Trost and Rodman each served for two years as Chair of the International Section of the National Council on Family Relations (NCFR). Several of the chapters were initially presented and discussed at the annual meetings of the NCFR, and we thank the members for their support.

All royalties earned by this book are being donated to the International Section of the NCFR. No payments have been made to the editors or to the contributors for their work on the book or for any of the expenses incurred in its preparation. We thank the contributors for the time and effort devoted to their chapters and for responding to requests for revisions. We also thank them for cooperating with the process of translation and copyediting.

For translation we thank Gabriela Mahn, Barbara Rodman, and Ronald Strom. For copyediting we thank Karin Gleiter, Mary C. Miller, Marie-Louise Sylvan, and Maria Szendrö.

We also appreciate the support of the University of Uppsala and its Family Study Center.

Editing the book and working with the contributors, translators, and copyeditors has been a constant challenge. We are grateful to have had this opportunity, and we are equally grateful that the task has now been completed!

Many others have also helped; we are simply unable to list all their names. We beg their indulgence.

Although the individuals and institutions mentioned above have been extremely helpful, responsibility for the views expressed in the book rests with the contributors and the editors.

The Editors

1
INTRODUCTION: THE ADOLESCENT DILEMMA

Hyman Rodman and Jan E. Trost

This book focuses on the dilemma posed by a child's transition through adolescence into adulthood. How much authority for decision-making should society turn over to adolescents during this transition? The process of adolescent development and adults' perception of that process will differ from society to society, and from one area of behavior to another. As a result, the policies adopted to deal with the adolescent dilemma will differ. Our primary focus is on decisions in the family planning area.

Social and cultural differences can fundamentally alter the nature of the adolescent dilemma, or even raise questions about its very existence. Some societies turn decision-making over to adolescents at a relatively early age; in other societies, parents or guardians maintain authority for a longer time. In some societies adolescence looms large as a period of turmoil; in others it may pass quietly or may not be recognized at all, children becoming adults through clearly defined and organized rituals, without an intermediate stage.

This book deals with European and North American national societies where the period of adolescence is socially recognized. Looking at a group of societies that differ widely in their cultural values with regard to family planning will make it possible to see the adolescent dilemma from a variety of cultural perspectives. Children depend on the nurturance of others for their physical survival and their social and psychological development. This nurturance is usually provided within the family--by parents, siblings, and other kin. As children grow older they become able to take responsibility for an increasing number of decisions. Conflicts between parents and children are usually resolved informally, within the family, but occasionally one of the parties may involve an outside agency, such as a judicial court. For example, a parent may charge a child with incorrigibility, or a child may sue a parent for financial support. There is at present no clear understanding of the implications of third-party involvement for parent-child relationships. Depending upon the society, third-party involvement is more or less possible, and its impact on family relationships may also differ from one society to another.

In some situations, the state unilaterally intrudes upon the parent-child relationship. For example, laws against child abuse may bring about an investigation of the family by professionals acting as agents of the state, and the state may remove children from their parents' care. Or the state may require minors to get parental permission for their marriages, for medical services, for paid employment, or for abortions.

Although the substantive issues and the procedures for dealing with them differ from society to society, the basic policy issue--how to structure minors' decisions and parental involvement--is constant. Looking at several societies permits us to explore their differences from a comparative perspective. It is, of course, unclear whether innovative and efficient policies from one country can be "translated" and adopted by other countries. As a first step, however, we are less interested in such policy diffusion than in providing a comparative framework within which the policy questions and choices available in any country can be seen more clearly.

The problem.   Young children need supervision and guidance from their parents or other adults. Adults are generally considered able to make decisions on their own. The situation of older children, however, is less clear. Developmentally, they are becoming more competent to make their own decisions free from parental control. However, since there is no magic developmental moment at which they move from dependence to independence, or from incompetence to competence, there are potential legal and policy problems. If law and social policy grant children the right to make their own decisions "too early," without parental involvement, they may exercise poor judgment and become vulnerable to manipulation by others. If, on the other hand, they are granted the right to make their own decisions "too late," their capability and right to make good judgments may be hampered by parental interference.

All societies face this dilemma--and we shall refer to it as society's adolescent dilemma. The dilemma is frequently overcome, or shortcircuited, informally.   As children grow older they develop the intellectual and social competence to make an increasing number of decisions. Parents and children typically negotiate the rate at which the parent gives up authority and control and the child assumes more responsibility. These negotiations between parents and children may go smoothly, or may engender much conflict. In some instances parents and children cannot resolve their differences by themselves and the state may be asked to resolve the conflict. We will be looking at the laws and policies in several societies in order to explore their varying ways of dealing with the adolescent dilemma.

Adolescents may want to engage in a variety of actions--to work, retain their own pay, live independently of their parents, drive a car, marry, enter into contracts, get medical contraceptive services, be treated for venereal disease, obtain an abortion. What are the laws and policies about such actions for children and adolescents? Is there an age of majority (adulthood) at which some or all of these activities can be engaged in independently, and prior to which there are restrictions? What are the restrictions? Does the age of majority differ for different actions?

In the family planning area, the following are examples of the questions asked: Do minors have the legal right to make their own family planning decisions, or does the state legislate parental consent requirements or some other form of parental involvement? What is the policy, for example, when a pregnant 15-year-old wants an abortion, but her parents object? What if the parents want the abortion, but the daughter objects?   What if the daughter wants to have the abortion without informing her parents? What about access to medical contraceptive services (e.g., a prescription for the oral birth control pill, or having an intrauterine device fitted)? Do the programs and services follow official laws and policies or do they occasionally or frequently circumvent them?

Since each society's treatment of minority/majority status may differ; and since each society's attitudes, policies, and practices about contraception and abortion for adults will differ; and since each society's values and policies about parental authority in general will differ-- the precise nature of the questions dealt with for each society will also necessarily differ.

What are the laws and policies about contraception and abortion generally (since it makes little sense to talk about minors' rights in a situation where adults' rights may be limited)?

What are the society's attitudes toward family planning (for adults and/or minors)?

What are the attitudes about parents' authority over their children? What are the attitudes and beliefs about children's competence and children's rights?

Can children (of what age) free themselves from the control of their parents? Can they go to live with another family despite their parents' objections? Can they live on their own despite their parents' objections?

Can the state (e.g., professional social workers acting for the state) intrude upon the family in order to investi- gate charges of child abuse or spouse abuse? What are the attitudes (and the laws) about family privacy and state investigation that are intended to protect individu- als from harm within the family?

In order to make clear to the contributors to this book what we expected, the contents of this chapter were shared with them before they wrote their chapters.

2
FAMILY PLANNING PRACTICES AMONG MINORS IN BELGIUM

Wilfried Dumon and Mieke Van Nuland

Introduction

The "adolescent dilemma" has never been acute in Belgium. For example, although in 1975 the minister of justice introduced a bill to reduce the age of majority from 21 to 18, the bill was never discussed, and was not re-introduced after a change of government. Nor have the limited legal rights of minors evoked much discontent among youth. Although they set a high value on autonomy, emancipation, and participation (Welten, 1977), young people consider their legal situation irrelevant, identifying their parents rather than the law as the most important barrier to their autonomy (Welten, 1977).

The only available study (Geeraert, 1977) of the relation between the attitudes and behaviour of youth and the attitudes of their parents and peers suggests that young people form their attitudes toward sexuality and family planning by referring to their peers, not to their parents. One may suppose, then, that young people will generally experience their parents as the only threat to their family planning rights.

After a short overview of the family planning rights of minors in Belgium, we will analyse in the following pages how Belgian youth use the rights they possess.

Deficient Use of Family Planning

Only two studies of sexuality and contraception among young people in Belgium have been made to date (Geeraert, 1977; Cliquet, 1981). Although both were limited to the Dutch-speaking community,[1] other research among youth in both the Dutch- and the French-speaking communities (Dooghe, 1981; Maroy and Rupuoy, 1981) suggests that the two groups are quite similar. In general, the results of the Flemish research will be taken as representative for Belgium as a whole.

The most important conclusion of the studies is that young people are permissive both in their premarital sexual behavior and in their attitudes toward such behavior. In 1975 about 75 per cent of unmarried 18-year-olds approved of premarital intercourse, and one-third reported they had had sexual experiences (Geeraert, 1977). The data of Cliquet (1981) indicate that the frequency of sexual experience among minors is still increasing.

Among 40 to 44-year-old married women, 49 per cent had intercourse while still minors, among 25 to 29-year-old married women, 74 per cent. Furthermore, a comparison of the generations shows that sexual activity starts at an ever younger age: While the median age at first intercourse was 21 years among 40 to 44-year-old married women, it had decreased to 19 years among 20 to 24-year-old married women, and 94 per cent of 16 to 19-year-old married women in 1975 had intercourse before marriage. Sexuality during adolescence and before marriage is now the norm in Belgium.

Sexually active minors do not want their activities to result in pregnancy (Cliquet, 1981). Since only their peers share their permissive attitudes (Geeraert, 1977), it is probable that pregnancy would lead to conflicts with their less permissive parents, teachers, etc. And because marriage remains the normative framework for reproduction, a great proportion of premarital pregnancies result in enforced marriages. In spite of the growing separation between marriage and reproduction,[3] and the increased acceptance of this separation, a majority (74 per cent) of minors still choose marriage as the best solution for a premarital pregnancy (Geeraert, 1977). It is clear that the enforced character of such marriages is in contradiction to the increased appreciation of marriage as an autonomous choice (Dumon, 1977). Half of the minors surveyed indicated that fear of an enforced marriage would motivate them to use family planning. Another important factor, mentioned by a third of the minors, was anxiety about the financial consequences of an enforced marriage between minors.

Although sexually active minors want and need family planning, their use of effective contraceptives is strikingly limited. Research (Geeraert, 1977) has shown that in 1975 20 per cent of sexually active young people used no contraceptives, 40 per cent used ineffective contraceptives,[4] and 40 per cent used effective[5] contraceptives at first intercourse. In recent years, there has been an increase in the use of effective methods, but the majority of youth still do not use effective contraceptives (see Table 1).

Why is it so? The absence of preventive family planning is even more remarkable since "curative family planning" occurs frequently in this age group. Data on abortions of Belgian women in Dutch policlinics[6] indicate that in 1977 about 5,000 Belgian women (15 to 19 years old) underwent abortion surgery, approximately one abortion per two births in this age group. This is in complete contradiction to the expressed attitudes of minors. When asked which solution they would choose if they (or their partner) were pregnant, only 14 per cent of young people (18 to 21 years old) said they would choose abortion (Geeraert, 1977).

The lack of preventive family planning and the frequent use of abortion are also remarkable because abortion is illegal in Belgium. It is therefore difficult to get information about where to go for an abortion, and necessary to make a trip abroad (to the Netherlands or Great Britain), as much as possible in secrecy.

In summary, although the sexual attitudes and behavior of minors are permissive, and young people do not want premarital pregnancies, the use of effective and preventive family planning is limited.

Such anxiety, while it may have an indirect effect on contraceptive use, it is not likely to be as strong a factor as anxiety about the more immediate consequences of facing one's parents in the event of an unintended pregnancy.

Causes of Deficient Use of Family Planning

An important cause of deficient family planning is that minors do not plan to have sexual relationships. They underrate the occurrence of sexual intercourse among their age-group (Geeraert, 1977), and do not expect to

Table 1. Contraceptive practice at first intercourse among women ever having had intercourse, in the Dutch community in Belgium, according to year of birth.

Year of Birth		1931-35	1936-40	1941-45	1946-50	1951-55	1956-59	1931-55
Ineffective	no c.p.	48	43	39	27	22	31	37
c.p.	C.I.	39	41	37	39	32	39	38
	P.O. (+C.I.)	10	12	14	18	14	10	14
Effective	Condom	3	3	6	7	14	9	6
c.p.	Pill (or I.U.D.)	0	1	4	8	18	11	6
Total (100%)		859	863	842	830	619	410	4,013

c.p. = contraceptives; C.I. = coitus interruptus; P.O. = Safe period; I.U.D. = Intrauterine device.

Source: Cliquet, 1981.

have sexual experiences before they are married. With this perspective, effective precautions are unlikely.

The consequence is that sexually active minors use no or ineffective contraception at first intercourse. The unlikelihood of sexual experiences decreases strongly after first intercourse, however, and precautions are then more frequent. This is confirmed by Geeraert (1977) and Cliquet (1981). But although the effectiveness of contraception increases if the frequency of intercourse increases (Geeraert, 1977), the proportion of minors who do not take precautions at later intercourse remains large (Table 2).

It is striking that researchers always revert to "attitudes" or "knowledge" to explain deficient contraceptive practice. From the fact that more knowledgeable adolescents have more effective contraceptive practices, Geeraert (1977) concludes that "knowledge" leads to effective contraception. Cliquet (1981) emphasizes the influence of "values" and "norms," and researchers in other countries find cognitive factors important (Schofield, 1965; Reiss et al., 1975; DeLamater and MacCorquodale, 1978; Thompson and Spanier, 1978). The Fishbein model (Fishbein, 1972; Fishbein and Jaccard, 1973), which has informed much socio-psychological research into contraception

Table 2. Contraceptive practice at first and later intercourse among sexually active minors.

		First Intercourse	Later Intercourse
Ineffective c.p.	No c.p.	19	15
	C.I.	25	21
	P.O. (+C.I.)	15	15
Effective c.p.	condom	16	11
	pill	25	38

c.p. = contraceptive practices; C.I. = coitus interruptus
P.O. = safe period; I.U.D. = intrauterine devices.

among adolescents,[7] assumes that behavior is determined by the attitudes of the actor toward the behavior in question, and his beliefs about what relevant others think he should do.

The central idea of these studies--that contraceptive behavior is caused by attitudes toward contraception-- underlies Belgian family planning policy. In 1972,[8] the Ministry of Public Health and the Family began a "Responsible Parenthood" project. Its purpose was to prevent unwanted pregnancies (in order to limit abortions), and to promote effective family planning, conscious and responsible parenthood, and a child-loving society (Ministry . . ., 1977). At the request of the secretariat of the High Council of the Family, staff members of the research institute within the Ministry of Public Health and the Family (C.B.G.S.: Population and Family Study Center) drew up a program in which the most important aspects of a policy concerning family planning were discussed (Beelkaen et al., 1973).

Three conditions were considered necessary to realize effective contraception among the Belgian population:

1. people must believe that contraception is a necessity;
2. "good" contraceptive methods (acceptable, effective, harmless, and unobtrusive) must exist;
3. it must be possible to use these methods in the right manner.

The authors of the program stated that, although the availability of contraceptives was not yet optimal, insufficient knowledge and lack of motivation were the major causes of deficient contraception.

Based on this advice, an information campaign concerning contraception was started in 1973. A first step was the large-scale distribution of an attractive brochure about "Contraception and Responsible Parenthood," in which a number of experts gave a clear and precise explanation of sexuality and contraception. Between 1974 and 1977 more than 850,000 of these free brochures were distributed by physicians, dispensing chemists, social organizations, schools, and universities.[9] In 1977 a new edition of the brochure was published.

The study of Geeraert (carried out in 1975) shows that minors who had read this brochure had a better knowledge of contraception than did minors who had not read it.[10]

More important, however, is the fact that only 9 per cent of 18-year-olds and 14 per cent of 21-year-olds had read it.   And although it can be supposed that distribution improved after 1975, the proportion of adolescents who have read the brochure remains very small.

The school is another important link in the information campaign. Sex education has become an essential part of the   curriculum   at   all   educational   levels,[11]   and information about contraception is taught in all secondary schools. Although informal conversations with teachers and pupils suggest that young people are learning more, and at younger ages, it is not clear that they acquire sufficient factual knowledge. Geeraert's data (1977) indicate that in general young people have imprecise knowledge, which they often obtain from their peers.

During the last ten years educational radio and television have broadcast some programs about sexuality and contraception. These programs were designed for various age groups, and were broadcast several times at the request of parents and teachers. It appears, however, that only a small percentage of adolescents have seen these programs.

Apart from the question whether the information campaign is reaching its target population, it remains doubtful that teaching factual knowledge and attitudes are the most effective ways to teach behavior. With respect to the   Fishbein   model,   some   authors   (Werner   and Middlestadt, 1979) have pointed out that--although there is   usually   a   relation   between   attitudes   toward contraception and contraceptive behavior--the causal influence can proceed in either direction. What is more, research (see for example, Triandis, 1968, 1971; Bem, 1972; Kiesler et al., 1969; Deutscher, 1966) is available showing that any correlation between attitude and behavior may be spurious, the behavior resulting from other   factors--for   example,   imitation.   Thorough knowledge and positive motivation may be necessary rather than sufficient conditions for the occurrence of a certain behavior.

Another difficulty in the case of contraceptive behavior is the fact that it is only negatively motivated (Faberij, 1975). The reward of contraceptive behavior consists only in the avoidance of unwanted pregnancy; it has no immediate positive value for the actor (Van den Bogaert, 1978).

This difficulty is confirmed by the following information concerning contraceptive accessibility.

In 1973 the Belgian government took measures to guarantee the practical accessibility of contraceptives. Displaying, selling, and transporting contraceptives were legalized. Medical regulation of the quality of contraceptives began, with the result that contraception has come to rest in the medical sector. The sale of contraceptives (with the exception of condoms and diaphragms) is reserved to pharmacists, and intrauterine devices and the pill can be obtained only by medical prescription. At first, centers for pre-matrimonial and family counselling were allowed to provide contraceptives to their clients, but after negative reactions from the medical establishment, this measure was annulled in 1975. Research (Marien, 1978; Samoy, 1978) has shown that these centers, together with the J.I.C. and J.A.C. centers,[12] certainly have a supervising and information function, but the number of young people who are helped in these centers is very small. In particular, youngsters who leave school early seldom make use of the services of these centers. Because reliable contraception can be acquired only by medical prescription or through a pharmacist, the availability of contraception is really a matter of the accessibility of the medical sector. A study of public health in Belgium (Nuyens et al., 1979) has indicated that the consumption of medical services is a learned behavior pattern. A person who has had frequent contact with the medical sector in the past--for example, because he or a family member has been seriously ill--will make more and earlier appeals to medical providers.

Health education is almost non-existent in Belgium, and young people have the fewest contacts with the medical sector; it can be assumed that they have fears about medical consultations concerning contraception. This is confirmed by data of Geeraert (1977): Young people find the pill difficult to obtain because in order to do so they must see a doctor. For this reason, most prefer the condom to the pill.

It is not clear whether doctors are unwilling to prescribe contraceptives for minors. Research is lacking, so we interviewed some strategic informants--the student doctor in Louvain and seven other young doctors in the Dutch-speaking community. Although they could not give detailed information about the number of doctors who do not want to prescribe contraceptives for minors, they reported that refusal seems to them relatively rare. It appears that the doctors who do refuse are generally old and practice in rural areas. It can be assumed, therefore, that the phenomenon of refusal will disappear in the long term. The interviewed doctors said that their younger colleagues gave the impression of being very willing to prescribe contraceptives for minors. Many young doctors say that they also give preventive advice: if they observe during a medical examination that a female patient is sexually active without contraceptive protection, they strongly advise her to use a contraceptive.

It is remarkable that most doctors have not previously seen the majority of minor women who come to them for contraceptive prescriptions. This could mean that minors are afraid of being refused or of being asked "annoying questions" by their family doctors, and therefore seek out other younger doctors from whom they assume a refusal will be unlikely. Whether minors use actual information or prejudices in their "definition of the situation" is not clear.

Information on the accessibility of "curative family planning", i.e. abortion, is also insufficient, although a number of studies allow us to draw some inferences. The illegality of abortion in Belgium suggests that its accessibility is quite limited. And although there is probably an increase in the number of illegal abortions in Belgium (Fastenaekens and Hubinont, 1977), a woman who wants an abortion usually has to travel abroad. Because the distribution of information on abortion is also illegal in Belgium, (some organizations nevertheless distribute the addresses of abortion clinics in the Netherlands) it is for most people difficult to acquire the necessary information. It is therefore surprising that the frequency of abortion among young women (about 1 per 2 births) is so high. This could mean that women who are under age are helped by adults (for example, their parents) to "go to the Netherlands." Indeed, although in 1973 54 per cent of the Belgian population rejected the legalization of abortion for other than medical reasons, the proportion who rejected abortion for minors was only 41 per cent (Dooghe and Vanderleyden, 1974). This could indicate that many parents would consider the pregnancy of their minor daughter as an exceptional case that would justify abortion.

In summary, four factors are implicated in the deficient family planning of minors (but further research is clearly needed):

1.   During their socialization, little or no attention is paid to teaching contraception as a behavior. Socialization is limited to factual knowledge and attitude formation.

2.   The use of reliable and effective contraceptives requires a willingness to use the medical sector. But because the use of medical services is also a behavior pattern and is neglected in the curriculum, we may assume that Belgian youth frequently avoid the medical sector.

3.   Although effective contraception assumes a thorough knowledge of existing methods, the ambitious information campaign of the government has reached only a small proportion of youth. The channels by which the information brochure has been distributed are used only by youngsters who receive higher education or who come in contact with the medical sector.

4.   Since the dominant ideology defines marriage as the institutional frame for sexuality (and procreation), young people consider it fairly unlikely that they will have premarital sexual relations. The result of such an attitude is that effective family planning is unlikely.

Implications for a Policy Concerning the Family Planning of Minors

The logical outcome of the frequent occurrence of unprotected intercourse--due to the lack of contraception or the use of ineffective means--is that the rate of premarital pregnancy among minors is relatively high. For example, Cliquet (1981) computed that in 1975/76 23 per cent of women in the age group 20-24[13] had become pregnant before they were 19, 16 per cent of them premaritally. And although the use of effective contraceptives is increasing, the probability of becoming pregnant while a minor continues to increase also. Of women who are now 40-44 years old, 9.1 per cent were pregnant by the age of 19, only 6.1 per cent premaritally.

We have mentioned already some reasons why young people experience premarital pregnancy at a minor age as problematic. Such a pregnancy has other consequences which are not foreseen by the persons concerned, but can be regarded as problematic in their planning of family life.

First of all, a premarital pregnancy may lead to unwed motherhood. And because Masui (1981) concluded in her study of unwed motherhood in Belgium that the majority of these mothers become pregnant during adolescence, it can be supposed that the chance of unwed motherhood is greater for a pregnancy during adolescence. In the second place, it has been indicated in both domestic (Cliquet, 1980) and foreign research (Chilman, 1980) that pregnancy at a minor age is followed by a higher average household size. Different studies have shown that marginality--both in the financial and in the social sphere--is a general characteristic of unwed mothers and households with many children (Masui, 1981; Dumon et al., 1978). Moreover, more problems are reported by such households (Dumon et al., 1982).

In the light of these findings, supplementary governmental measures concerning the family planning of minors are necessary:

1.   Contraception should be taught as a behavior pattern. The most obvious method is the presentation of behavior models, for example in film and television. Because of the personal character of family planning, other learning processes--social learning, role-playing, etc.--are not possible.

2.   The fear of medical examinations and the use of medical services to obtain contraceptives can be lowered in the same way. The use of the medical sector is a behavior pattern that can be learned by means of role-playing, the presentation of attractive models, and the positive sanctioning of medical consumption.

3.   Information must be distributed through more effective channels. Assuming that the transfer of knowledge starts at a young age and is focused on facts, the school seems to offer the best possibility for reaching the greatest population.

4.   As far as possible, adolescents must be made aware of the fact that sexual experience is proba-

ble for them, and that family planning is therefore necessary.

Footnotes

1. Geeraert studied a sample of 800 unmarried young
   people (18 to 21 years old) of both sexes. Cliquet
   studied a sample of 4,463 married and unmarried
   women between 16 and 44 years of age; the age group
   of 16 to 19 year old women contained only married
   women.
2. Geeraert showed that youngsters from rural areas were
   more restrictive toward sexuality (in attitude as well as
   in behavior). Therefore, it can be assumed that minors
   are more restrictive in the rural French-speaking
   community.
3. In 1962 97.9 per cent of all births were legitimate; in
   1977 96.9 per cent.
4. Ineffective contraception: use of coitus interruptus, or
   the rhythm method.
5. Effective contraception: use of the condom, the pill, or
   an intrauterine device.
6. The registration of abortion patients indicates that 25.5
   per cent are 15 to 19 years old (Schnabel, 1976). And
   based on an estimate of the number of Belgian women
   who had abortions in 1977 (Van Praag, 1978; N =
   20,000), it can be assumed that about 5,000 women
   between 15 and 19 years of age had abortions in 1977.
   The estimation of Van Praag seems to us the most
   reliable (see also Verheye, 1981).
7. Jaccard and Davidson, 1972; Fishbein and Jaccard,
   1973; Vinokur-Kaplan, 1978; Werner and Middlestadt,
   1979; McCarthy, 1981.
8. The government's declaration of policy of 20 January
   1972 mentioned for the first time the necessity for a
   policy concerning family planning (Van Praag, 1979).
9. The Dutch edition consisted of 556,000 copies, of which
   540,000 were distributed. The French edition consisted
   of 390,000 copies, of which 341,000 were distributed.
   About 10,000 brochures were printed for the German-
   speaking community.
10. Geeraert writes that the fear of a medical exami-

nation concerning contraception is lower for readers of the brochure. However, this does not indicate that the brochures reduce the fear, because doctors were an important channel in their distribution.

11. In State-aided schools, lessons about sexuality and contraception are given in courses on "morality" and "biology," in the Free schools in courses on "religion" and "biology".

12. J.I.C. and J.A.C. centers are centers for youth information and advice.

13. This age group contains both married and unmarried and both sexually active and inactive women.

References

Balkaen, J. et al., "Nota betreffende anticonceptiebeleid in Vlaanderen", in: **Bevolking in Gezin,** 1973, 1, 177-197.

Bem, D.J., "Self-perception theory", in L. Berkowitz (ed.), **Advances in Experimental Social Psychology vol., 6,** New York, 1972, 1-62.

Chilman, C.S., "Social and Psychological Research Concerning Adolescent Childbearing: 1970-1980", **Journal of Marriage and the Family,** 42 (1980) 4, 793-805.

Cliquet, R.L., **The Flemish Survey on Family Development, 1975-76: A Summary of Findings,** World Fertility Survey no 24, London, 1980.

Cliquet, R.L., "Geslachtsverkeer, voorbehoeding, zwangerschap en geboorte voor het huwelijk in Vlaanderen", in **Bevolking en Gezin,** 1981, 3, 317-351.

Cliquet R.L., en R. Schoenmaeckers, **Van toevallig naar gepland ouderschap,** Studies en Documenten no 6, C.B.G.S., Ministerie van Volksgezondheid en van het Gezin, Brussel/Kapellen, 1975.

Cliquet, R.L. en Thiery, M. (red.), **Abortus Provocatus, een interdisciplinaire studie met betrekking tot beleid-salternatieven in Belgie,** Studies en Documenten no 2, Ministerie van Volksgezondheid en van het Gezin, Brussel/Antwerpen, 1972.

DeLamater, J. and P. MacCorquodale, "Premarital Contraceptive Use: A Test of Two Models," in **Journal of Marriage and the Family,** 40 (1978) 2, 235-248.

Deutscher, I., "Words and Deeds: Social Science and Social

Policy," in **Social Problems,** 13 (1966), 235-253.

Dooghe, J., **De jongeren en het verbruik,** OIVO/CSUR/FO-PES, U.C.L., Louvain-la-Neuve, 1981.

Dumon, W., **Het Gezin in Vlaanderen,** Leuven, 1977.

Dumon, W. en J. van Houtvinck (eds.), **Marginalisering en Wezijnszorg. De één-oudergezinnen,** Programmatie van het Wetenschapsbeleid, Brussel, 1978.

Dumon, W. en J. van Houtvinck (eds.), **Preventie van Structurele Marginalisering van Onregelmatige gezinnen,** 2 vol., National Onderzoeksprograma in de Sociale Wetenschappen, Brussel, 1981.

Faberij, I., **Anticonceptiegedrag, deel 1: Theori en opzet van een onderzoek bij 1.200 Nederlandse vrouwen en mannen,** NISSO-onderzoeksrapport no 12, Zeist, 1975.

Fastenaekens, C. et Hurinot, P.O. (eds.), **Réflexions sur l'avortement,** themanummer, Revue de l'Université de Bruxelles, 1975, no 2-3.

Fishbein, M., "Toward an understanding of family planning behavior," in **Journal of Applied Social Psychology,** 2 (1972), 214-227.

Fishbein, M. and J.J. Jaccard, "Theoretical and Methodological Considerations in the Prediction of Family Planning. Intentions and Behavior," in **Representative Research in Social Psychology,** 4 (1973), 37-51.

Geeraert, A., **Seksualiteit bij Jongeren.** Studies en Documenten no 8, C.B.G.S., Ministerie van Volksgezondheid en van het Gezin, Brussel/Kapellen, 1975.

Jaccard, J.J. and A.R. Davidson, "Toward an Understanding of Family Planning Behaviors: An Initial Investigation," in **Journal of Applied Social Psychology,** 2 (1972), 228-235.

Kiesler, C.A., B.E. Collins and N. Miller, **Attitude Change: A critical analysis of theoretical approaches,** New York, 1969.

Marien, S., **De centra voor prematrimoniale, matrimoniale en gezinsconsultaties.** Sociologisch Onderzoeksinstituut, K.U., Leuven, 1978.

Mardy, C. et D. Ruouoy, **Les jeunes et la consommation,** CRIOC/CSUR/FOPES, U.C.L., Louvain-la-Neuven, 1981.

Masui, M., **Buitenechtelijk Moederschap in Belgie. Een morfologische verkenning,** Technisch Rapport no 40, C.B.G.S., Ministerie van Volksgezondheid en van het Gezin, Brussel, 1980.

Masui, M., **Ongehuwd Moeder. Sociologische Analyse van**

een wordingsproces, Studies en Documenten no 16, C.B.G.S., Ministerie van Volksgezondheid en van het Gezin, Brussel/Kapellen, 1981.
McCarthy, D., "Changing Contraceptive Usage Intentions: A test of the Fishbein Model of Intention," in **Journal of Applied Social Psychology,** 11 (1981), 192-211.
MINISTERIE VAN VOLKSGEZONDHEID EN VAN HET GEZIN, **Bewust Ouderschap. Bericht over Informatieverspreiding,** Brussel, 1977.
Nuyens, Y. et al. (red.), **Eerstelijnsgezondheidszorg** 1 H., Nationaal Onderzoeksprogramma in de Sociale Wetenschappen, Brussel, 1978.
Reiss, I.L., A. Banwart and H. Foreman, "Premarital contraceptive usage: A study and some theoretical explorations," in **Journal of Marriage and the Family,** 37 (1975), 619-630.
Samoy, E., **De Jongeren Informatie- en Adviescentra,** Sociologisch Onderzoeksinstituut, K.U. Leuven, 1978.
Schofield, M., **The Sexual Behavior of Young People,** London, 1965.
Schnabel, P., "Poliklinische abortus: een vergelijking tussen Nederlandse en Belgische abortusclienten," **Bevolking en Gezin,** 1976, 2, 183-194.
Thompson, L. and G. Spanier, "Influence of Parents, Peers, and Partners on the Contraceptive use of College Men and Women," in **Journal of Marriage and the Family,** 40 (1978) 3, 481-492.
Triandis, H.C., **Attitudes and Attitude Change,** New York, 1971.
van den Bogaert, G., **Profiel van de Vrouw in Belgie,** Studies en Documenten no 9, C.B.G.S., Ministerie van Volksgezondheid en van het Gezin, Brussel/Kapellen, 1978.
van Praag, Ph., "Poliklinische abortering van Belgische vrouwen in Nederland," in **Bevolking en Gezin,** 1978, 2, 273-282.
van Praag, Ph., **Het bevolkingsvraagstuk in Belgie,** Studien en Documenten 12, C.B.G.S., Ministerie van Volksgezondheid en van het Gezin, Brussel/Kapellen, 1979.
Verheye, C., **Analyse van de poliklinische zwangerschapsonderbreking bij Belgische vrouwen in Nederland op grond van gegevens afkomstig van de permanente regis-** Volksgezondheid en van het Gezin, Brussel/Kapellen,

1981.

Vinokur-Kaplan, D., "To have-or not to have-another child. Family Planning Attitudes, Intentions and Behavior," in **Journal of Applied Social Psychology,** 8 (1978) 1, 29-46.

Welten, V.J., "Adolescenten en jong-volwassenen in twee culturen: Vlaanderen en Nederland," in **Jeugd en Samenleving,** 7 (1977) 11/12, 712-785.

Werner, P.D. and S.E. Middlestadt, "Factors in the Use of Oral Contraceptives by Young Women," in **Journal of Applied Social Psychology,** 9 (1979) 6, 537-547.

Zelnik, M., Y.J. Kim and J.F. Kantner, "Probabilities of intercourse and conception among U.S. teenage women, 1971 and 1976," in **Family Planning Perspectives,** 11 (1979) 3, 177-183.

3
THE FAMILY PLANNING RIGHTS OF MINORS IN CANADA: THE CASE OF ONTARIO

Doris E. Guyatt

Canada is a federation of ten provinces and two northern territories. At the time of confederation in 1867, responsibility for the various aspects of Canadian society was divided between the provincial and federal governments as stated in The British North America Act, an Act of the British Parliament. This basic division of responsibility was continued in the recent Constitution Act of 1982 which severed the tie to the British parliament and repatriated the constitution.

Family law for the most part is within the jurisdiction of the provinces. Because of cultural differences between provinces, particularly between Quebec whose residents are mainly French speaking and whose legal system is based historically on that of France and the other provinces whose residents are mainly English speaking and whose laws have developed from England's legal system, family law has varied somewhat from one province to another. Therefore, the major focus of this paper will be the situation with regard to the rights of minors in Ontario, the largest and most populous province in Canada.*

Throughout Canada, as in other western societies, the

----

* The population of Canada as determined by the 1981 Census of Canada was 24,343,181, of which 8,625,107 or one-third resided in Ontario.

21

fundamental purpose of family law has been to support our traditional family structure. Generally speaking, the law reflects the dominant cultural norms. As the role of the family has undergone significant changes in recent years, as evidenced by the change in women's roles, the redefinition of parental roles, the increase in marital breakdown and the rise in the number and proportion of single-parent families, it has become more difficult to determine what is the cultural norm with regard to a number of family issues (Catton 1979, pp. 247-250).

Currently there is little consensus as to the best method of childrearing and the appropriate relationship between children and their parents, particularly as the children mature and their capacity increases to make sound judgments about matters related to their own welfare. Most of the authority for making decisions respecting children traditionally has been lodged with parents but the degree of parental control has declined over the past century so that the state now has wide powers to intervene in the parent-child relationship.

Children's Rights in General

While children have the same rights as adults with regard to such broad areas as freedom from discrimination, freedom of speech and even greater rights than adults to protection from abuse or neglect, they do not have the right to be treated in the same manner as adults in specific state-regulated areas such as the right to vote, to serve in the armed forces, to drive, to drink alcohol, to marry and so on. Further, their right to act independently of parental control and/or guidance varies according to the issue at hand.

"All of these legal differences are premised on the assumption that children lack the judgment, maturity and conceptual powers necessary for full adult privileges and responsibilities" (Landau 1982, p. 4). During the past decade, a number of psychologists and educators have questioned the validity of this assumption. They note that different jurisdictions have granted the same rights at different ages. For example, in Canada the provinces have different ages for drinking, driving, leaving school and marrying. There is no clear rationale given for the choice of a particular age for various legal rights. In Ontario, without parental consent, a child may drink at nineteen, drive at sixteen, leave school at sixteen, and marry at eighteen.

In her recent book on family policy in Canada, Eichler (1983) noted:

Children's rights depend, at the most basic level, on the definition of a child. That is by no means a simple or straightforward matter in Canada---children reach adult status at different times for different purposes in Canada, and across provinces. As noted, children can marry at different ages---until 1981, a female of the age of twelve years and a male of the age of fourteen could get married with parental consent in Quebec! (It is now age eighteen for both sexes in Quebec.) The age of majority and accountability is usually eighteen years of age, but Saskatchewan recently raised the legal drinking age to twenty-one.

A federal government study of divorce in Canada (Statistics Canada 1983, p. 201) states that in regard to custody, parental rights were of more importance histori-cally than those of the children. Now it is common to speak of children's rights and to base decisions concerning custody on what is in the child's best interest. Although this appears to be a sound philosophy, it is not an easy matter to discover what is the best interest of a parti-cular child and who should make such decisions.

In Ontario, the Children's Law Reform Act (R.S.O. 1980, as amended 1982, Chapter 20, Sec. 65) states that in deciding an application for custody of a child, "a court where possible shall take into consideration the views and preferences of the child to the extent that the child is able to express them." This is a new move to include in law a child's right to be heard. This law is meant apparently to apply to children under sixteen because the following section states, "Nothing in this part abrogates the right of a child of sixteen or more years of age to withdraw from parental control."

A consultation paper issued by the government of Ontario (Ontario 1982, The Children's Act, p. 38) concer-ning a proposed Children's Act, which sets out the rights of children with regard to child welfare services, dis-cusses the confusion that arises among service providers because of the lack of clearly defined children's rights.

In Ontario, the law pertaining to the consent of minors is unclear and confusing. As a result, service providers are frequently uncertain as to whether they are permitted by law to serve children without their parents' consent. The situation most likely to pose problems for service providers, such as counsellors or therapists, is that of an adolescent who, in seeking a service for himself, specifies that he does not want his parents to know that he needs help. Service providers may thus be placed in the unenviable position of having to decide whether to serve the child anyway, without the parents' consent, or to contact the parents and possibly risk not having the child receive a needed service. Greater legislative clarity would, in such situations, benefit all the parties involved.

This paper recommends (The Children's Act, pp. 42-43) that where a child twelve or over initiates the provision of counselling services, his parents' consent should not be required but that the counsellor be required to discuss with the child the desirability of informing or involving the parents. In cases where the child refuses, the counsellor would be obligated to respect his wishes.

Landsberg (1982, p. 191), a well known Canadian journalist, in discussing adolescent rights, questions whether children should be able to get confidential treatment for drug abuse, venereal disease, pregnancy, or abortion. She asks, "Aren't parents then abandoning their responsibility to nurture and protect? Aren't youngsters being asked to shoulder an intolerable heavy burden of decision-making?" However, after considering arguments on both sides, she concludes that clearer laws would mean the difference between despair and a fruitful life for thousands of Canadian youngsters.

The need for change with regard to children's rights continues to be the subject of much debate. Recent amendments to legislation at both the provincial and federal levels indicate that the necessary change has begun as shown, for example, by amendments to Ontario's Child Welfare Act (R.S.O., 1980, as amended 1981) to allow independent representation for children, by Ontario's Children's Reform Act (R.S.O., 1980, as amended 1982) to ensure that children are consulted about custody and guardianship and, at the federal level, by the proposed Young Offenders' Act (Canada, Bill C-61, 1981) to increase procedural safeguards for children before the courts. Under the Canadian Charter of Rights passed in

1982, legislation which does not provide the same procedural rights for children as for adults may now be challenged in Court (Landau 1982, p. 5).

Family Planning Rights of Minors

An area which is particularly illustrative of the confusion which exists around the rights of minors is that of their rights to family planning services. As both family law and laws concerning health care are areas of provincial jurisdiction in most regards in Canada, the example of the situation with regard to minors in the province of Ontario will be discussed from this point on.

In Ontario, as in most other jurisdictions in Canada, the Age of Majority and Accountability Act (R.S.O. 1970, as amended 1971) lowered the common law age of majority from 21 to 18 so that all parental authority terminates at that point. The legislation leaves a vacuum concerning who may consent to medical treatment on behalf of an incompetent adult (Code, undated). Unless a committee has been appointed under the Mental Incompetency Act (R.S.O. 1980) or an order has been made by a judge of the Supreme Court of Ontario, no medical treatment of an incompetent adult can be legally authorized.

Accordingly, a competent adult of 18 or more years may obtain birth control pills or an intrauterine device from a physician or may consent to surgical procedures such as therapeutic abortion and sterilization. The rights of a person under age 18 are less clear. There are no age restrictions with regard to the purchase of condoms or contraceptive foams and jellies from a drug store, but with respect to the more effective methods of contraception which require a physician's services, access for minors is more difficult.

The basic issue concerning rights to family planning services is the matter of competency to consent to medical treatment. When is a minor competent to consent to treatment? Who can consent for an incompetent person? To what procedures may consent be given by a minor or by the person with legal responsibility for a minor?

The Common Law Regarding Consent

The common law in Ontario has always protected the inviolability of individuals. Any intentional touching of another without his consent constitutes a violation of his person. This is recognized in law as the tort of battery and to defend himself against allegations of battery a physician must obtain his patient's consent to medical treatment. An exception is made in emergencies in which event the common law permits physicians to provide necessary medical attention to an unconscious or incompetent person to preserve his health.

The elements necessary for a valid consent are:
o that the physician has given his patient sufficient information about the nature and consequences of the intended procedure to allow the patient to come to a reasoned decision, i.e., to give an informed consent;
o that the patient is mentally competent;
o that the consent is truly given;
o that it is not obtained through mis-representation;
o that no express instructions of the patient override the implied consent; and
o that the consent is in relation to the procedure actually performed (Ontario Interministerial Committee on Medical Consent 1979, p. 8).

In the absence of statutory law in Ontario which regulates the age at which medical consent may be given by a minor, by common law there is no fixed age at which a person is considered competent to consent to the provision of health care services. Because of this, physicians who provide birth control information and devices to minors without consulting parents are uneasy about their potential legal jeopardy. Case law has supported the physician's right to provide medical treatment to a consenting minor if he has ascertained that the minor has the capacity to understand the nature and consequences of the proposed treatment and all other aspects of a valid consent have been met. It is the intelligence of the patient and the adequacy of the information given him that determines the validity of his consent.

This was determined by the Supreme Court of Ontario in the case of Johnston vs. Wellesley Hospital in 1971. At that time, the common law age of majority, namely 21, was in force. Johnston was a 20 year old who consented to a cosmetic operation on his face without his parents' consent. They subsequently laid a charge of assault on the basis that Johnston being a minor lacked the capacity to consent. The judge dismissed the case referring to an earlier judicial ruling "that an infant who is capable of appreciating fully the nature and consequences of a particular operation or of particular treatment can give an effective consent thereto, and in such cases the consent of the guardian is unnecessary...." (Code, undated, pp. 6-7).

The Public Hospitals Act Regulations on Consent

There appears to be a consensus among physicians that at age 16 a person is competent to give consent in the absence of any signs to the contrary. This position may have been given some credence by the passing of new regulations to the Public Hospitals Act (R.S.O. 1970) in 1975 which established sixteen as the age for medical consent and consent to surgery in public hospitals. However, legal opinion is that these regulations apply only to hospitals and provide no protection for individual physicians who provide medical services to minors in or out of a hospital. Contradictory as this may seem, for physicians the common law with regard to consent still applies.

In addition to creating the myth that age 16 is the legal age for consent to medical treatment, the revisions to the Public Hospitals Act have tended to create a myth that minors under 16 are not competent to give consent in any circumstances. This, of course, is not the case for at common law, there is no fixed age at which a person is considered incompetent to consent to the provision of health services.

Consent in Other Provinces

In other provinces, generally the common law still governs. However, four provinces have enacted statutory medical consent provisions--Quebec, British Columbia, New Brunswick and Saskatchewan--but the age of consent varies from 14 in the first to 18 in the last.

The Interministerial Committee on Medical Consent

In Ontario late in 1978, the non-therapeutic sterilization of mentally incompetent young people on the authority of their parents' consent became an issue. The law was unclear as to whether parents had the authority to consent on behalf of their retarded children.

The Ontario Minister of Health placed a moratorium on these procedures and established an interministerial committee to study the problems of consent to surgery and other medical procedures for minors (under 18) and the mentally incompetent.

After an extensive public consultation, the committee prepared recommendations and draft legislation which was widely circulated for public comment. The recommendation of the committee was as follows:

The age of 16 should be established as the age of consent to health care services. A rebuttable presumption of incompetency to consent should exist below that age... This approach would permit the treating of persons under the age of 16 on their own consent, and without parental involvement, only where the presumption is rebutted. The presumption is rebutted when a health care provider determines the young person has the ability to both understand and appreciate the nature and consequences of the proposed procedure (Ontario Interministerial Committee on Medical Consent 1979, pp. iv, xiv).

In the case of consent to health care services on behalf of a person determined to be incompetent, the committee recommended that for ordinary procedures, a gradation of relatives available and willing to give consent should be authorized to consent on behalf of the incompetent person. Where there are no such relatives, the Public Trustee should be authorized to provide consent.

Certain procedures, however, should be excluded from those for which substitute consent alone is sufficient authorization. These include non-therapeutic sterilization, non-therapeutic experimentation, non-therapeutic transplantation, and psychosurgery for behaviour control. In these latter procedures, the Committee recommended that the parent or relative's consent along with the doctor's report of the proposed procedure should be forwarded to a central committee of medical and other experts for approval. An appeal to the court from a decision of the committee should be permitted.

This draft Health Care Services Consent Act aroused the concern of special interest groups who lobbied successfully to prevent its implementation as law. These groups included the Right to Life and certain religious groups that oppose not only abortion but also sterilization and most other contraceptive methods. As a consequence, the moratorium on the performance of non-therapeutic sterilization for mentally incompetent minors was extended and continues to this date. No other statute regarding age of consent has been proposed since and the common law described earlier continues to govern the provision of health care to minors.

The need for changes to ensure that family planning services are readily available to persons under the age of 18 is clearly demonstrated by the number of births out of wedlock to women in this age group. In 1981 in Ontario, there were 2,274 births out of wedlock to minors. A further 4,069 women under 18 were aborted that year.

The Situation With Regard to Abortion

While age of consent to medical contraceptive services is governed by provincial law, the right to obtain an abortion is regulated by federal legislation. In Canada, induced abortion cannot be legally performed unless several conditions are complied with which are set forth in the federal Criminal Code (R.S.C. 1970, Chapter c-34):

o The procedure must be done by a qualified medical practitioner.

o The medical practitioner must be a physician who is not a member of a hospital's therapeutic abortion committee.

o The abortion must be approved by a therapeutic abortion committee set up by the board of the hospital to consider questions related to pregnancy termination in that hospital.

o The committee must consist of three qualified medical practitioners.

o The procedure must be done in a hospital accredited by the Canadian Council on Hospital Accreditation.

o All provincial statutes regarding authorization or consent must be met (Canada Committee on the Operation of the Abortion Law 1977, pp. 85-86).

The section of the Criminal Code regarding abortion does not specify any age of consent. Therefore, a minor of any age who is not otherwise legally incapable may give a valid consent to the procedure. In Ontario, because the Public Hospitals Act sets the age of consent for medical and surgical procedures in hospital at 16, this becomes the age at which minors may give consent to a therapeutic abortion.

In practice, however, most hospitals with therapeutic

abortion committees require the consent of a parent or guardian to a therapeutic abortion on an unmarried minor of any age. Even in Ontario where the Public Hospitals Act sets the age of consent at 16 some hospital committees use the age of majority instead.

A survey conducted by a federal Committee on the Operation of the Abortion Law in 1977 found that although there is no known legal requirement in the case of a married woman for the consent of the husband to a therapeutic abortion, more than two-thirds of the hospitals surveyed required the husband's consent and in the case of a woman who had never married, a few required the consent of the woman's father (Canada Committee on the Operation of the Abortion Law 1977, p.32).

In Ontario, there are no provincial guidelines as to the criteria a therapeutic abortion committee in a hospital should establish for approving applications of abortions. Consequently, practice varies across the province depending upon the policy established by the board of the hospital and the members of the abortion committee. Right to Life groups in some communities have attempted to take over hospital boards in order to set policies that rigidly exclude applications for abortion under almost all circumstances. Therefore, although a minor may have the right to consent to an abortion, she may be denied access to the procedure by a restrictive abortion committee policy or by the lack of an abortion committee at the hospital in her community. As it is not mandatory for hospitals to set up a therapeutic abortion committee, many hospitals operated by religious orders decline to do so. Currently, of 155 hospitals in Ontario offering obstetrical and gynecological services, only 70 have therapeutic abortion committees and it is not publicly known whether abortions are performed at all 70 hospitals.

Because hospital abortion committees across the province set varying rules---most have quotas, some won't take women from out of town, some approve abortions only if the woman is suicidal---access to therapeutic abortion services is limited. The federal committee set up to examine the operation of the abortion law in Canada concluded that the procedures set out were not working equitably across the country and that there were sharp disparities in the distribution and the accessibility of therapeutic abortion services which caused dangerous delays and sent many women across the border into the United States to obtain medical services (Canada Committee on the Operation of the Abortion Law 1977, p. 17).

In the case of a competent minor who does not wish to have an abortion although her parent has given authorization for the procedure, legal opinion supports the position that if a minor is competent to give consent to the abortion, she would also be competent to refuse it. Even in the case of a retarded pregnant fifteen year old girl who refused an abortion, the parent would not have authority to give consent unless the abortion was clearly necessary to safeguard the health of the patient (Sharpe, undated).

At the time of writing, the abortion law in Canada is being challenged by a private physician, Dr Henry Morgentaler, who has attempted recently to set up free-standing abortion clinics in two provinces--Manitoba and Ontario--to provide ready access in these provinces to abortion without the dangerous delay caused by the hospital abortion committee procedure. Morgentaler for some eight years has been operating an abortion clinic in Montreal, Quebec in defiance of the law after three Quebec Court hearings in which juries found him not guilty of contravening the federal law. The Supreme Court of Quebec has accepted the verdict of the people that the operation of Morgentaler's clinic is not illegal and a number of other similar clinics are now operating freely in that province.

Morgentaler is basing his defense in the upcoming Court cases against him in Manitoba and Ontario on the grounds that enforcement of the abortion section of the Criminal Code (Section 251) would be illegal because the section conflicts with Canada's new Charter of Rights which guarantees the right to life, liberty and the security of the person. No doubt he will be required to carry his case to the Supreme Court of Canada to determine once and for all whether the current abortion law is unconstitutional.

Similar challenges to Canada's abortion law have been initiated in The Supreme Courts of Manitoba and Quebec by the Coalition for Reproductive Choice in Manitoba, Inc. and the Canadian Abortion Rights League of Ontario on the grounds that by forcing a woman to have an unwanted child, the law constitutes cruel and unusual punishment. It is difficult at this point in time to predict the outcome of these court cases for women in general and for minors, in particular, whose rights are even less clear.

The Treatment of Venereal Diseases

An area for which there has been statutory law in Ontario with regard to age of medical consent is the treatment of venereal diseases. Until February of 1983, the Venereal Diseases Prevention Act (R.S.O. 1980, Chapter 521)prevented persons under the age of 16 from providing a valid consent to the examination or treatment, or both, of venereal disease (Ontario Interministerial Committee on Medical Consent 1979, p. 13). This Act has now been repealed and replaced by the Health Protection and Promotion Act, 1983 (Statutes of Ontario, 1983, Chapter 10) of which Part IV on Communicable Diseases, in Section 23, specifically places responsibility on the parent for treatment of a person under 16 years of age as follows:

> Where an order by a medical officer of health in respect of a communicable disease is directed to a person under sixteen years of age and is served upon the parent of the person or upon any other person who has the responsibilities of a parent in relation to the person under sixteen years of age, the parent or other person shall ensure that the order is complied with.

The Act also requires a private physician to report suspected cases of a communicable disease as soon as possible to the medical officer of health in his area. It is silent, however, with regard to the necessity for the physician to obtain the consent of the parents of the adolescent for treatment. Presumably, the common law with regard to competency to consent still applies in this situation and the doctor may treat his young patient if he has ascertained that the minor has the capacity to understand the nature and consequences of the proposed treatment. In practice, many private physicians would do this.

The wording of Section 23 of the Health Protection and Promotion Act seems to give the medical officer of health some discretion as to whether to serve an order on the parents of a minor with a communicable disease. If the adolescent is cooperative, behaves responsibly and obtains treatment, the medical officer of health does not appear to be required to notify the parents.

While the wording of the relevant section of the new Act may provide some flexibility for the physicians involved, it does not state clearly the right of a competent minor to consent to medical treatment for venereal diseases. Therefore, it does little to encourage minors to seek treatment. Many teenagers will continue to go without treatment rather than risk having their parents informed.

This is obviously a situation in which it would be in the best interest of both the minor and the public to allow a competent minor the authority to consent to treatment. Although the Act in name purports to promote health, in fact its failure to address this issue may contribute to the spread of venereal disease. This appears to be a compromise on the part of a government that wishes to improve access to medical treatment for minors but fears the impact of strong lobbying groups which support parental control of minors in all areas related to sexual activity.

Summary

In conclusion, although the common law in Ontario provides for a competent minor to give consent to most family planning services, the lack of statutory law which establishes age of consent makes many physicians leery of providing medical services without parental approval. In the few instances where statutes clearly set the age of consent at 16, this tends to have the unfortunate effect of denying service to children below that age. The principle of parental control over minors is supported at the expense of the well-being of the children.

Recent government efforts to develop a law governing consent to medical treatment for minors and for the mentally incompetent ended in failure because of strong opposition on the part of certain special groups. However, the need to bring about changes has been recognized and the growing support in Canada for children's rights may in time result in legislation which establishes the rights of competent minors to consent to family planning services.

References

The Constitution Act, 1982. **The Criminal Code.** Revised Statutes of Canada 1970, Chapter c-34, Section 251.
The Young Offenders Act, Bill C-61, 1981.
1977. **Report of the Committee on the Operation of the Abortion Law.** Ottawa: Supply and Services Canada, Catalogue No. J2-30/1977.
Catton, Katherine. 1979. "Children and the Law: An Empirical Review." Pp. 179-280, in **The Child in the City: Changes and Challenges,** edited by Michelson et al. Toronto: University of Toronto Press.
Code, Michael. Undated paper. **The Existing State of the Law in Ontario with Respect to Consent to Medical Treatment.** Prepared for the Ontario Interministerial Committee on Medical Consent.
Eichler, Margaret. 1983. **Families in Canada Today: Recent Changes and Their Policy Consequences.** Toronto: Gage Publishing Ltd.
Landau, Barbara L. 1982. **The Rights of Minors to Consent to Treatment and to Residential Care.** York University: Osgoode Hall Law School, L.L.M. thesis.
Landsberg, Michele. 1982. **Women and Children First.** Toronto: Macmillan of Canada.
McKie, D., C., B. Prentice, and P. Reed. 1983. **Divorce: Law and the Family in Canada.** Ottawa: Statistics Canada, Catalogue No. 89-50E.
Ontario. Interministerial Committee on Medical Consent. Sept. 1979. **Options on Medical Consent.** Toronto: Ministry of Health.
Dec. 1979. **Options on Medical Consent-Part 2.** Toronto: Ministry of Health.
1982. **The Children's Act: A Consultation Paper.** Toronto: Ministry of Community and Social Services.
The Age of Majority and Accountability Act. Revised Statutes of Ontario 1980, Chapter 7.
The Child Welfare Act. Revised Statutes of Ontario 1980, Chapter 66, as amended 1981.
The Children's Law Reform Act. Revised Statutes of Ontario 1980, Chapter 68, as amended 1982, Chapter 20.
The Health Protection and Promotion Act. Statutes of Ontario 1983, Chapter 10.
The Mental Incompetency Act. Revised Statutes of Ontario 1980, Chapter 264.

The Public Hospitals Act. Revised Statutes of Ontario 1980, Chapter 410.

The Venereal Diseases Prevention Act. Revised Statutes of Ontario 1980, Chapter 521. Repealed 1983, Chapter 10.

Price, Matt. 1981. **Medical Consents and Child Welfare.** Paper prepared for the Ontario Association of Children's Aid Societies, Toronto.

Sharpe, Gilbert. Undated. **Current Medico-Legal Controversies in Patients' Rights.** Paper given at International Conference on Controversies in Law, Medicine and Health Care.

Undated. **Legal and Ethical Aspects of Health Care For Children: Sterilization and the Incompetent Minor.** Paper given at McMaster University, Faculty of Health Services.

4
THE FAMILY PLANNING RIGHTS OF MINORS IN CZECHOSLOVAKIA

Z. Matejcek and S. Radvanová

Background Information on Czechoslovakia

The Czechoslovak Socialist Republic (CSSR) is a federation of two national states with equal rights, the Czech Socialist Republic (CSR) and the Slovak Socialist Republic (SSR). It has about 15 million inhabitants, with roughly one third in the SSR. Differences in language and culture are not large, especially when compared with other European multinational states. The Czech regions were somewhat more economically advanced before the war, but more rapid growth in Slovakia in recent decades has led to a steady reduction in the differential in living standards between the two republics. The birth rate has been somewhat higher in Slovakia than in the Czech Republic, while divorce and abortion rates have always been slightly lower. In recent years, strong pronatalist measures on the part of the government have increased the fertility rate (births per 1,000 people) from around 15 in the late 1960s up to 19.4 in 1974. Since 1974, however, there has been a slight decline in the fertility rate. In 1982 the fertility rate in the CSR was 13.7; in the SSR, it was 18.2. (The divorce rate per 1,000 people in 1982 was 2.70 in the CSR and 1.30 in the SSR.)

For the purposes of this study, the fertility of women in the youngest age group is of particular interest. Statistics for the last forty years are shown in Table 1. The table shows a relatively rapid increase in the fertility rate of adolescent girls after 1970, with the peak in both republics in 1977 and 1978, and a slight decline in the

37

following years.

Subsequent tables and statistical data in this report refer to the whole federation, and thus reflect nationwide developmental trends, irrespective of local deviations (see Tables 2, 3, 4, and 5). The tables generally indicate that the government's pronatalist measures had not yet had much effect on marriage and fertility rates by 1971, but that they had taken effect by 1975.

Governmental Population Commission

The State Population Commission was established at the time of abortion liberalization in 1957 as an advisory body of the Federal Government on population questions. In 1971, it was upgraded to a higher level Governmental Population Commission, consisting of federal and national deputy ministers of the respective ministries, representatives of the Trade Unions, the Union of Czechoslovak Women, the Union of Socialist Youth and the mass media, along with the heads of research institutes concerned with population problems. The main task of the Commission is to observe and evaluate population developments and to make suitable recommendations to the government. In addition, the Commission puts forward suggestions for research on certain phenomena and popularizes the objectives of government population policy through educational institutions and mass media.

The Adolescent Dilemma in Czechoslovakia

The need to "get free of parental authority" is generally regarded as one of the basic psychological needs of adolescents for attaining social autonomy. Development from infancy to adulthood goes from the point where

Table 1:   Fertility Rates in CSR and SSR: Number of Live Births per 1,000 Women Age 15-19

	Mother's age	1937	1960	1970	1975	1977	1979	1982
CSR	15-19	14.9	44.0	49.0	61.2	61.5	55.5	50.9
SSR	15-19	28.7	50.5	39.2	46.0	47.7	47.5	46.5

individuals are subject to complete parental and social control, to the point where they exercise full adult autonomy based on social responsibility. Under normal circumstances, the period of adolescence tips the scales notably in the direction of autonomy--and the dilemma is between rushing this shift too quickly or checking it until too late. But what is early and what late might be indicated only by comparative longitudinal studies--which are not available so far. We shall therefore try to show what legal basis there is for the increasing autonomy of adolescents in our country and what the government policy is in the sphere of family planning.

The process of socialization begins in infancy and in individual cases takes on quite different forms and proceeds with varying speed. What has been said about adolescence in general applies to adolescents in the CSSR too: they are moving towards complete adult autonomy. But where is the tipping point in this continuum? In order to find out, all sorts of questionnaire surveys and psychosocial and sociological studies have been conducted. Summarizing and comparing their findings with those, for example, in the USA and particularly in Scandinavian countries, we see much less aggressive attitudes of "protest" in our youth and less vigorous assertion of their autonomy rights. Teenage communities, with their specific ideology, including the freedom of sexual and partner relationships, have not taken root and spread in Czechoslovakia. Drug and alcohol abuse in minors does, of course, arouse the attention of the administrative bodies and medical institutions, but it has not become a mass phenomenon so far.

What with the ten-year compulsory school attendance and the large number of secondary school and university students, school is a very important environment for adolescents. It is organized along the lines of a "working place" and is traditionally an authoritative institution with great social prestige. Attaining a certain level of education is a fundamental precondition for professional and social career advancement. This exerts a strong conforming and consolidative pressure on young people.

Another important stabilizing factor is the full employment of adolescents (if not "employed" by school). In itself, this factor creates conditions for some autonomy of adolescents in an important sphere of social life (improved professional qualification, specialist instruction, wages and the possibility of using them freely, and so on). On the other hand, not working, not holding a paying job amounts to violation of the law and is therefore criminal.

The society is traditionally pedocentric and the parents' concern with the child's welfare is great. Studying in clinical practice how adolescents assess their position in the family, we note a prevalent loyalty to parents. A typical finding from surveys of adolescents about parental attitudes and practices is a great positive interest of the parents in the children and a relatively high parental directivity. These two factors are highly correlated. This means that the minors commonly associate parental authority and control with parental warmth and interest. They do not view authority and control as a manifestation of hostility and for the most part do not experience them as oppression.

Of course, with this background, it holds true even in the CSSR that parents consider adolescents' freedom excessive, and that adolescents on the contrary believe there is too little of it. It does not appear, however, as if this discordance at a general level exceeds the bounds of a healthy, developmentally stimulating confrontation of generations. In individual cases it may happen that the disagreement becomes unmanageable within the family and calls for help of the court, which then exercises the legal norms.

Table 2:   Age-Specific Marriage Rates: Number of Marriages per 1,000 Unmarried Women/Men

		16	17	18	19	20
Women	1971	7.4	28.9	134.2	206.4	285.9
	1975	9.4	34.5	151.4	192.5	221.3
	1979	7.9	32.1	160.6	232.4	281.1
Men	1971		0.6	17.6	37.8	64.7
	1975		1.2	25.4	44.5	60.2
	1979		0.9	22.5	40.5	52.5

Table 3: Age-Specific Divorce Rates: Number of Divorces per 1,000 Married Women/Men

		16-17	18	19	20
Women	1971	2.5	5.6	11.0	14.7
	1975	5.6	6.8	12.3	16.5
	1979	3.6	7.8	14.3	15.4
Men	1971		2.8	6.2	10.9
	1975		4.2	8.5	15.4
	1979		1.5	8.8	14.9

Table 4: Marital Status of Youth per 1,000 Women/-Men, by Age: 1970 and 1979

			16	17	18	19	20
Women	1970	single	996	997	887	737	571
		married	4	23	113	261	423
		divorced	0	0	0	2	5
		widowed	0	0	0	0	1
	1979	single	997	977	882	726	560
		married	3	23	118	272	435
		divorced	0	0	0	2	5
		widowed	0	0	0	0	0
Men	1970	single	1 000	999	990	958	908
		married	0	1	10	42	91
		divorced	0	0	0	0	1
		widowed	0	0	0	0	0
	1979	single	1 000	999	988	955	911
		married	0	1	12	45	88
		divorced	0	0	0	0	1
		widowed	0	0	0	0	0

Minority and Majority Status

In Czechoslovak civil law, majority status is defined by the Civil Code, Law No. 40 of 1964. Majority is attained to the full extent at the age of 18. Otherwise, before reaching this age, majority may be attained only upon marriage, for the court may permit a minor over 16 years of age to contract marriage. Majority attained upon marriage then remains valid even when the marriage is dissolved or annulled before the person reaches the age of 18.

Czechoslovak law does not recognize any other way of attaining majority. The declaration of majority of an authorized body, frequently possible in other legal systems, is not possible in Czechoslovakia. Similarly, it is not possible, in individual cases, to change the age necessary for attaining majority or to annul an already attained majority on some legal grounds.

Attaining majority is a prerequisite for full liability to legal obligations. By liability to legal obligations is meant the fitness to attain rights and assume responsibilities through one's own legal acts. To a limited extent, such a liability exists even in minors. The Czechoslovak Civil Code does not specify any additional age limits for minors to determine the extent of their liability for some legal acts. Rather, the minor's liability is defined by the Civil Code only generally as a liability to such legal obligations as are adequate to his intellectual and moral maturity corresponding to his age.

Table 5: Age-Specific Fertility Rates of Young Married and Single Women: Number of Births (Live and Stillborn) per 1,000 Women

		15	16	17	18	19	20
Married	1971		918	734	504	438	383
Women	1977		946	936	596	494	428
	1979		1 000	880	599	517	436
Single	1971	2	5	10	12	14	17
Women	1975	2	5	9	12	14	16
	1979	2	5	11	13	16	18

The reasons for which liability to legal obligations may be limited or for which the citizen may be deprived of it are strictly defined by law. Examples are, permanent mental disorder or excessive use of alcohol or narcotics. The court always appoints a guardian to a citizen deprived of or limited in his liability to legal obligations, who then acts as his legal representative.

Majority status is a general concept of Czechoslovak civil law, respected and built upon by other divisions of the law. A different situation, however, obtains in the case of liability to legal obligations. Some divisions of the law set concrete age limits for different legal acts of minors, that is, at some particular age the minor attains liability for a certain legal act. The Labour Code, for example, recognizes the liability of persons over 15 years of age to a contract of service; and some administrative regulations (e.g., driving licence for some motor vehicles, rights and duties concerning identification papers) also use an age limit of 15 years.

According to Czechoslovak law, citizens who have reached the age of majority are charged with legal responsibility--they assume rights, duties, and obligations as a result of their behaviour, legal or illegal. Legal responsibility arises not only in the sphere of civil law and criminal law, but also in administrative law and other legal branches. As far as a citizen under age 18 is concerned, the assumption of responsibility depends on various conditions specific to individual divisions of the law.

Criminal liability of persons under 18 years is set down by Criminal Law No. 140 of 1961. A person who at the time of committing a criminal offence has not reached 15 years of age is not held criminally liable. Criminal liability of minors commences with the day following their attaining the 15th year of age. When punishing a person who was 15 and has not exceeded 18 at the time of the criminal offence, the court reflects the special concern for youth by a socialist society by making use of the educational purposes of criminal prosecution. For example, if a minor is sentenced to a correctional institution due to a criminal offence, the sentence would be served in an institution which makes it possible for him to continue his work apprenticeship or to obtain some other type of work qualification.

Legal position of a minor in the family. The scope of the basic rights and duties of minors, particularly in relation to their parents and other relatives and persons functioning as "substitute" parents (adoptive parents, foster parents, or guardians), is limited by Family Law No. 94 of 1963 and related regulations.

The basic rights and duties of parents to their children are preeminently the right and duty to bring up the child, to represent him, and to manage his affairs (especially his financial affairs). These rights and duties fall only to a parent of a minor child. In addition, the parents have a maintenance duty to the child. Fulfillment of this duty continues up to the time when the child is capable of self maintenance. Maintenance duty may thus come to an end even before the child's coming of age, or more often it may extend into his majority. This is particularly the case when the child is studying for his/her future profession.

Czechoslovak family law does not expressly give the parents the right to determine the minor's place of abode. However, the right and duty to bring up the child quite clearly entails having the child living with the parents or the right to place him with another person or in an institution. The right to determine the child's place of abode enables the parents to bring up the child and take care of him. The parents are thus entitled to turn to state authorities for help if necessary for the proper exercise of their parental rights and duties and the state, by law, is obliged to help them. The regulations issued by the Ministry of Interior require the police to assist parents in finding and returning children who have run away from home. In fact, until coming of age the child cannot live outside the parental home without the parents' consent. Also a minor cannot acquire the right to use a flat--such a contract, if made by him, would be invalid. In some cases it may happen that a minor assumes the right to use a flat directly by law (e.g., by inheriting the flat). For a minor to live in the flat is, however, possible only when a person of age lives there together with him and if the parents agree to this arrangement.

Labour legislation makes it possible for the minor, after he has reached the age of 15 and finished compulsory school attendance, to make a contract of service or apprenticeship, which is valid without the parents' consent. In theory and practice, however, such a contract cannot be valid if it runs counter to the parents' right to determine the child's place of abode.

The minor has a legal liability to such legal obligations as are adequate to his intellectual and moral maturity corresponding to his age, and within this scope he may enter into civil law contracts. A contract contrary to such prerequisites is invalid. The Civil Code does not make such contracts by minors conditional upon parental consent. However, a legal act that exceeds the minor's maturity and liability must be made only by the minor's parent or legal representative. Any claims of the minor that stem for his/her contract of service of apprenticeship, such as payment for work, belong directly to the minor. The parents cannot dispose of such income. Family law, however, requires the child living together with his/her parents not only to help them according to his abilities, but expressly to contribute financially to cover common family needs, provided he has an income from his own work.

Unlike the civil law, some legal regulations, especially in administrative law, require the parents' consent for some actions by minors (e.g., application for a passport, enrollment in various courses of extracurricular education, sports activities, etc.).

Marriage of minors. Before attaining majority at the age of 18 the Czechoslovak citizen cannot contract a valid marriage. Nevertheless, family law allows an exception to this rule. The court may grant a marriage to a minor over 16, providing the marriage is motivated by important reasons and if it is in keeping with the social purposes of marriage. In practice it is the minor woman's pregnancy that is the prevailing reason for the court to grant permission to marry, and the very high fertility rates of young married women, shown in Table 5, confirm this.

With marriage, as stated earlier, a minor attains majority status. If the minor's marriage that has been approved does not take place, the minor does not attain majority and cannot enter into a marriage with some person other than the one mentioned in the court's decision.

If a minor over 16 has contracted a marriage without the court's permission, it will be invalid and the court has to annul it. Prior to this, though, the invalidity of the marriage may be rectified if the minor reached the age of 18 or if the wife became pregnant.

Even though the law does not expressly say this, its wording clearly yields itself to the interpretation that only one member of the couple may be granted permission to marry. If both are minors such permission of the court is out of the question.

The law explicitly says that a marriage contracted by a minor under 16 does not materialize at all. That means that under no circumstances may the court make an exception for such a minor.

Sexual abuse. The Czechoslovak legal system forbids, under criminal law sanctions, sexual intercourse with persons under 15 years. Criminal Law No. 140 of 1961 prescribes that whoever has sexual intercourse with a person under 15 years or sexually abuses such a person in any other way will be sentenced to imprisonment of 1 to 8 years. More severe punishments are reserved for cases in which this criminal offence is committed against a person under the guardianship of the offender who thus takes advantage of the victim's dependency. The severity of punishment increases when the criminal offence inflicts heavy injury to the victim's health and if it were to cause death the offender will be imprisoned for 10 to 15 years.

Severe punishment is also reserved for those guilty of the criminal offence of rape against a woman under 15 years. The criminal offence of rape can be committed only on a woman.

For minors who are over 15, but under 18 years, the criminal charge of sexual abuse would be applied only against an adult who abuses the dependency of the minor entrusted in his care. In such cases, the degree of punishment is considerably lower--the offender may be imprisoned for up to two years.

The criminal offence of sexual intercourse with a person of the same sex is committed by a person who, after reaching the age of 18, has sexual intercourse with a person of the same sex under 18 years of age.

The above shows that criminal law, in principle, does not punish sexual intercourse of persons over 15 and under 18 years of age; in other words, they are permitted sexual relations. Legal protection of these minors--over 15 and under 18--confines itself to situations where it is necessary to protect a minor against sexual behaviour which in the legislators' view involves social risk. These minors have to be protected against the risk of sexual abuse by a parent or guardian or of homosexual intercourse by any adult. Protection without exception is laid down for children under 15 years.

Education and supervision. Educational measures, imposed by state authorities, are part of the sociolegal protection of the child. The competence of National Committees includes the following educational measures: suitable admonishment of the minor or his parents or the citizens interfering with his education, or delegation of this admonishment to another social organization; supervision over the minor which is conducted in the place of residence or work in coordination with the school or various social organizations. Finally, they may place the minor under restrictions to prevent harmful effects on his education; for example, they may preclude him from visiting public places and entertainment which in individual cases and in view of his person may be unsuitable for the minor. These measures may also be imposed by the court.

It falls exclusively within the court's competence to restrict parental rights, to deprive a parent of his rights, and finally to place a child in educational care substituting for the parents' education--whether it is substitute care of a family type or institutional education. Family law prescribes precisely formulated reasons for each of these measures. Once the proceedings have been concluded, the court passes judgment. If the parental rights of one of the parents are limited or terminated, this does not affect the rights of the other parent. Parental rights would then be concentrated in the other parent who would continue to exercise them alone. If both parents are deprived of parental rights, the court must appoint a legal representative or guardian for the minor; the guardian assumes the parental rights and duties in lieu of the parents.

Protection of minors' rights. Czechoslovak family law defines relatively broadly the relation of society toward children in the sphere of exercising parental rights and duties. It explicitly mentions the "share of society in the exercise of the parents' rights and duties" and lays down the scope of concrete rights and duties of state authorities through which society's participation is effected.

In the first place, of course, it is the general duty of citizens, social organizations and state authorities to draw attention to serious violations of parental rights and obligations towards children. Similarly, there is the right to let the parents or even a state authority know of the children's objectionable behaviour. The competent authorities whose duty it is to bring about correction by concrete measures are National Committees, the court, and some other authorities, such as the Public Prosecutor's Office. Steps to limit parental rights, however, may be taken solely by the court.

Contraception

Statistics on termination of pregnancy by induced abortion show that up to the age of 16 its annual incidence in the whole of the CSSR is limited to fewer than 100 cases. In the 16th, and then the 17th, year of age it rises sharply. Questionnaire surveys, conducted mostly among university students in Prague and other large cities, agree in showing that sexual activity in a large majority of young women begins between the ages of 17 and 19. These findings suggest that the lower age limit for contraceptive need is about 16.

Both male and female contraception is in use by minors. Male contraceptives are commonly available--condoms are relatively cheap and are sold at chemists' and from occasional vending machines. As to female contraception, adolescents have ready access to chemical contraceptives, e.g., suppositories such as Antiko, without a medical prescription. Oral hormonal contraceptives-- the pill (Antigest, Biogest)--and IUDs (DANA) have been produced in the CSSR since 1966, and before that they were imported. Their price is subject to regulation by the Ministry of Health, as is their marketing. Both of these contraceptive methods, as well as estrogenic contraception (one pill after sexual intercourse) and luteal supplementation (minipills with a low content of gestagen), are available to adolescents and adults only on a medical prescription.

The contraceptive DANA has to be inserted only by gynecologists in hospitals. Hormonal contraception is also prescribed exclusively by a gynecologist. In keeping with

WHO recommendations the Methodological Instruction of 1977 by the Ministry of Health advises the use of other than hormonal contraceptives during early adolescence. However, in sexually active girls, gynecologists are guided by the finding of whether the menstruation cycles are stabilized and ovulatory. In the affirmative case, pills are routinely prescribed. Unlike other prescribed drugs, which are completely free of charge, pills have to be paid for. Their price, though, is so low that the economic aspect by no means restricts their use. The question of IUD use in adolescents has so far remained unresolved among specialists. The MIMH of 1977 does not recommend the use of intrauterine devices in teenage girls unless there are special reasons in exceptional cases.

Questionnaire reports and statistics show that the role of contraception in adolescent birth control in the CSSR is as yet very small. Lack of information among young people is still given as one of the main reasons for the limited use of contraceptives by adolescents, in addition to the ambiguous standpoints adopted by health workers and the whole of society towards adolescent contraception. Placing hormonal contraception under medical control is no doubt a limiting factor. On the other hand, it reflects the social prestige and responsibility vested in the Health Services for dealing with population problems.

Legally it has not been quite cleared up whether to inform the parents of an underage girl about the medical prescription of contraceptives. The routine practice, however, is such that the gynecologist does not report this circumstance to the parents on his own initiative.

After an earlier period of enthusiasm about female contraception, sexual and parenthood education, as we shall see later, refocused on education towards responsibility of young people in the sphere of sexual behaviour. As to contraceptives, the greatest publicity is in the first place again given to male contraception (the sheath or condom). Nevertheless, surveys show that in the contraception of both adults and adolescents coitus interruptus is by far the most frequent method. In health care education, artificial termination of pregnancy is strongly opposed, especially in first pregnancies in young girls. Contraception is advocated as a means of prevention of these abortions. Of late, their number has in fact mildly declined. It is being considered whether to set up a special advisory service for contraception problems under the Health Service, similar to those in some other countries. So far, though, it has not been introduced.

Abortions

Artificial termination of pregnancy was legalized in the CSSR in 1957. The law says that "permission for termination of pregnancy may be granted on medical grounds or for other reasons deserving special consideration." The "other reasons" have been established in practice to include a broad range of economic and social grounds. Among those concerning adolescents in particular is the "difficult situation arising from the pregnancy of an unmarried woman." Not all the abortions applied for by women are granted. To decide whether to allow the abortion or not is the task of special Abortion Committees which come under the National Committees (the local bodies of state power and administration). The procedure is as follows: To request an abortion the pregnant woman has to forward an application either personally or through her physician to the head of the gynecological department of the Health Centre in her district of residence. If she does not withdraw her application after being informed of the possible consequences of the abortion, her request is placed on the agenda of the Abortion Committee, usually consisting of a gynecologist, a social worker, and the local representative of the Trade Unions or the representative of the Union of Women. If the District Abortion Committee does not approve the application, the pregnant woman has the right to appeal to the Regional Abortion Committee, which makes the final decision. (A district is an administrative unit with about 100,000 residents; a region is an administrative unit with more than 1,000,000 residents.) About 8 to 10 per cent of the requests are turned down by the District Committees. After appeal to the Regional Committees the number of denied requests is reduced to 2 to 3 per cent. (In a study of children born to women denied abortion, which will be mentioned later, only the children belonging to these 2 to 3 per cent of twice rejected applications for pregnancy termination were observed.)

The request for abortion is turned down most often

because of a failure to meet one or another condition laid down by the Health regulations, e.g., that the pregnancy must not exceed 12 weeks' duration and that the period since the previous abortion is not less than 12 months. In underage girls denials due to the latter reasons are very rare; the former circumstance, however, comes up relatively often, owing to lack of information, inexperience, and the inhibition and embarrassment of a "prematurely" pregnant girl.

For a termination of pregnancy made on other than medical grounds, the Abortion Committee levies a charge to partially cover the care expenses. The charge is relatively small--it amounts to roughly one sixth of the average monthly pay in the CSSR and certainly is not a limiting factor in abortions. (Moreover, this charge may be dropped in exceptional cases.)

The proceedings of the Committee are considered confidential, although through the very existence of the Committee it can hardly be completely anonymous. This principle of confidentiality is observed even in underage girls. In view of the legal position of minors, however, the Committee could insist on the parents' approval, as the abortion is a serious medical intervention. The routine practice is such that the Committee takes into account the nature of each particular case and applies the principle that the girl must not be exposed to psychological or social harm by divulging the fact of abortion. It has been estimated that parents are involved in more than 50 per cent of all cases. However, if a girl does not want her parents to be informed, the Committee will respect her decision.

An important legal provision is that the abortion may be performed only with the consent of the pregnant woman. The law does not set any age limit for the validity of this provision. This means, for example, that parents cannot legally force an underage girl to have an abortion if she does not wish to. They cannot decide for the pregnant girl even if she is under 15. The pressure on a minor to have an abortion, from parents or other people, is thus limited. On the other hand, the question of whether to deny the request for an abortion and let the pregnancy continue is largely left to the discretion of the committee which may (but need not) invite the underage girl's parents to the proceedings. It may even invite the man who, according to the woman's report, caused the pregnancy or, if it is a minor male under 18, his parents. The general tendency is to preserve the pregnancy and to create conditions for the child's acceptance into the family or to arrange for its adoption.

The proportion of abortions performed on adolescent girls (in relation to the total number of terminations made in women of all age categories) has risen from 9 per cent in 1963 to a maximum of 14 per cent in 1971; since then it has shown a mildly declining tendency. Abortion can be categorized as spontaneous, as induced for medical/health reasons, or as induced at the woman's request for other than health reasons. Among married women, the last category makes up about half of all abortions; among young, unmarried women it makes up the vast majority of all abortions.

All legal abortions must be carried out in gynecological departments of hospitals during the first trimester, using primarily dilation and curettage procedures. Hospitalization usually lasts two days. With the improved technique of vacuum aspiration, which is increasingly coming into use, the period of hospitalization is reduced to several hours. This substantially enhances the chances of keeping the abortion of a minor secret.

Gynecological departments keep a detailed record of the consequences of abortions. Reliable statistics of mortality following abortion are also kept. For the period between 1973 to 1979 the mortality ratio has dropped to 0.8 per 1,000,000 pregnancy terminations.

Illegal abortions are relatively rare nowadays. Estimates suggested about 3,500 illegal abortions per year in the late 1960s in the CSSR. The record number of illegal abortions induced by the pregnant woman herself or by another person is in an annual range of about 50 in the late 1970s. Before 1957 several thousand illegal abortions were recorded annually and considered criminal.

Guidance

By Government Decree No. 267 of 1973, the preparation of young people for marriage and parenthood has been assigned as a task concerning the whole society to all institutions concerned in some way with the education of the younger generation. By Law No. 121 of 1975 the bodies of state administration are obliged to organize marriage guidance centres and all citizens are granted the right to marriage and premarriage guidance service free of charge.   A network of premarriage and marriage guidance centres has been set up, with teams composed of psychologists, physicians, lawyers, social workers and other specialists functioning nowadays in almost every district.   Some 20 per cent of these centers' capacity is devoted to premarriage guidance, covering preeminently advisory, educational or even psychotherapeutic work with teenage engaged couples. Annually this amounts to about 10,000 clients in the whole of the CSSR. In fact, if a minor wants to marry, she (or he) must be marrying an adult, and must have permission from a court.   As a matter of course, the courts refer both partners to guidance centres for advisory services from specialists. The 1980 statistics indicate that ten times more adolescent girls than boys under age are clients of marriage guidance centres.

With few exceptions, the reason for applying for a marriage licence, if one of the partners is under 18, is the continuing pregnancy of the girl. The following practice is being increasingly adopted: The court will ask the premarriage and marriage guidance centre to assume care and supervision of the engaged couple, and will require this couple to produce a certificate that they have visited the centre.   Although permission to marry is not conditional on this certificate, this procedure nevertheless places pressure on the young couple to participate in the educational experience of the centre. The centre invites the partners for several individual interviews and then puts them through a preparatory course for marriage and parenthood. Only when they have finished the course do they get the certificate for the court.   As a result the instruction becomes more or less compulsory.

Parenthood Education

Building on Decree No. 71 of 1966, the Ministry of Education gradually issued detailed instructions on parenthood and sex education to primary and secondary schools to be implemented as teachers became more familiar and comfortable with the subject.   Since 1973 parenthood education has been functioning as an integrated system which penetrates all school subjects. At the level of primary school it is divided into three stages according to the children's ages--6 to 10 years, 11 to 12 years and 13 to 15 years. One objective is to provide knowledge on sensitive topics to elementary school children before they encounter misinformation elsewhere. In secondary schools, sex education and instruction in the use of contraceptives are subsumed under parenthood education which is deemed to cover the whole spectrum of premarital and marital relations. Specialist staff members of marriage and premarriage guidance centres give increasing numbers of lectures to children in primary and secondary schools.

Parenthood education continues beyond the school years and also takes place outside the schoolroom. Special efforts are made to convey a sense of responsibility to adolescents. Out-of-school education of children and adolescents is for the most part conducted by departments of Health Education of the Health Service system in the CSSR. They direct their educational and instructional activity particularly at adolescents of preconception age. They make extensive use of the mass media which have been strongly encouraged by the Governmental Population Commission to disseminate information on population matters and to play an important role in adolescent education. Health education also prepares the lecturing staff of the so-called Socialist Academy, which is entrusted with public educational activity and which holds lectures, courses, and seminars for teenagers, young married couples, parents-to-be, and others. Topics covered range from contraceptives and love relationships to child care and education.

Parenthood education is to a large degree synonymous with the term family planning, for its aim is to make young people realize how many children they want to have and when. At the same time, it is intended to show young people a positive approach to parenthood and to prepare them for their future maternal and paternal functions. This is the reason why great emphasis is laid on education, while technical instruction (such as the use of contraceptives) is less emphasized. The aim is for young people, through their personalities, to carry into their family of procreation those preconditions deemed essential for healthy family life--which is the basic prerequisite for the healthy development of the new generation. In this sense, parenthood education is also part of the effort to reduce the high divorce rate, which is dangerously on the increase especially in teenage marriages. Thus, although parenthood education is incorporated into the government's pronatalist policy, the government is less concerned with increasing the birth rate than concentrating on the quality of relations and assuring the best possible conditions for the rearing and educating of children.

Research

We have mentioned earlier that the government's present policy is especially concerned with educating young people for healthy family functioning and creating the best possible conditions for the healthy development of children. "Healthy development of the young generation" is also the name of one of the principal tasks of a state research plan which has already been in progress for several 5-year-plan periods. Under this plan, a research project, "Children born from unwanted pregnancies," has been implemented and has received considerable publicity. A total of 220 children born in Prague to women twice denied abortion for the same pregnancy and 220 matched controls were subjected to extensive study. While differences between the "unwanted" and the control children nine years after birth were not dramatic, they were consistent and cumulatively impressive in disfavour of the unwanted children. The follow-up at the age of 14-15 and then again at 16-18 revealed that the differences continued to persist into adolescence, becoming more statistically significant over time. This suggests that "unwantedness" during early pregnancy constitutes a risk factor for the subsequent development of the child. By the time he or she reaches reproductive age it again creates, in the personality of the once unwanted child, risk conditions for his or her own family of procreation. The negative factors associated with "unwantedness" may thus perpetuate themselves.

Another major task of the state research plan involves projects dealing with so-called problem families, including children from families of alcoholics and a number of problems closely connected with the reproductive behaviour of adolescents. At present, two studies are taking place: a longitudinal follow-up study of children born illegitimately in Prague in 1970 (more than 300 children born mostly to teenage mothers are under observation) and a study of marriages contracted by adolescents who are observed by marriage guidance centres.

The conclusions which will soon be drawn from the research findings will become a matter for legislation and will be put into social practice through the agency of the Governmental Population Commission, the highest body for government population policy. In this case it means they will be integrated into the system of educational and instructional programs designed for the young.

Summary and Conclusions

According to Czechoslovak law, majority status is attained only at age 18 or through a court-sanctioned marriage. Persons who have attained majority status have full legal responsibility, depending upon the situation. According to the Civil Code, minors have legal responsibility for their actions only to the extent that their intellectual and moral maturity, and their age, renders them competent to undertake such responsibility. But no specific ages are mentioned in the Civil Code. Other divisions of the law, however, do specify particular ages at which minors have legal responsibility for certain actions. According to criminal law, for example, legal responsibility for criminal acts begins at age 15. Labour law gives minors the contractual right to work or to undertake an apprenticeship at age 15, and to retain their own earnings. Minors below the age of 15 are provided blanket protection against heterosexual or homosexual intercourse and against sexual abuse. Between the ages of 15 and 18, minors are granted more limited protection and a greater degree of responsibility in the area of sexual behaviour. They have legal access to medically prescribed contraceptives and to abortions, usually on a confidential basis. Whether to involve parents in these family planning decisions, however, has not been fully settled, and cases are dealt with on an individual basis, although the Abortion Committee will usually respect the minor's wishes.

The right--in the legal sense of the word--of adolescents to family planning is without doubt of utmost importance. But even more than this right are the attitudes and beliefs which form the motivational basis for people's actions. Therefore we do not think it appropriate to tell adolescents about their rights without any further explanation and instruction. Nor do we believe it suitable to confine guidance only to education by fear, for example, by emphasizing all the disadvantages of an unwanted pregnancy. It is crucial that young people should adopt a positive outlook on marital and family life and, hand in hand with this, that they should accept responsibility for shaping it. The concluding passage of the report on children of unwanted pregnancies (Dytrych et al., 1975), which we should like to quote, is a sort of proclamation of our educational and self-educational family planning program for adolescents:

"It is necessary to develop and cultivate the basic psychological needs of young people so that their parenthood and life with children become a source of positive gratification. Prevention of unwanted pregnancy consists in the awareness of young people that it is extremely important for them not to throw away their rare and unique chance to enjoy a full marital life, having children that they want to have at the optimum time. This presupposes their knowing about this possibility and incorporating it into their own system of 'expectations from life'."

References

Brablcová, V. et al.: Marriage, Family, Parenthood. **Horizont,** Praha, 1977. /In Czech/

David, H.P.: **Family Planning and Abortion in the Socialist Countries of Central and Eastern Europe.** The Population Council, New York, 1970.

David, H.P., McIntyre, R.J.: **Reproductive Behaviour: Central and Eastern European Experience.** Springer, N.York, 1981.

Dunovsky, J., Koluchová, J., Radvanová, S.: Education of Children in Substitutional Family Care. **SPN,** Praha, 1980. /In Czech/

Dytrych, Z., Matejcek, Z., Schüller, V.: Unwanted Children. **Zprávy VUPs,** Praha, 1975. /In Czech/

Havránek, F.: Fertility and Possibilities of Contraception in Adolescence. **Cs. Gynekol.,** 41:304-308, 1979. /In

58   MATEJCEK & RADVANOVA

Czech/
Matejcek, Z., Dytrych, Z., Schüller, V.: Children from Unwanted Pregnancies. **Acta phychiat. scand.**, 87:67-90, 1978.
Matejcek, Z., Dytrych, Z., Schüller, V.: Follow- up Study of Children Born from Unwanted Pregnancies. **Int. J. Behavioral Development**, 3:243-251, 1980.
Matejcek, Z.: Mental Health Services for Children in Czechoslovakia. **Int. J. Ment. Health**, 7:40-45, 1978.
Matejcek, Z., Márová, Z., Radvanová, S.: Education of Children in Uncomplete Families, **SPN**, Praha, 1977. /In Czech/
Pávek, F.: Children Seen by a Judge. **SPN**, Praha, 1978. /In Czech/
Radvanová, S.: About Marriage, Family and Children. **Panorama**, Praha, 1978. /In Czech/
Schiller, J. et al.: Comments to Family Law, **Orbis**, Praha, 1970.

5

FAMILY PLANNING RIGHTS OF MINORS IN DENMARK: THE LEGAL SITUATION AND MINORS' USE OF ABORTION

Erik Manniche

As one of the Nordic countries, Denmark has always remained on the periphery of cultural and ideological movements in continental Europe. Christian ideas of sexual morality were never solidly integrated into Danish behaviour, nor were they ever accepted as majority values. Through the centuries they have been adopted only by the Royal Court and the upper classes. The peasantry, constituting until late into the 19th century about 95 percent of the population, let their behaviour be guided by old agrarian customs, which allowed great freedom between the sexes and sexual relations between unmarried (but betrothed) couples. Tolerance was in certain respects greater in Denmark than on the European continent--always assuming that you followed the old rules. Tolerance did to some extent also extend to adolescents (Manniche and Svalastoga, 1969; Manniche, 1979.

Thus, whereas in other cultures--e.g., those of the European continent and North America--one may today speak of a "sexual revolution" taking place just after the middle of the 20th century, this term does not truly apply to Denmark or to the rest of Scandinavia (Christensen, 1982; Christensen and Gregg, 1970; Trost, 1979).

Yet in recent years Denmark has experienced considerable change in several elements of the family system. There has been a decrease in the marriage rate, and a corresponding increase in the occurrence of unmarried cohabitation; a general decrease in the birth rate, and an increase in the rate of children born outside marriage, corresponding to the increased occurrence of unmarried cohabitation; an increase in the divorce rate; and--since 1973--for all practical purposes, "free abortion" and the disappearance of illegal abortion. Further, over the last approximately 20 years, a high degree of attention has been directed to the condition of women, especially with respect to disadvantages they have suffered relative to the status of men.

Basic attitudes towards sexuality may not have changed very much--such change would be very difficult to document--but matters of sexual behavior are dealt with much more openly than they were 25 or 30 years ago not only in the public sphere (schools, media) but also and perhaps especially in the families. And during approximately the last generation changes have occurred in the values surrounding sexual activities, in that the traditional permissiveness has been gradually extended to youngsters below the age of 18 years. Consequently, the law of 1973 "accepted" or at any rate recognized the existence of sexual activities (including coitus) among minors--that is, in Denmark, persons who have not yet reached the age of 18 years.

The 1973 law on abortion apart, the majority of the changes mentioned above were not accurately predicted by social scientists. Indeed, social scientists were inclined to consider the family system, inclusively perceived, as one of the most stable elements in society. Thus, the societal background to the presentation in this chapter involves considerable and unanticipated changes in the general family and social systems, changes regarding both behavior and norms--and in that time sequence.

Below we shall describe the family planning rights and behavior of minors in Denmark, presenting first the major provisions of present Danish law regarding induced abortion, then showing to what extent the relevant sections of this law have been used by minors in recent years and discussing some of the data adduced in this connection.

Solid empirical data are available on minors' use of abortion services. Data are unfortunately lacking, however, with respect to minors' use of contraception. Only one major piece of research has been done recently in Denmark on family planning, a series of studies carried out by the Danish Family Planning Association on the family planning patterns of pregnant women (Danish

Family Planning Association, 1980; Braestrup, 1971, 1974). These studies did include minors, but not a sufficient number to permit generalizations. They do suggest that among the minors who got pregnant some 15-20 percent did not use any contraception; that the method most commonly used among them is the condom; and that they use contraception very much less than do adult women.   No study exists addressing itself specifically towards minors.   Thus we cannot give a general and empirical description of this aspect of minors' rights to use family planning; we can merely observe that for all practical purposes they have, from the age of 15, the same rights as adults.

The best explanation for the lack of any major or special studies of minors' contraceptive behaviour may be that the topic, in Denmark, is regarded neither as being particularly interesting nor as constituting a "social problem." In this connection it may be in order to mention that the data describing minors' use of abortion facilities stem not from special studies but from routine statistical registrations.

Induced Abortion Among Minors

For present purposes, the main points of Law 350 of 13 June 1973 regarding induced abortion are these:

A woman who is a resident of Denmark may, at no cost to herself, have her pregnancy terminated on conditon that it be done prior to the expiration of the 12th week of pregnancy.   She must be informed of the possibilities under the law of receiving various sorts of assistance to complete the pregnancy and to give birth instead of aborting. If she is married, her husband's consent is not necessary; the decision to obtain an abortion is the sole privilege of the woman.

After the 12th week, a pregnancy may be terminated only if one of a number of conditions is met: for instance, if the abortion is necessary to avert danger to the woman's life or to avert a serious impairment to her physical or mental health; for eugenic reasons; if the woman is very young; or if one of a number of other specific grounds is met.   About five percent of the abortions performed among minors occur after the 12th week; among adults the corresponding percentage is about two and one-half.

If the woman is not yet 18 years old, her parents (or other guardian) must give their consent. When general circumstances indicate it ("naar omstaendighederne taler derfor," § 6 part 2 of the law), a standing committee consisting of a psychiatrist and a gynaecologist may disregard the refusal of the parents, or for that matter may decide not even to seek their consent. Such situations are rare.

The law also provides that any medical officer can refuse, on grounds of conscience, to perform an abortion. In such cases the woman is referred to another hospital or hospital unit. Hitherto, this medical privilege has not caused any problems or difficulties for women who wish abortions (Meyer and Mogensen, 1981). The existence of this clause in the law may be seen as a majority concession to minority opinion. Nurses do not have the same categorical right to refuse; in case of conscientious objections, they have to work in some other unit in the hospital.

It should be understood that since the introduction of free legal access to induced abortion in 1973 and the generally increased openness around the topics of "sex" and contraception two developments have taken place: (a) illegally induced abortion has disappeared - the pheno-

Table 1: Induced abortions per 1.000 women aged 15-49, Denmark 1973-1983.

year	general abortion rate	year	general abortion rate
1973	14.2	1978	19.7
1974	21.2	1979	19.1
1975	23.7	1980	19.0
1976	22.7	1981	18.5
1977	21.6	1982	17.2
		1983	16.6

menon does not exist in Denmark, and (b) after an initial increase in the rate of legally induced abortion 1973-75, due to conversion of illegal to legal abortion, the general rate of induced abortion has steadily and without interruption declined - this is shown in table 1.

Since space is limited the description of how minors use the provisions of the law will emphasize presentation of empirical data rather than detailed interpretation and discussion. It should be borne in mind that in some cases we are talking about quite small numbers. Since considerable changes have taken place in very recent years we shall present data for two points in time viz. 1979 and 1983 so as to indicate the direction of developments.

Counselling and easy - and in many cases free - access to contraception notwithstanding, a total of 2.962 minors in Denmark became pregnant in 1979 and a total of 2.014 in 1983. These numbers represent 3.2 % and 2.6 %

Table 2: Outcome of total number of conceptions in 1979 and in 1983, for general female population and for females below age 18. In percent.

	General population		Females below age 18	
	1979	1983	1979	1983
Birth	65	65	21	18
Induced abortion	25	25	69	72
Spont. abortion	10	10	$10^{a)}$	$10^{a)}$
Est. number of pregnancies	92.907	77.555	2.962	2.014

a) The rate of spontaneous abortion for females below age 18 has arbitrarily been set as identical with the figure estimated for the general population.

respectively of all pregnancies in these two years.

The outcome of these pregnancies has been calculated in table 2. For purposes of comparison we have also shown the outcome of all pregnancies in Denmark. The table shows that the birth/abortion proportions are reversed between minors and adults. The best explanation seems to be that among minors pregnancies are to a much greater extent unwanted than they are among adults.

Table 2 also shows that while the total number of pregnancies has diminished by only 17 % from 1979 to 1983, the number of pregnancies among minors has diminished by all of 32 %, nearly double the general rate.

If we look at the absolute numbers for minors, for the years 1979 and 1983, there were 628 births and 354 births, respectively, and 2.034 and 1.459 induced abortions. These numbers of births and of abortions correspond to the following percentages of all births and abortions in the two years:

	1979	1983
minors' contribution to total number of		
births	1.1	0.7
abortions	8.8	7.0

Both as regards births and abortions the proportions accounted for by minors have decreased, by 44% and 28 % respectively, suggesting more effective contraceptive behavior. The rate of abortion for minors varies with degree of urbanization, as it does for adults, but not as much as it did 10-15 years ago.

Information on the live births to minors is presented in table 3, again for the years 1979 and 1983, and the total numbers of births are also shown. The percentage of non-marital births among minors (88-90%) is more than twice that in the general population (41%). This difference is partly explained by the fact that the legal marrying age for females (as for males) is 18, although dispensation may be given to girls who have reached the age of 15. It is probably much more important to note that marriage below age 18 is contrary to popular norms and values - it is considered to be "too early"; indeed, early marriages are not regarded very positively.

The decrease in the absolute numbers of births and

abortions among minors can only in small part be explained by the difference in size of the birth cohorts 13-
17 years prior to 1979 and 1983, respectively. The age-
specific abortion rate for those aged 17 and below has
during this period gone down from 18 to 12 (cf. table 4),
and the age-specific birth rate for those aged 15-19 has
gone down from 18.1 to 10.6 - reductions by about 33%
and 41% respectively.

The decrease not only in the total population but
especially among minors both in births and in abortions
(and thus in total number of pregnancies) might be attributable to reduced sexual activity esp. coitus among
minors or it might be due to more effective contraceptive
behavior. The latter explanation seems more plausible
than the former. The children appearing in the statistics
for minors for 1983 would have been born c. 1966-1969; as
a conjecture, difficult or impossible to test, it may be

Table 3: Live births to minors in 1979 and 1983, marital
and non-marital, by age of mother. Absolute numbers.

age of mother	1979		1983	
	marital	non-marital	marital	non-marital
13		2		2
14		6		
15	4	33	1	12
16	15	132	9	76
17	55	381	25	229
total	74	554	35	319
All live births				
in Denmark	41.198	18.266	30.203	20.619

Source: Befolkningens bevaegelser, 1979 and 1985.

that they from childhood on have experienced a more open sexual atmosphere in their home and family life than those born a mere 4 - 5 years earlier - such openness being a consequence of influences impinging upon their parents during and after the late 1960s.

The age-specific abortion rates and the absolute numbers of abortions for 1979 and for 1983 are shown in table 4. The main points to observe are that the rate for minors is lower than for any other age category below age 40, and that the 1979 - 1983 decrease in abortion rate is much stronger among minors (33%) than in any other age category.

The apparent explanation for the differences in age-specific abortion rates is that the amount of sexual activity carried out by teenagers is indeed very much lower, and much more irregular, than in the older age categories (Manniche and Holstein, 1969). The average

Table 4: Age specific abortion rates and absolute numbers of induced abortions in age categories, for 1979 and in 1983.

Age category	1979		1983		Decrease in rate 1979-83
	Rate	Numbers	Rate	Numbers	
17 & below	18	2.034	12	1.459	33
18-19	31	2.216	26	2.077	16
20-24	29	5.318	29	5.319	0
25-29	25	4.558	23	4.202	8
30-34	22	4.502	18	3.423	18
35-39	19	3.109	15	2.971	21
40-44	9	1.324	8	1.218	11
45-49	1	132	1	122	0
Total	19	23.193	17	20.791	11

age at first sexual intercourse, for both males and females, is 16 to 17 years. (Hertoft, 1976)

The matter of the age-specific abortion rate for minors
is brought up here since, prior to the enactment of the
1973 law, both medical and political people expressed the
fear that abortion might be used as an alternative to
contraception, especially by the very young. Events since
1973 seem to have shown this fear to be unfounded,
especially if the number of abortions is seen in relation to
the numerical size of the age category--as is traditionally
done. Neither among minors nor among adults can any
support be found for the view that abortion is generally
used instead of contraception to prevent or regulate
births. Thus, it has been estimated that more than
200,000 pregnancies are prevented annually by means of
contraception, and the abortion figures should be seen in
relation to this figure of more than 200,000 prevented
pregnancies. (Matthiessen, 1976)

However, if the number of abortions were simul-
taneously set in relation to the number of acts of sexual
intercourse occurring in each age category, we might get
a very different picture--and for many purposes a much
more realistic or relevant picture. We would hypothesize
that, if an induced abortion rate were calculated on the
basis of sexual activity, minors would show a much higher
rate. In other words, one might find that some minors do
"use abortion" as "contraception". The results one gets
and the conclusions one draws seem to hinge on the
particular "rate" or "ratio" employed. This is an example
of the classical problem in the sciences: how do you
index? The much higher relative frequency of abortions
versus births, among minors as compared to adults, as
shown in Table 2, points in the same direction: that the
traditional focus upon "abortion rates" is not entirely
satisfactory.

Table 5 is presented in order to illustrate the argument
given above. The age-specific abortion rates that are
generally accepted are shown in column 2. Since we have
only fragmentary and unsystematic knowledge of the
relative frequency of coitus in different age groups both a
"high" and a "low" estimate of coitus frequency are shown
in columns 3 and 4. These estimates are based on several
very different, and for the most part local, studies of
coitus frequency. The majority of these studies suggest

that the "low" estimate may be closer to reality than the "high" estimate. Ideally such estimates should also take into account the probability of impregnation (per coitus) as dependent upon age and upon frequency of coitus.

It is nearly certain that neither set of estimates of coitus frequency is accurate, and it really does not matter. However, the distributions do appear plausible, and the general tendency of differences between the age groups also seems believable. Whether you take the high or the low estimates of coitus frequency, the result is a rather different rate of abortion than the one that is customarily presented. And, above all, a very different conclusion must be reached with respect to contraceptive effectiveness among sexually active minors, and indeed among sexually active teenagers in general: namely, that they are much less effective or careful than are adult women.

If in addition to differential coitus frequency rates you also took into account that ovulation among teenagers

Table 5. Age-Specific and Age/Coitus-specific abortion rates in eight age categories, Denmark, 1979.

Age	Age Specific Rate	Estimated Coitus Freq*		Age-Coitus Specific Rate	
		High	Low	High	Low
15-17	18	1	0.8	18.0	22.5
18-19	31	3	2	10.3	15.5
20-24	29	15	8	1.9	3.6
25-29	25	17	8	1.5	3.1
30-34	22	15	8	1.5	2.8
35-39	19	12	7	1.6	2.7
40-44	9	6	3	1.5	3.0
45-49	1	3	2	0.3	0.5

*Time unit: 1 month.
Source: Manniche 1983

(esp. 14-17 year olds) seems to be quite irregular this conclusion would in all probability be further strengthened.

The extent of recidivism among those who abort is seen in table 6, for different age groups. Recidivism may be taken as an indicator of the extent to which any certain group of women load up the abortion statistics. The table shows recidivism within 12 and 24 month periods. The highest rates of recidivism are found among those aged 20-24 and 18-19 years of age while the minors place themselves slightly below the average rates.

Finally, we wish to mention that the law of 1973 also provides for free sterilization as a family planning measure. But on this point minors are not put on an equal footing with others. The law requires that candidates for

Table 6: Percentages of women having a legally induced abortion in one calendar year and a repeated abortion within 12, respectively 24 months thereafter. Shown for 1980(-81) and 1982(-83) and for 1980(-82) and 1981(-83).

age of woman	1980 (-81)	1982 (-83)	1980 (-82)	1981 (-83)
-14	1.7	3.8	2.5	2.8
15-17	4.1	4.5	8.5	7.5
18-19	5.4	5.5	11.5	10.7
20-24	6.1	6.3	11.7	11.3
25-29	5.2	4.6	9.7	9.6
30-34	4.7	3.7	8.6	8.1
35-39	2.6	2.8	6.1	5.7
40-44	1.9	2.0	3.4	3.6
45-	-	0.7	0.7	0.6
All	4.6	4.5	9.1	8.7

Source: Statistik om praevention og aborter, 1:11:1984.

sterilization, be they male or female, have reached the age of 25 years. The idea behind this requirement is that some degree of maturity should be reached before deciding upon something as critical as sterilization.

In Denmark, in contrast to some other national cultures, more men than women let themselves be sterilized; and there is a correlation between social status and male sterilization: the higher the social status, the greater the ratio of male to female sterilization (Kristiansen and Skovbjerg 1976, Manniche 1985).

Summary

From an absolutely restrictive policy as regards induced abortion Denmark has slowly (since 1866) and step by step moved towards free abortion, which was legally established in 1973. Since free abortion was introduced abortion rates have steadily diminished. The rate of induced abortion among minors was until a few years ago of about the same magnitude as that for adults; today the rate for minors is only about two thirds that for adults when calculated on numerical sizes of age categoires; however, if rates were based on sexual activity in age groups the rate of induced abortion for minors would undoubtedly be a good bit higher than the rate for adults.

Compared to rates of other countries Danish rates are not high, they are rather low. And when compared to the total abortion rates in countries where access to legally induced abortion, as well as to contraception, is restricted or absent Danish rates are extremely low indeed. One conclusion would be that free access to contraception **and** to induced abortion will reduce the (total) number of induced abortions.

However, in view of the easy access to contraceptive knowledge and facilities the Danish rates for minors as well as for adults may be considered still to be too high.

References

Braestrup, Agnete, Use of Contraception by Young Mothers in Copenhagen, **Journ. of Biosocial Science**, 1971, 3, pp. 43 - 60.

Braestrup, Agnete, Teenage Pregnancies in Denmark 1940-71, **Journ. of Biosocial Science**, 1974, 6, pp. 471 - 475.

Christensen, Harold T. and Christina F. Gregg, Changing Sex Norms in America and Scandinavia, **Journal of Marriage and the Family**, 32, 1970, pp. 616 - 627.

Christensen, Harold T., Women's Sexual Liberation Viewed in Cross-Cultural Perspective, **Sociological Micro-journal**, Vol. 16, 1982.

Danish Family Planning Association, **Gravide kvinders familjeplanlaegningsmönter**, Copenhagen, 1980.

Hansen Kristiansen, Jette E., og Hanne Skovbjerg: Mandlig kontra kvindelig sterilisation, **Ugeskrift for Laeger**, 1976, vol. 138, no. 6, pp. 380 - 1.

Hertoft, P., **Klinisk sexologi**, Copenhagen 1976. Revised and updated edition Copenhagen 1980. Italian edition has appeared, English edition 1983 (Academic Press).

Manniche, Erik, en Björn Holstein: Huwelijk met de eerste seksuele parter, **Tijdschrift voor Sociale Wetenschappen**, 1969: 3, Gent 1969.

Manniche, Erik et Kaare Svalastoga: La Familie en Scandinavie, **Sociological Microjournal**, vol. 3, 1969.

Manniche, Erik, Sukanjiabia ni okeru kazoku ni tsuite, **Komyunitei 55:** Kakkoku kazoko no ataras hi i ugoki, Tokyo 1979.

Manniche, Erik, Om alderspecifikke og alders/coitusspecifikke abortrater, **Orientering om fremtidsforskning** 1983:4, Institute for Futures Research.

Erik Manniche: **The Family in Denmark,** IPC Press, Helsingoer, Denmark, 1985.

Matthiessen, P.C., Abortudviklingen i de nordiske lande, **Ugeskrift for laeger 1976,** vol. 138 no. 6, pp. 351 - 3.

Meyer, Bente Elsass and Dorthe Mogensen, Praevention og abort, in **Årbog for kvinderet**, 1981, Copenhagen 1981, p.106.

Jan Trost: **Unmarried Cohabitation**, Västerås, (Sweden): International Library, 1979.

5

THE FAMILY PLANNING RIGHTS OF MINORS IN DENMARK: CONTRACEPTIVE COUNSELLING AND SEX EDUCATION

Lisbeth Shore Paludan

In order to better understand the family planning rights of minors in Denmark, a brief description of national health services provisions may be useful.

There is no Ministry of Health, in which health services can be organized, nor are there definite boundaries between those sections of the health services which are the responsibility of the state and those of the counties and municipalities.

In principle, the state lays down laws and rules for the various functions and planning of the health services and the National Health Insurance Scheme, the counties are responsible for the curative health services and related functions, whereas the main tasks of the municipalities are in the areas of nursing and preventive medicine.

The state's responsibilities within the health services sector are carried out by several ministries. The chief responsibility is entrusted to the Ministry of the Interior - the Board of Health within this Ministry is the supervisory authority for the health services sector. The National Social Security Office, under the auspices of the Ministry of Social Affairs, administers the National Health Insurance Scheme. The Ministry of Education is responsible for the education of academic health personnel, and (of interest here) is also responsible for proposals for legislation regarding sex education in the public schools.

Age of Majority

An amendment to Act 312, June 1972, reduced the age of majority from twenty to eighteen years. Minors under the age of eighteen are legally in the custody of a parent or legal guardian, unless they are married; however, minors who intend to marry must have the legal consent of a parent or legal guardian.

With regard to health services, the situation is somewhat different; at the age of sixteen, minors become independent members of the National Health Insurance Scheme, and in principle, have a right to choose a general practitioner in their area of residence. Since April 1976, an agreement between the Organization of Practicing Physicians and the National Health Insurance Act stipulates that contraceptive counselling may be provided free of charge for patients by their general practitioner; for minors this may be done without parental consent. A girl under the age of sixteen, if living at home, is still covered by her parents' Health Insurance Scheme. Although the law stated she may receive counselling and consultation regarding contraceptive methods--including prescriptions for pills and the fitting of a diaphragm or IUD-without parental consent, she must still have parental permission to use the Health Insurance Scheme card for a consultation with her general practitioner.

Legislative Provisions

In the mid 1970s, two legislative changes were made which affected the accessibility to minors of counselling and teaching regarding sexual matters. The first was Law 313, June 26, 1975, of the Public School Act, stipulating obligatory integrated sex education in the public schools, as will be discussed later in this chapter.

The second concerns the Social Welfare Act, which decentralized the administration of health services. According to Act 282, paragraph 11, enacted April 1, 1976, each county is responsible for providing access to counselling in contraceptive methods to persons under the age of eighteen. This counselling is provided free of charge either from their general practitioner or the county contraceptive counselling clinics, without parental consent.

County Contraceptive Counselling Clinics

To help implement this Act, the Ministry of the Interior prepared guidelines for the organization, personnel criteria, and responsibilities of the counselling clinics, which are maintained under the auspices of the counties' Health and Social Welfare administration. The guidelines do not state how counselling should be provided, but state that each clinic must employ a physician knowledgeable in contraceptive counselling, preferably a gynecologist/obstetrician (Circular, 1976).

By the end of 1979, there were 35 clinics throughout the country. In twelve of these clinics counselling was supplemented by the free distribution of contraceptive devices under limited circumstances. Three clinics provide free contraception to clients below the age of eighteen, while others distribute contraception to all clients during the first visit. In general, the principle of providing contraception free of charge depends upon the age, education and social situation of the client. However, a pre-requisite for utilizing the offer of free contraception is adequate information about its existence. The level and type of public information varies greatly from county to county. The county of Copenhagen, for example, has advertised its clinic facilities in the press, although usually without mentioning that contraceptive devices are free of charge.

Two of the counties with the most extensive clinic systems published brochures in 1978. The cover of these brochures stated that 'contraceptive devices are free of charge (at the clinics) if you are under the age of 18'. Copies were distributed to schools and other institutions in the counties.

Table 1 provides information on the number, rate, and percentage breakdown of clients visiting county clinics in 1979, by age and sex.

Compared to the total number of clients, those in the youngest age groups (under 20) constitute only 28% of the female and 4% of the male clients.

A comparison of counselling clinic clients and general practitioner clients shows that most had consulted the general practitioner; only 5% of the total had visited the counselling clinics in 1978. Of these, however, the majority of the clients were minors who had not previously consulted their general practitioners. The majority of the counselling clinic clients are women between the age of 16-29 years.

Many counselling clinics have been closed in the past few years, but at least one clinic in each county remains open. The clinics were considered too expensive to maintain in relation to the limited use being made of them. Furthermore, the desired decentralization of the hospital sector would necessitate that general practitioners take the task of counselling upon themselves.

Similarly, distribution of contraceptive devices free of charge to minors has been discontinued in many clinics, due to financial cutbacks and to 'too little demand'.

In a study (Paludan, 1985), interviews with 14-15 year old pupils indicate little awareness of the existence of counselling clinics in their county. Some girls stated that to 'appease' their boyfriends they made clinic appointments, which they then did not keep. The very few who had visited the clinic described it as cold and impersonal, and most preferred consultation with their general practitioner.

Table 1. **Clients visiting country clinics, Denmark, 1979,**

| Age | Percentages | | Rate per 1 000 | |
	Females	Males	Females	Males
14-15	5.4	2.0	18	0
16-19	22.7	2.0	41	0
20-24	26.2	13.3	38	0
25-29	20.4	5.8	30	0
30-34	13.8	18.0	18	0
35-39	7.1	8.6	11	0
40-44	3.0	20.7	6	0
45-49	1.2	29.4	2	1
Total	26 597	255	21	0

Source: Knudsen, Board of Health, Medical Statistics, 1980.

Contraceptive Knowledge and Practice

Youth are in a favourable position to learn about contraceptive practices because the Danish health services provide free contraceptive counselling through general practitioners or through counselling clinics. Access to counselling and contraception could assist them in being able to make independent, responsible choices. But there may be psychological barriers to responsible contraceptive behavior.   Several studies among school youth in Denmark have suggested that lack of knowledge of how to obtain and use contraceptives only plays a minor role in explaining why these in fact are not utilized effectively.

In one study (Bernsted et al., 1978) regarding youth and contraceptive knowledge and practice, it was found that 75 percent of both boys and girls had knowledge of at least 4 methods of contraception, but lacked knowledge regarding anatomic and physiological factors, such as conception and ovulation, which are preconditions for utilizing contraceptive methods with responsibility.

In a study of abortion-seeking teenagers (Wittrup 1980) it was concluded that the technical knowledge teenagers had regarding contraception was quite good, but that this, in and of itself, was not sufficient.   There are emotional factors which must be considered, and attitudes which must be acknowledged and dealt with, in order to prevent them from acting as barriers to actual contraceptive usage.

For example, in the Paludan (1985) study, teenage girls have stated that contraceptive devices such as a diaphragm or condoms 'could never' be carried along to a party because this would make it appear that she was 'looking for it'. It seems that acceptance of oneself as a sexual being is part of a maturing process in which youth strongly adhere to the social mores of their peer group. Those who 'go steady' may utilize safe contraceptive methods, such as pills, without as many social sanctions as those who do not have a steady partner. Being prepared for a sexual encounter, for example when going to a party, apparently removes the element of spontaneity which perhaps must indeed be present amongst those youth who have not fully matured and accepted the sexual aspects of their physical and emotional selves.

How then is it possible to prepare youth for a more adequate integration of sexuality as an aspect of their approaching maturity, so that this also includes responsible contraceptive practice?   Although sexual matters are most often discussed among peers, one study (Hessellund 1977) has indicated that teachers play a dominant role among school-age teenagers as a source of knowledge regarding sexuality. This was especially true for boys, whereas girls often named their mothers as an important source of both concrete knowledge and emotional support.

Sex Education in the Schools

The schools' role is important. In the 1960s, the Danish Parliament established a working committee to draw up new guidelines for sex education in the public school system. In 1970, Parliament passed a law for obligatory sex education in the schools, and the following year, guidelines were established for carrying this out (Circular, 1972).

On June 26, 1975, a new Public School Act was passed; paragraph 6 of this Act established sex education as an integrated subject. The school must provide information regarding genital anatomy, conception, contraception and venereal disease, but being an integrated part of the syllabus, this information is intended to be conveyed during the course of teaching in other subjects, and during the Home Room class. Integrated sex education is to begin no later than the third grade. Subsequently the school **may** offer more comprehensive teaching in the 6th or 7th grade, and again in the 9th grade. At this level, a more comprehensive subject coverage is voluntary for both teachers and pupils. On the one hand, integrated sex education permits questions regarding sexual matters to be dealt with as they arise, as a natural and integrated facet of class discussion. On the other hand, it becomes a difficult subject to administer and coordinate in the teaching syllabus. In reality, it is often left to individual teachers to determine the extent and content of their teaching on the subject.

The legislative goal of sex education is stated as an ideal: the purpose is for pupils "to acquire knowledge of sexual matters so as to learn to take responsibility for their own lives and to demonstrate consideration for others". But in practice a number of problems arise, some of which are institutional, some pedagogic, and still others psychological. In the final analysis many of the problems have an underlying political dimension because of differences within the adult population about what they want to include under sex education. Each county and each school principal, in fact, is left alone to administer the teaching and fulfill the requirements stipulated by the Act.

In the ongoing investigation mentioned previously, interviews with 8th and 9th grade teachers and pupils suggested several problem areas in sex education taught in school. Briefly, some of these were stated as: 1) the problem of establishing rapport between teachers and pupils, 2) the divergence of level of maturity and knowledge in the class, 3) lack of sufficient/appropriate teaching materials, 4) differences in attitudes and values about sex education among pupils' families and teachers.

What does teaching pupils 'to take responsibility for their lives and demonstrate consideration for others' imply? Is it a technical matter concerning contraception and venereal disease, or is it also a matter of discussing attitudes and emotions?

Some of these questions have in part been answered by the interviewed 8th and 9th grade pupils in their heartfelt wishes for more 'emotional' discussions. In the earlier grades, they claimed, they had learned enough about technical aspects of sexuality; now they expressed a need for discussion and support regarding the radical changes in their bodies and emotional lives. As some stated, 'Right now we're in puberty - now it's relevant and important to talk about our problems growing up'.

The Danish history of social consciousness and openness provides many opportunities for its young citizens to make responsible decisions as they mature. Some of the barriers to implementing the knowledge they may receive, to utilizing the comprehensive health care available, may lie in the fact that they are at an age where reason and responsibility are at times overshadowed by the task of grappling with the changes in their own beings. The institutional framework, which demonstrates a willingness to provide for the needs of the young, is one thing; the pedagogic and psychological barriers are quite another. Sex education and counselling must take these factors into account if they are to fully reach the country's youth.

References

Bernsted, L., et at. :   **School youth and contraception: Knowledge, attitudes, practice,** Copenhagen 1978.
Circular regarding rules for sex education in the public schools, Ministry of Education. Copenhagen. June 1972.
Circular regarding rules for contraceptive counselling clinics, Ministry of the Interior, 1976.
Hesselund, Hans: **Socio-sexual experiences of school youth.** Ålborg, 1977.
Knudsen, L.:   **County contraceptive counselling clinics,** Board of Health, Medical Statistics, 1980.
Paludan, Lisbeth Shore: **'Sex education among youth'.** Institute for Social Medicine, Copenhagen 1985.
Wittrup, G.:   How could 29 unwanted pregnancies have been prevented? **Folkeskolen,** 1980.

6

THE FAMILY PLANNING RIGHTS OF MINORS IN FRANCE*

Béatrice Koeppel

Introduction

Before describing the law in France relative to minors as it concerns contraception and abortion, it seems opportune to set forth the main lines of the legislation which regulates the child-parent relationship.

If one looks at the provisions of the "Code civil" relating to minors one sees that in France children are subject to the authority of their two parents up to the age of 18, unless they have been emancipated by a judicial decision or by marriage.

It was not always so. In the first place it was only in 1974 that the age of civil majority was lowered from 21 to 18. The code of 1810, reflecting the influence of Roman law, subjected the child up to the age of civil majority to the authority of the father. The law of 1970 embodied the development of custom and jurisprudence in substituting for the idea of paternal rights that of parental rights, and the new article of the "Code civil" precisely defines these rights: "authority appertaining to father and mother in order to protect the safety of the child, his physical and moral health".

----

*I wish to thank Madame Henriette Girault, jurist at the Centre de Vaucresson, whose advice on legislative and judicial matters was very important in the preparation of this chapter. The author alone, however, is responsible for the present formulation of the material.

The second paragraph of the same article adds to the idea of rights that of duties: "in regard to him they have the rights and duties of guardianship, supervision and education".

The need to protect children from parental abuse and to prevent their exploitation in employment has been recognised for a long time. Since the nineteenth century the law has operated in this way.

Since 1935, to the provision of sanctions against abuse have been added provisions to protect the child, and then in 1958 provisions to help parents who are unable to fulfil their parental obligations. Under the present law, parents who abuse their powers, who do not fulfil their obligations or have difficulty in doing so, may be deprived of their parental rights or may receive help. There may be a declaration that the child has been abandoned and an intervention by a judge of the children's court and the local services. (The minor himself may ask for the intervention of the court or the preventive services.)

Children have then, from birth, a right to moral and physical welfare and education.

In addition to these general rights, other particular rights are recognized during the adolescent years. When he or she reaches 16 years of age, a minor can have a bank account, receive a salary, be a member of a labour union (unless his/her parents object) and his/her private life is protected by acknowledging the confidentiality of his/her correspondence.

An adolescent has the right to give an opinion when important decisions are made concerning his or her future. For example, since 1976, a child of 13 or older cannot be adopted without his consent; the children's court has an obligation to hear the child before arriving at a decision. In contrast it is possible but not obligatory for the divorce judge to hear the minor before deciding which parent should have custody of the child and what the visiting arrangements should be for the non-custodial parent. In this type of conflict between parents, the courts are tending increasingly to consider the preferences of adolescents.

These new tendencies are a recognition that adolescents are developing toward adult independence, but they seem quite modest to those who demand recognition of more definite and more extensive rights: for example, to choose where one lives, to choose one's life style, to leave home, and to have an active sexual life. In effect, a minor must live with his parents or with the parent having legal custody. A person who has sheltered a runaway can be prosecuted and punished even though no sexual relationship has occurred. Parents have, in principle, the power to put the minor into a profession or occupation and to decide on his religion. But a number of administrative rules in the area of schooling and health care very seriously limit the freedom of parents in their choices and their authority is also limited by the social context.

The law normally reflects the state of society. One should not be surprised that in the area of minors' rights-- and especially the rights of adolescents--there should appear the same types of contradictions that are found among alternative ways of life in a period of profound social change.

On the other hand, youngsters acquire freedom of action earlier than did preceding generations, but they remain financially dependent on their parents longer: school is compulsory until the age of 16 and vocational training demands several more years of study. Parents are often still fulfilling their financial obligations long after their children have reached the age of majority.

On the other hand, recognition as an adult, and the independence that goes with it, are still the result of motherhood for women, or, for both men and women, a result of marriage and of the exercise of a profession. There are no rights without responsibilities.

To give adolescents rights implies also giving them responsibilities and duties, but in today's society one might well wonder how they could fulfill such responsibilities and duties.

It is in this context--of contradictions among changing moral values, a new judicial orientation, and traditional family relations--that laws about contraception and the right to abortion exist. These laws may be seen as challenges to parents' responsibilities to look after their children: only recently has it been accepted that minors may have sexual relationships without being married and that they can have access to methods of birth control. These new laws have been passed, however, in order no longer to punish private sexual relationships and in order to avoid the abandonment or relinquishment of children born to mothers so young that they cannot take care of their children.

These new laws imply a recognition of the sexual emancipation of adolescents, but they are not yet integrated into family life or the social context as a whole. We will thus look further at three areas:

1.   Minors' access to contraception as influenced by French laws and morals.
2.   The right to abortion.
3.   The contradictions and conflicts that result from these legal innovations.

Access to Contraception

Until 1967 there was in France no possibility for minors to obtain contraceptives. In July of 1966 the annual congress of l'Union Nationale des Associations Familiales (U.N.A.F.), although declaring itself in favour of better dissemination of information about family planning and education in the areas of sexuality and morals, nevertheless recommended that providing contraceptives to adolescents under 18 years of age should be prohibited. In the same year, la Confédération Nationale des Associations Familiales, concerned that many girls between the ages of 14 and 18 were becoming pregnant, discussed at length the role parents should play in the moral education of their children. The confederation felt that families should prepare children for marriage and for their parental roles by instilling in them respect for love and for the value of personal relationships. The confederation worried that, although parents are responsible for family life education, they may lack vision, authority, and a responsible attitude. But, though urging parents to provide better sexual education for their children in the framework of preparing them for marriage, the confederation did not recommend that adolescents be given information on contraceptive matters. In 1966 the French were still generally opposed to the use of contraceptives by minors.

In spite of this social climate, the Parliament in December 1967 passed the Neuwirth Law[1] which made contraception legal for all women, including minors. That contraception was legal, however, did not mean it was easy to obtain contraceptives. They had to be prescribed by a physician and dispensed by a pharmacist, and neither physicians nor pharmacists respected the privacy of minors. Those whose parents forbade them to use contraceptives were effectively prevented from obtaining them.

A number of organizations, e.g. le Planning Familial and le Conseil Supérieur de l'Information Sexuelle, were opposed to such restrictions on minors. They set up clinics where doctors would prescribe the pill without requiring parental approval. Still, minors faced problems when their parents disapproved: they might have difficulty paying the physician's bill or receiving social security reimbursement for the prescription. Moreover, a conflict over contraception could be grounds for the parents to turn custody of their daughter over to the Juvenile Court.

Sex education in the schools began in 1973 as a result of a governmental decision. Courses in human reproduction are given in the fifth and sixth levels; some teachers include instruction about contraceptive methods in the courses. The fact that l'Education Nationale deals with this subject has made parents more at ease in discussing birth control with their children. They have tended to look at birth control as a technique everyone should know about and they have begun to teach their adolescent children about sexual matters in the same way that they are instructed in history and geography.

In 1972 a campaign to legalize abortion was begun by le Mouvement Francais pour le Planning Familial and le Mouvement de Libération de la Femme, which presented statistics on serious illnesses and deaths resulting from illegal abortions. Minors are heavily represented in these statistics, and professors of medicine and other academically trained people declared that parents made a serious mistake when they did not educate their children in the use of contraceptives.

In April 1972, birth control centres were established. They were sponsored by municipalities in order to give women information and advice for a nominal fee.

In 1974 the law on birth control was considerably changed.[2] Women gained the right to be reimbursed for contraception through the social welfare system. Minors, however, could receive birth control at no charge, and no longer needed parental consent. Birth control centres also had fewer legal constraints. But in spite of minors' having the right of privacy at birth control centres, and not being charged medical and laboratory fees, few took advantage of these arrangements at first. It was difficult for young girls to overrule the restrictions of their parents. Many wanted to begin taking the pill even before their first sexual encounter but they had never been to a physician without the knowledge of their parents. Since Wednesday afternoons are school holidays, le Planning Familial started an open house on Wednesdays at which young girls could talk freely about their sexuality, and gradually began to avail themselves of contraception also.

Parents are afraid of the unforeseen. Their anxiety is greatest when their daughters go on vacation alone. Some youngsters travel without their parents to foreign countries in order to learn a foreign language, others go to vacation resorts. Some parents give their daughters the pill prior to vacation in order to protect them, but many girls are pregnant when they come home. The dilemma for parents is either to refuse to give their daughters freedom and mobility or to give them the same freedom and access to education as boys have while encouraging them to use contraception to prevent an unwanted pregnancy or a traumatic abortion.

A study carried out by l'Institut Francaise d'Opinion Publique (IFOP) in 1980 on a sample of 1250 French men and women aged 18-50 years reported their opinions on the use of birth control by adolescents.[3] The following were seen as negative factors:

Contraception stimulates young people to have sexual experiences too early	38%
Contraception provokes a lack of morals	27%
Some birth control methods reduce sexual pleasure	22%
Contraception reduces the poetic element in the development of love for young people	20%
The pill changes the natural functioning of the body	20%
Birth control forces adolescents to act like adults	16%
The availability of contraception encourages women to have extra-marital experiences	20%
Birth control is a threat to the respect for life	10%

According to the same study, 27 per cent of the sample thought it would be "totally normal" for their minor daughter to wish to take the pill, 35 per cent thought it would be "somewhat normal," 16 per cent "somewhat abnormal," and 15 per cent "not at all normal." (Seven per cent did not answer this question.) That adolescents want to use the pill is recognized by almost two-thirds of the respondents. In regard to birth control, people are more tolerant the younger they are, and the more middle-class their environment. The most hostile are to be found especially among practicing Catholics.

These attitudes explain some of the problems of the family planning and family counselling centres. The choice to attend such a centre often results from very young couples' taking responsibility for each other, or from minors' having received a modern education, or from young girls' fear of discussing these matters at home.

In most cases the mother suggests that her daughter visit a physician, where questions can be discussed that are not open for discussion at home. The father does not often involve himself in these matters, but retains the right to set a curfew for the child and to give an opinion on his daughter's choice of partner. The ambivalence of the mother is evident in her wish both to prevent her daughter from engaging in sexual relations and in her desire to guard her daughter's health by authorizing the use of contraceptives. The physician is the link between the past and the future. He counsels both mother and daughter, and he can mediate in the family if a conflict arises.

Parents know that young people begin having sexual relations earlier and earlier. A national study of 5,000 high school pupils in 1980[4] showed that 20.6 per cent had their first sexual relationship between 15 and 16 and 15.6 per cent between 17 and 18. One boy out of ten and two girls out of ten used contraceptives; the rest relied on wishful thinking: "If I really do not want to have a child, I will not become pregnant."

The Right to Abortion

The movement to legalize contraception stems partly from parental fears about their young daughter's pregnancy. It was disturbing for parents to think that their own young daughter, still under their authority, might herself become a mother. In France, a young unmarried pregnant woman is a prime example of misfortune, of failure, of shame. Minors are aware that their pregnancy can meet with hostile reactions, indignation, and social ostracism. They might be forced to leave school, sometimes to leave their homes for single mothers centres. In the best of cases the girl is forced to marry her child's father or the infant is accepted as another sibling in the family.

Before 1975 many young girls went abroad with their mothers in order to have abortions, though only wealthy families could afford this expensive solution. Others tried to find secret abortions in France, which were also sometimes very expensive. Secret abortions caused deaths, illness (salpingitis), and serious bleedings. Those performing them were sometimes incompetent people who did it for money. Fearing their parents' reaction, minors tried to hide their pregnancy and when they could conceal it no longer had to choose between a very dangerous abortion and keeping a baby neither they nor their parents wanted.

Gradually a political movement was mobilized in order to repeal the law of 1920 and demand the legalization of abortion. The law forbade abortions for all women, including adolescents, unless the mother's life was in danger. But contraception had not decreased the number of illegal abortions and homes for single mothers were still filled by young women rejected by society. Both abortion and the birth of a baby could mean that a minor's good relations with her family were at an end. The parents often quarrel. Sometimes the mother or a close relative feels sorry for the girl and consoles her, sometimes the parents accuse themselves of incompetence. Until she is 16, a minor is looked upon as a child receiving food, housing, and clothes from her parents. When a child gives birth to a child it seems to be "unnatural." The girl is dependent on her parents; on whom should her child be dependent? Should it perhaps be regarded as a half-brother or half-sister in her family, a child taken care of by the whole family where the grandparents at the same time are both parents to their daughter and non-biological parents to their grandchild?

Some private associations and militant organizations (e.g., le Groupe d'Information Santé and le Mouvement

pour la Libération de l'Avortement et de la Contraception) started performing illegal abortions in 1972. Only
minors who had the assistance of liberal parents were able
to gain access to these abortions. Finally, in 1975[5], a
liberalisation law was adopted for a trial period of five
years. This law permitted abortion but only on specific
grounds: the woman had to be in an emergency situation
and the abortion had to be carried out prior to the tenth
week of gestation. An unmarried minor, in addition, must
have the permission of someone having parental authority
over her.

Even this law did not solve all problems. Some young
girls informed their parents at the last moment, immedia-
tely prior to the tenth week; they were still so young that
their periods were normally irregular, or they lacked
information, or they simply did not believe they could be
pregnant. It was not easy to admit that they had had a
sexual relationship. When a young woman requests an
abortion late in her pregnancy, she runs the risk of being
refused because there is not enough time to complete the
preliminary requirements. How is it possible for her to
return to a harmonious family life after such an experience? The pregnancy is perceived, by the young woman
and by the family, as a double fiasco. In such difficult
situations, the Children's Court can become involved and
place the minor in a home for unmarried mothers.

The atmosphere, as in all periods of crisis, can be
almost impossible for those involved. The parents must
suddenly confront many things at the same time: their
daughter's sexual relationship, the announcement of a
possible birth, the knowledge of her secret activities, and
her brutal change of status. The girl is hindered in her
wish for independence, she is forced to abide by the
decision of her parents, and she has, in a traumatic way,
to accept questions concerning her intimate life: Does she
want to have this child? Why has she not used contraception? How long has she had a sexual relationship?

Minors are sometimes tormented by these questions and
by the abortion process. Abortion in France involves
formalities and hurdles for minors. The permission of one
of her parents is compulsory. When this permission is
received, the minor will be forced by the specialist to
wait: the law demands two visits with one week between
them. The reason for this waiting period is to give the

woman time to reflect on the abortion. During this period she is informed about the medical risks[6] of the procedure and about the rights of unmarried mothers. For minors this can be a time of great conflict and confusion. Finally, before the abortion can be performed, the minor must give her consent, and she must do so without the presence of her parents.

The cost of an abortion is still very high and is not reimbursed by social welfare or the insurance system. This can increase a young girl's feeling of guilt toward her parents. Abortions are also difficult because everything happens in a hurry. Private clinics are overloaded and turn down many requests. Many hospitals are not able to perform abortions; the head physicians have the right to refuse abortions at their hospital. Physicians in France also use the clause of conscience: a physician is never forced to carry out an abortion, though he must inform the patient of his refusal at her first visit.

In 1980 the abortion law that had been on trial for five years became a French law. Still, women have had to pay very dearly for their lack of information about birth control. They have suffered through the difficult administrative procedures for obtaining an abortion, and this has been especially harsh for minors who do not find acceptance and understanding of their situation. A 1980 study[4] shows that in France only 15 per cent of sexually active young people have received information about contraceptives. An information campaign has recently been launched by the government, and announcements are posted at schools and in other places frequented by young people publicizing family planning and abortion services.

Too many minors, in seeking an abortion, have lost weeks through misinformation and bureaucratic delays: "I went to a physician, who asked me to go to a certain hospital. There I saw a gynecologist and a psychologist for a short while and they gave me one week for reflection. Then I was called and told that an abortion was impossible because of a lack of space."[7]

It is easy to imagine the confusion of a minor who, after having decided with her family that she will have an abortion, is not allowed an abortion. Confusion is rife for the minor and her family as they alternately fear the abortion and then fear the unwanted birth. Anger and depression are common and family harmony is difficult to maintain.

Le Planning Familial (MFPF) and some unions (including the union of judges) have demanded that parental permission should not be necessary for a minor to have an abortion. MFPF believes that everything should occur in the same place: medical examinations, financial assistance, and processing of the application. Interviews should be supportive and aimed at reducing feelings of guilt. Some family planning clinics provide social support to minors who have applied for abortions by placing them in groups to discuss their motivations and to exchange ideas. Minors have increasingly made use of the services of clinics that can certify the need for a legal abortion with a minimum of bureaucratic red tape.

When a minor is living in a conflict-laden environment, the Children's Court can intervene to prevent potential danger of abuse for her baby. Homes for unmarried mothers more and more accept young mothers who have failed in their attempts to gain abortions. Most of these come from disadvantaged social classes. Their lack of money delays their pursuit of abortion and their difficult living conditions can lead to a lack of communication between parents and daughters. Sometimes, too, having a child at an early age allows such girls to escape from the control of the parents, who may be exploiting them.

Birth Control and Abortion for Minors:
Contradictions and Conflicts

The first contradiction is that the minor, in order to obtain an abortion, must ask for the permission of her parents, who possibly did not know that she was sexually active. Minors can obtain contraceptives from family planning clinics and their privacy will be respected, but if they become pregnant the parents learn about the private lives of their daughters.

Another contradiction is that, although giving birth makes a minor an adult, the decision to give up her child makes her a minor once again. But whatever decision an unmarried minor makes--whether to keep her child or give it up for adoption--she is exercising parental authority. And this authority too is paradoxical. For example, she can decide to put her child in a hospital and give permission for its care, but she cannot do this for herself. She would have to have permission in order to have an abortion, but not in order to give birth to a child or to relinquish it for adoption.

Family conflicts can arise from the strong feelings that individuals in French society have about such issues as motherhood and abortion. On the one hand, motherhood is equated with adulthood and responsibility; on the other hand, the pregnant adolescent has acted irresponsibly and may become even more dependent upon her family, especially her mother.

Abortion is not well accepted, and the pregnant girl and her parents may have different ideas about whether an abortion is advisable. Under such circumstances there may be considerable pressure upon the "deviant" daughter to follow the wishes of her parents. The daughter may want to bear and keep the child, only to be persuaded by her parents to have an abortion. Or the parents may refuse to give consent for their daughter's abortion. In the latter case, if she is determined to have an abortion, she may do so through covert action. She would have to be placed under the guardianship of the Children's Court for two days and the expenses would have to be borne by the local administration. Such duplicity, of course, can heighten family tensions.

Outside agencies are playing a larger role in dealing with adolescent problems[8]. Many pregnant minors are seeking outside help, in some cases because they have been rejected by their parents. Educational institutions, social agencies, and the courts are thus being confronted with problems that stem from adolescent sexuality, contraception, pregnancy, and abortion.

Girls who are under the jurisdiction of the courts--including delinquent girls--are often abortion recidivists. Some, at the age of 17, have already had three abortions. They may wish for a child as a way of gaining adulthood, but they are also afraid of the problems a child would cause. Because these minor girls have so few resources, judges and social workers advise them to have abortions.

Parents in France are very anxious about the health of their minor children. They look upon the physical integrity of the child as extremely important. As a result, they may prolong their protective attitude toward minors. Every person who is not a member of the family may be seen as posing a potential physical or moral threat to the minor. Both early childbirth and abortion are viewed as dangers to the minor's health; abortion is also an affront to the value placed on motherhood. These attitudes make it difficult for parents to accept their daughter's sexuality or her use of contraceptives. However, especially after an abortion, they may come to accept contraception as the lesser evil. The law certainly reflects a preference for contraception: after an abortion a woman must be informed about contraception.

Conclusion

Only recently has much attention been paid to the sexuality of minors. Many parents, themselves poorly educated in matters of sexuality and birth control, have been relieved that outside agencies have increasingly taken on more responsibility for the sexual education of their children. Parents are disturbed by studies showing that the first sexual experience occurs, on average, during the 17th year[9] and that one out of three abortions is performed on a minor. Apprehensive about changing morals, they have often preferred to have only limited knowledge about their minor children's sexual activities. An unwanted pregnancy and a potential abortion, however, is a signal of alarm that shatters the family's equilibrium. The parents resume their rights and responsibilities and once again become directly involved in caring for their children's health and welfare.

Family autonomy has been breached by the development of resources for minors outside the family. Family planning and family education centres provide advice and guidance to minors and contribute to minors' independence. Without meaning to be, they are meddlers in the family. The sexual life of minors is no longer a matter solely for parents and children. Minors' recently gained rights to birth control and abortion have disturbed traditional family values and have had unexpected and largely unexplored effects upon families, and especially upon the relationship between parents and children.

Footnotes

1. Law No. 67-1176, December 28, 1967. Code de la Santé Publique, p. 832, Dalloz.

2. Law No. 74-1026, December 1974 (Article 3 and following). Code de la Santé Publique, p. 832, Dalloz.

3. IFOP opinion poll, Jan. 30-Feb. 6, 1980, for the magazine ELLE and FR3, March, 1980.

4. Carried out and published in 1980: "Dossiers de l'Etudiant", April, 1980. Quota sample was selected by age, grade level, sex, and place of residence.

5. Law No. 75-17, January 17, 1975. Code de la Santé Publique, p. 1, Dalloz.

6. Law No. 79-1204, December 31, 1979. Code de la Santé Publique, p. 53, Dalloz.

7. Interview cited in "Contraception, Avortement, Droit des Femmes", Editions Tierce, Paris, 1979, p. 94.

8. J.P. Rosenczveig, "Y'a de l'abus", in Justice (Syndicat de la Magistrature), special issue on minors, Oct.-Nov., 1980.

9. "La première expérience sexuelle des Francais". Sample survey of 1,000 individuals over age 18 carried out and published by la SOFRES, 1980.

THE FAMILY PLANNING RIGHTS OF MINORS IN HUNGARY

Péter Józan

Introduction

Hungarian law defines the age of majority as eighteen; those who are younger are considered minors, if they are not married. Adolescence, the important period between childhood and adulthood, is defined in Hungary as lasting from fourteen to eighteen years of age. Of course this periodization is arbitrary, since no physical, mental, or social measurements will correspond exactly to these ages and mark the turning points of these three stages in life. Nevertheless using calendar years to classify the different stages in life is not without foundation. Human experience shows that around fourteen and eighteen years the accumulated changes in the developing human being mark not only quantitative but also qualitative differences among a child in the early teens, an adolescent, and a young adult in the late teens. The " family planning rights of minors" is neither an accurate nor a felicitous phrase in the Hungarian context. All people under eighteen are minors if they are not married and only a few of them are interested in planning the number and spacing of their children. The "birth control rights of adolescents" is a more apt phrase to describe minors' legal status in this field.

The Demography of Adolescents[1]

In a country with a 1983 population of 10.7 million, there are 2.2 million children (ages 0-13) and 553,000 adolescents (ages 14-17), 20.6 percent and 5.2 percent, respectively, of the total population. Among adolescents, the proportion currently married is 1.2 percent. There are a negligible number of married adolescent males; married females represent 2.5 percent of the adolescent female population. (In comparison, the relative number of married people is 51.6 percent in the total population and 83.7 percent in the 35-39 age group, where it is highest.)

In 1981 there were 1.4 marriages per 1,000 non-married 16- to 17-year-old males and 32.4 marriages per 1,000 non-married 14- to 17-year-old females. In the male population the net marriage rate was 69.0 per thousand, in the female 101.8 per thousand. Marriage is most frequent among males aged 25-29 and females aged 20-24; in comparison to these groups the rates for adolescents are very small.

Naturally, the frequency of marriage is insignificant among 14- to 15-year-old females. Marriage is much more frequent among 16- to 17-year-old females, who, if they marry, are generally already pregnant. The net marriage rate in the 14-15 age group increased until recently. It grew steeply in the 16-17 age group between 1970 and 1975, but has been decreasing since then (see Table 1). It

Table 1

Marriages per 1,000 Non-married Adolescent Females

Age	1970	1975	1980	1981
14	0.4	0.8	1.1	0.8
15	4.2	5.3	5.8	5.8
16	28.5	54.3	51.0	47.2
17	64.8	102.8	89.2	84.6
14-17	23.1	40.9	34.7	32.4
20-24	280.0	267.3	241.7	238.4
Total	107.5	124.2	106.1	101.8

is worth mentioning that the decline in marriages among the 16-17 age group has followed changes in adults' attitudes toward marriage with about a five-year time lag.

The data on the use of oral contraceptives have to be handled cautiously since their reliability is questionable. However, it can be said that since its introduction the pill has been adopted most widely in the age group under 20, and in 1981 about 38 percent of females between the ages of 17 and 19 protected themselves against pregnancy with this kind of contraception. This rate is about six times as high as it was in the early seventies. It is not known how many minors use the pill, but it is quite plausible that the upward trend in oral contraceptive consumption is present for them also.

The abortion rate changes erratically among minors and no clear-cut trend can be seen in the use of this means of birth control (see Table 2).

Table 2
Abortion Rate per 1,000 Females

Age	1971	1975	1980	1981
14	0	0	0	0
15	4	6	7	7
16	15	15	12	17
17	34	25	31	29
20-29	120	51	42	41
15-49	69	36	31	31

Table 3
Live Births Per 1,000 Females

Age of Mother	1970	1975	1980	1981
14	2.0	2.9	3.7	2.6
15	5.0	9.3	9.9	9.1
16	13.1	24.6	28.9	26.1
17	37.7	56.0	60.1	56.2
20-29	135.6	160.4	127.2	125.2
15-49	56.6	72.8	57.6	55.7

Age-specific fertility rates increased remarkably until recently among adolescent females. Nevertheless in 1981 they began to decline (see Table 3) and it is highly probable that they will continue to do so. Age-specific fertility rates in the 14-17 age group are naturally rather low in comparison to the fertility rates in the 20-29 age group and to the general fertility rate (Table 3). Yet marital fertility is extremely high among adolescents (Table 4)--good evidence that teenage marriages are in a sense forced ones.

The Rights of Minors in General

There is no law on the family planning rights of minors per se. Yet over the last three decades an elaborate system of laws and orders has been developed which regulates, on the one hand, the rights of the minors and, on the other, family planning in general. If the law does not order otherwise, what is valid for the adult population regarding family planning is valid also for minors. The particular position of minors has been taken into consideration in drafting the laws and orders; it is assumed that minors need extra protection since their means to defend themselves are less efficient than are those of adults.

One of the main reasons for changes in the rights of minors is that a new relationship between child and parent has been developed. In other words, the legal status of minors has changed within the family. The traditional

Table 4
Live Births per 1,000 Married Females

Age of Mother	1970	1975	1980	1981
14*	-	-	-	-
15	600	833	598	706
16	403	491	472	479
17	408	469	432	415
20-29	175	212	161	159
15-49	76	97	74	71

*Note. The rate cannot be defined realistically because of the small number in the denominator.

paternal authority has ceased to exist legally and has been replaced by parental care. The state has broader powers to intervene in family life in the interest of the child. Last but not least, discrimination against children born out of wedlock no longer exists. In every respect they have the same rights as those born in marriages. The meaning of the new legal relationship between parent and child is that parental rights can be exercised only in the interest of the minor, whose welfare (physical, mental, and moral) is a general obligation of his parents.

The law on marriage, family, and guardianship,[2] as it stands now, was enacted by the National Assembly in 1974. This basic law regulates by and large all the relevant issues regarding family life. Particular detailed issues are addressed by legal decisions at several levels of government: the Presidential Council, the Council of Ministers, and Ministers of portfolios.

Since minors are either legally incapable or have only limited capacity, their rights are correspondingly restricted. Take, for example, the right to marry. A man may marry at 18, a woman at 16 years of age. In exceptional cases, and after consultation with the parents or legal representatives of a minor, the State Authority on Guardianship may permit a man of 16 or a woman of 14 to marry.

It is the right of the parents to decide a child's place of residence up to his sixteenth birthday. After that, a child may leave the parents' home with the permission of the State Authority on Guardianship even without his parents' consent, if this serves his interests. If a child wants to live abroad permanently, the consent of his parents must be ratified by the State Authority on Guardianship.

In the case of preparation for career or profession, it is necessary to know the opinion of the child. Taking into consideration all the relevant factors, among them the child's opinion, the parents choose a suitable career or profession. If there is no agreement, the State Authority on Guardianship decides the issue. At sixteen years of age, a minor may be an employee or a member of a cooperative without his parents' consent. A child who is fourteen years old may use his earnings in his own right.

Minors cannot enter into contracts and cannot take legally binding oaths. In general, minors cannot get driving licenses although in exceptional cases those who are 17 years old may if they pass a thorough physical and psychological examination.

The interests and health of children are also protected by rules in the Code of Labour. During the school year, a fourteen-year-old may be employed only if he has already finished primary school. During the summer this restriction is lifted, though a minor may not be employed in heavy, physical work. In general, minors cannot work for more than one month, since they must have at least four weeks rest during the summer. Persons under sixteen may be employed for the first time only with parental consent. Any contract made without such consent is null and void. The minister of health defines dangerous and extremely heavy jobs in which minors must not be employed. A factory medical officer also has the right to temporarily forbid the employment of a minor in any job that he considers harmful. Before being employed a minor must have a thorough medical examination, the results of which determine whether he may be employed. Yearly medical examinations are compulsory for minor employees.

Since accidents are disproportionately frequent among adolescents because of their inexperience and sometimes careless behaviour, education on the prevention of factory accidents is compulsory, and protective measures are applied in workshops that employ minors. Minors may not work the night-shift, between 10:00 p.m. and 6:00 a.m., and those under sixteen may not work overtime.

For healthy development, adolescents need more vacation than adults. In addition to their basic leave, those under sixteen have twelve days' leave and those under eighteen, six days' leave. It often occurs that an employed minor finishes his secondary education in an evening school or participates in some form of open school. In order to ensure that he finishes his studies, his employer is obligated to give the minor as much as one hour a day extra leave to allow him to get to school on time. Furthermore those minors who work before they have finished school are given extra leave in order to study for their exams.

Family Planning Rights of Minors

Before the pill was introduced in the late 1960s, "family planning" per se was unknown in Hungary. At the present, it is a household phrase. In 1966 the first knowledge-attitude-practice study was conducted. In 1977 this type of study was repeated within the framework of the World Fertility Survey. In other studies the fertility, family planning, and birth control behaviour of marriage cohorts have been followed through the first 12 years of marriage, to the end of the normal fertility history. In addition, women have been asked about the impact of family planning measures on their lives in the context of population policy. Another source of knowledge is abortion statistics covering all pregnancy terminations since the mid-1950s.

In fact, family planning was practiced in most social strata even before the term was translated into Hungarian. The usual methods were coitus interruptus, the condom, the diaphragm, spermicides, and very rarely the rhythm method. If an unwanted pregnancy occurred an induced abortion was performed by either a physician or a midwife, although strictly speaking it was illegal. According to some estimates, 100,000 to 150,000 induced abortions were performed yearly in the beginning of the 1950s.

Between 1953 and 1956 very strict anti-abortion laws were in force. A pregnancy might be terminated legally only in the case of rape, incest, or grave danger to the woman's health.

In 1956 a permissive abortion system was introduced when the Minister of Health ordered that abortions might be performed up to the 12th week of pregnancy in cases of health risk or social indication. Because of a lack of effective contraception, the abortion rate increased year by year, until in the 1960s there were more abortions per thousand women of propagative age than there were live births. By the early 1980s, however, more than 80 percent of married women of propagative age practice family planning. (There are no reliable data on the family planning of unmarried women, much less on that of minors.)

In 1973 the Council of Ministers' Decision on the Tasks of Population Policy introduced measures to ensure the simple replacement of the population. It was thought then that a higher fertility rate could be reached by providing different types of incentives. At the same time, the decision explicitly recognized the utmost importance of family planning. It is generally accepted that population policy and social policy are strongly interrelated. Therefore, an elaborate system of financial, health, and other measures has been developed to help couples in family planning and in raising children.

The family planning rights of minors are as follows:

Oral contraceptives may be prescribed for those who are at least sixteen years old. (It is believed to be undesirable to encourage the use of the pill among those under sixteen years old, since the pill contains hormones which may have an impact on the development of the neuroendocrine system.) Until she is eighteen years old, however, a young woman must have a medical examination before obtaining the prescription.[3] The doctor advises her about the effects of the pill and its possible side effects, and each woman taking it must be registered. The usual practice is to prescribe a six-month supply in advance, but no more than a two-month supply will be issued at any one time in pharmacies.

An IUD may be fitted only by an authorized specialist in a recognized health institution.[4] It is the method recommended for women (regardless of age) who have already been pregnant, and for other women for whom pregnancy is undesirable because of ill health or the risk of complications. In other circumstances, an IUD may not be given to a minor.

Before inserting an IUD, the physician must fill out a record of gynaecological treatment, on which the patient must certify that she has been informed of the possible side-effects of the IUD. The Directive calls for a schedule of follow-ups. The patient should be given a control examination after the first menses following the insertion of the IUD; after this, the control examinations must be carried out each six months.

Traditional contraceptives may be bought in pharmacies, and condoms in vending machines; there are no restrictions on their purchase by minors.

In 1973, the Council of Ministers' Decision on the Tasks of Population Policy and the Minister of Health's Order on Judging Applications for Termination of Pregnancy[5] revised the system of induced abortions in order to decrease harmful effects on the health of women. As a consequence of this revision and later modifications, permission to terminate an unwanted pregnancy is automatically granted in any of the following circumstances:

a.   the abortion is justified for medical reasons;
b.   the woman is unmarried or lives separately permanently;
c.   pregnancy is the result of a criminal act;
d.   neither the pregnant woman nor her husband has a rented flat or apartment in a condominium or house;
e.   the pregnant woman is at least 35 years old.

In the following cases, permission for an abortion must be given by a three-member committee headed by a physician:

a.   the woman has two living children, and the infant to be born would be at risk;
b.   the husband is a conscript or in special service in the armed forces;
c.   the woman or her husband is imprisoned;
d.   the abortion is strongly justified by social factors.

An induced abortion may be performed through the 12th week of pregnancy.

If the pregnancy termination is requested by a minor, her legal representative must be consulted. The Committee's permission is a substitute for the consent of the legal representative. If a minor does not want to terminate her pregnancy, against the will of her legal representative, she may either not attend the committee hearing nor keep her appointment at the hospital. Although these possibilities for the minor are not explicitly noted in the regulations, in practice her decision is accepted. An abortion may be performed for a minor until the 18th week of pregnancy.

The Council of Ministers' Decision stated that biological, health, ethical, and moral knowledge are necessary for establishing harmonious, desirable human relations and a well-balanced family life, but that modern family planning is not sufficiently wide-spread, especially among young people. Therefore, in all forms of public education, measures should be taken to prepare people for family life, and lectures should be presented for people no longer in school. Since September 1974, family life and sexual education have been incorporated into the curricula of all institutions of education, beginning in the primary schools.

When persons apply to be married, they must go to a physician who gives them advice on the protection of the family and women, and they must take part in a family planning consultation. If necessary, the proper method of contraception is taught to them and they are provided with contraceptives in a way prescribed by law. The registrar is obliged to refuse permission to marry to persons who do not present written certification that they have taken part in this compulsory consultation. Since 1974, couples who are marrying for the first time and who are under 35 years of age participate in family planning counselling before marriage.

Family planning advice is provided to the whole interested population at counselling institutions throughout Hungary. Counselling specialists staff a network of these institutions in county centres, in cities and towns, and in factories having medical offices.

Minors are obliged to participate in family planning education in order to learn its methods and to be aware of their rights.

Footnotes

1. If it is not otherwise stated, all demographic figures are data from the Hungarian Central Statistical Office.
2. A családjogi törvény (Law of the family) Közgazdasági és Jogi Könyvkiadó, Budapest, 1982, p. 542.
3. Directive No. 13/1974. Eü.K.13.
4. Directive No. 22/1973. Eü.K.17.
5. 4/1973/XII.1./Eü.M.E.K.special number.

8
FAMILY PLANNING SERVICES IN IRELAND WITH PARTICULAR REFERENCE TO MINORS

Kathleen O'Higgins

This description of family planning services in Ireland will set out the historical background to current attitudes and values, present relevant demographic data, describe present laws concerned with family planning and abortion, plus the services provided, and give some data on the rights of minors generally, together with their family planning rights specifically.

Historical Background

First the historical background. I make no claim of comprehensiveness but will attempt to describe the historical context of the attitudes and values held by people in Ireland today, with some account of the country's social and cultural character.

In looking at the historical background one must go back to the early 19th century. People in Ireland at that time generally married whom they pleased, and early marriage with large families was the norm. This situation was aided by the prolific potato, the staple diet of the population: one did not need much land to grow sufficient potatoes to feed a family. Rising corn prices allowed the tenant farmer to till a smaller and smaller part of his land for rent, since a given rent could be earned on less land. Holdings for sons were carved from the parents' farm without lowering the previously accepted standard of living and more holdings meant more and earlier marriages, more and larger families. Only a minority of young people went abroad to Britain or America or even to Irish towns at that time.

The subdivisions of farms with a rapid growth in population through early, haphazard, and happy-go-lucky marriages was, however, a dangerous practice. By the 1830s many holdings were so reduced and the land so exhausted that, with a run of bad seasons, the seriousness of the situation was brought home to the peasant farmer. Almost half of the Irish rural population of 1841 had holdings of less than 10 acres. The division of holdings was curtailed and a stream of emigration started. The Great Famine of 1845 to 1847 was probably the key factor in changing the system of inheritance[1] and thus the rate of marriage. As Connell (1968, p. 116) said, the Famine "dramatised the risks of improvident marriage and halted the division of land that had made these marriages possible".

It is this link between marriage and personal living standards, of which people in Ireland and elsewhere became increasingly aware in the 19th century, that Kennedy (1973) believes to be the crucial variable in the onset of high levels of permanent celibacy and late marrriage age. The subordination of the gratification of the sex urge and desire to have children to the desire to maintain or to achieve a certain minimum standard of living and social status is also found in Arensberg and Kimball's (1968, p. 225) classic study of family and community in Ireland in the 1930s. They comment, "instances of families of brothers and sisters who stuck together celibate until old age, are more often examples of the force of failure to find a mate of acceptable status than of any other cause". And Humphreys (1966, p. 243), writing about urban young people in Dublin in the 1950s, says, "considerations of social advancement on the part of both boys and girls effectively and increasingly operate, according to the testimony of the New Dubliners, to delay marriage on all levels except among the poorer labourers".

But why should people subordinate their desire for marriage and children to economic and social status? Kennedy (1973) would say that to answer this question requires a knowledge of the links between the family as a social institution and the economy. The fragmentation of agricultural holdings before the Great Famine gave way to the stem family system in which only one could inherit. Kennedy describes the consequences thus:

Regardless of the variations of the stem family system, the demographic consequences were essentially the same. The custom of only two children per family being permitted to marry locally under stable agricultural conditions (the one who inherited the land and the one who married the neighbour's heir) resulted in some siblings who never married and hence never became part of the legitimate childbearing population. These persons did not marry because they could not support a family at the same level of living which they shared as a member of a landholding family. If they left the family farm and married without the means of supporting a family they became landless labourers and were constantly downwardly mobile. In more general terms, we can say that the stem family system resulted in a willingness to place economic considerations over desires for universal marriage and childbearing and in a tolerance of never married adults in all age groups with no implication of individual sexual deviance (p. 152).

Also, to keep the holding at an acceptable level to support the heir and his relatives, the bride had to bring enough land with her to support herself and any offspring. The arranged marriage thus became commonplace in Ireland. "This unaccustomed scarcity of land (after the 1845-1848 Famine) is, I think, the most powerful of the forces which tended, in succeeding decades, to disseminate the 'arranged marriage'," says Connell (1955-56, p. 89).

Kennedy argues that "in Ireland after the 1870s, as in several other European countries, there was an increased awareness of the association between marital status and one's own personal standard of living. The motivation to postpone marriage and remain permanently single in Ireland was especially intense, however, because the gap between desired and actual standard of living probably was greater in Ireland than in any other European country" (p. 209). Ireland was, and continues to be, one of the economically least developed countries in northwestern Europe, yet the aspirations of the Irish were and are focused on standards in England and the United States, two of the most highly industrialised nations in the world. Remaining unmarried in Ireland had long been considered an alternative to emigration; as the rate of emigration declined after the 1880s, the rate of celibacy rose.

I have been concentrating on rural residents for the most part, but what of urban residents? Four out of five people in Ireland lived on the land in the 19th century. Ireland was not a rapidly industrialising country; indeed, its urban population declined between 1851 and 1891. This meant fewer urban jobs and consequently less upward social mobility. Religious discrimination against Catholic workers, the overwhelming majority of the workforce, by non-Catholic managers and employers, exacerbated their difficulties in earning a decent living, so they remained single or postponed marriage.

The argument has been put forward that the position of the Catholic Church and the great reverence shown to priests and nuns contribute to the high rates of postponed marriage and permanent celibacy in Ireland.   O'Brien (1954, p. 224) says, "Another factor tending to deepen and extend the wholesale practice of celibacy in Ireland is the enormous reverence for the priesthood and the religious life which obtains among the Irish. It is without parallel anywhere on earth ... With veneration for the religious life comes unwittingly but inevitably veneration for the celibate state with which the religious life in the Catholic West is always associated."

Kennedy (1973, p. 145), however, argues that the special character of present-day Irish Catholicism is the result, and not the cause, of the high proportion of single people in the population. He points out that the Church encouraged early marriage, and the sexual puritanism for which Irish Catholicism is known today is actually a very strong emphasis on the dangers of sex among unmarried persons. "Single persons," says Kennedy, "accepted the puritanism of their clergy because it helped them avoid emotional involvements which might lead to marriage" (p. 146). He quotes Inglis (1965, p. 202): "The temptations that years of celibacy imposed on (the unmarried Irish) could obviously only be resisted with the help of a powerful moral code; priests felt it necessary to push sexual licence to the head of the ordinary sins against which they preached; and also to seek in every possible way to remove the occasion of sin, such as mixed gatherings for dancing or other relaxations, which elsewhere would have been thought innocent enough."

There is, therefore, an association between the devotion of the Irish to Catholicism and their stern attitudes to pre-marital sex. As Kennedy has pointed out, the importance given to sins against chastity by the priests, and the special relationship existing between priests and people in Ireland, no doubt acted as strong deterrents to behaviour that might lead to the conception of children outside marriage.

The rate of illegitimacy in Ireland has always been low relative to other countries, even though marriage was late by international standards. The low rate of illegitimacy cannot be attributed to an innately weak sexual drive, or to widespread sterility, contraception, or abortion. Contraception and abortion, as will be seen, were rare in Ireland and when people did marry they had large families. The low rate of illegitimacy is probably partly attributable to the shamefulness attached to pregnancy outside marriage which has been a feature of Irish society for centuries. "Pregnancy outside marriage was a shameful matter to the girl and her family," says Connell (1968, p. 62). "(It) promised a wretched future for the child and herself..." Begging and prostitution were the only means of support open to mothers of illegitimate children. The source of the harshness of Irish attitudes towards illegitimacy are difficult to trace, since such harsh attitudes are not a typical feature of peasant societies and neither illegitimacy nor having an illegitimate child was an impediment to marriage in most peasant societies.

In spite of the wretched future facing an unmarried pregnant girl in Ireland in the early 19th century, Connell (1968, p 63) says there is little evidence of the practice of abortion: "... critics of the Irish were too many and too insistent for all to have been dissuaded by literary convention from exposing what, had they the evidence, they and their readers would have thought utterly reprehensible."

This then is the historical background to the attitudes and behaviour of the Irish today, 95 per cent of whom are Roman Catholics. Even though traditional standards, and more particularly old taboos, are crumbling faster than we are building up a modern ethic to replace them, a substantial number of people in Ireland retain their orthodox attitudes and values, and present legislation is based on the more orthodox viewpoint.

Recent Demographic and Attitudinal Data

Kennedy has noted that even in the 1960s "the extreme degree of postponed marriage in Ireland is perhaps that nation's most widely known contemporary demographic characteristic. While the Irish willingness to remain single receives the best publicity, at least in English speaking countries, Ireland actually is the most extreme example of a general European pattern." Since Kennedy wrote, however, some dramatic changes have occurred. Walsh (1980) points out that during the 1960s and early 1970s Ireland rapidly lost many of the demographic characteristics that had set it apart from its neighbours, and experienced a marriage boom sufficient to render obsolete the old pattern of high levels of permanent celibacy and extremely late age at marriage. This sharp rise in Irish nuptiality may not be permanent: the crude rate of 7.4 per thousand registered in 1971, 1972, and 1973 fell to 6.1 in 1977. The fall may be connected to the deteriorating economic climate, though other factors such as cohabitation have been mentioned as contributing causes. The hearsay evidence suggests a growing number of couples cohabiting, but it seems to be still a relatively small number.

Although the marriage rate may increase and consequently the incidence of permanent celibacy decrease, no great change would appear to be occurring in the attitudes of a large number of people toward pre-marital sex. A survey of moral values of Catholics in the Republic of Ireland carried out by the Research and Development Unit of the Catholic Press and Information Office (Nic Giolla Phadraig, 1977) found that pre-marital sex was regarded as "always wrong" by 71 per cent of a national random sample of the Irish adult population from the electoral registers in 1973-74. Eleven per cent considered pre-marital sex as "generally wrong" and 9 per cent considered it "right". Eight per cent were ambivalent. Almost half of those viewing pre-marital sex as "always wrong" and more than one in four thinking it "generally wrong" gave as their reason that it is "against the law of God/the Church". One in three respondents believed that the use of contraceptives, even within marriage, is "always wrong" and a similar proportion saw it as "generally wrong". Over half of those who viewed "using contraceptives" as right (about one-third of the total sample) were of this opinion only in the context of family planning for married people.

Two studies of attitudes toward contraception carried out in recent years by Hibernia Review/Irish Marketing Surveys, Ltd., found a change between 1971 and 1974. In the 1971 study, males were proportionately more in favour of the legalisation of the sale of contraceptives than were females (39 per cent of males in favour, 29 per cent of females in favour). In the 1974 study, the percentages overall in favour had risen and, since the female proportion had risen much more than the male, the percentages were very close (55 per cent of males in favour, 52 per cent of females in favour). Social class was found to have a linear relationship to attitudes towards legalisation of contraceptives, with higher social classes expressing more favourable attitudes. All social classes, however, showed extensive moves in a pro-legalisation direction and, as might be expected, the younger the person the more liberal his/her attitude. Seventy per cent of 16-24 year olds and 74 per cent of 25-34 year olds were in favour, while 43 per cent of 45-54 year olds were in favour and, of those over 55, only 30 per cent.

Another 1974 study carried out in Ireland was that of Wilson-Davis (1974), who used a national stratified sample of 754 Irish women aged 15-44. His findings were similar to those of the Hibernia study: older women were more conservative than younger women regarding the availability of contraceptives, and favoured their being restricted to married couples on prescription or on medical grounds only.

On the question of abortion, which is illegal in Ireland under the Offences Against the Person Act of 1861, over 95 per cent of those interviewed in the Catholic Press and Information Office study regarded having an abortion as wrong - 74 per cent as "always wrong". Only one per cent of respondents saw abortion as generally right. As we see elsewhere in this chapter, however, the rates of Irish women going to the United Kingdom for abortions are rising.

Family Planning

A short review of some of the main events leading up to the present law, which legalised family planning services and contraceptives, may be useful. This law was published in 1978, passed in 1979, and went into effect in 1980.[2]

In 1935 the Criminal Law Amendment Act forbade the importation, display, or offering for sale of contraceptives and also their importation for personal use. There was no notable objection to the passing of this law.

Between 1962 and 1965 the steroidal pill developed by Rock and his colleagues appeared on the market. The importation of this pill as a contraceptive would have been illegal. It was therefore prescribed and legally sold on the Irish market as a therapy for irregular cycles, but not as a contraceptive.

In 1967, the Minister for Justice introduced the Censorship of Publications Amendment Act. This released on the market most publications advocating or giving information on contraception methods which had previously been banned by the Censorship Board as "indecent" or "obscene".

In 1969, the Fertility Guidance Company Limited opened its first clinic. Only verbal advice on contraception was given. The pill was prescribed as a "regulariser", but clients had to import other items prescribed for themselves.

In 1971 the Fertility Guidance Company opened a second clinic. A bill for the legalisation of contraception was introduced into the Senate (the Upper House) but was refused a first reading. In the same year a private citizen, Mrs. Mary McGee, sued the Attorney General and the Revenue Commissioners for the confiscation of some spermicidal jelly which she had attempted to import. This case failed and was appealed to the Supreme Court.

In 1972 an identically worded bill to that introduced in the Senate in 1971 was introduced in the Dail (Lower House) but was refused a first reading.

In 1973 a second Member's Bill received a second reading in the Senate, but was defeated the following year. Mrs. McGee won her case in the Supreme Court; the decision made the importation of contraceptives for personal use legal. The first vasectomy performed in a clinic was performed at one of the Fertility Guidance Clinics, the company now renamed The Irish Family Planning Association Limited (IFPA). After the Supreme Court decision the IFPA was able to import contraceptives, diaphragms, and creams and distribute them to clients who were asked to make a donation towards the cost.

In March 1974 the Government introduced its own bill to legalise contraceptives, but it was defeated because the Prime Minister and six of his deputies voted against it. The IFPA was charged under the 1935 Criminal Law Amendment Act with the promotion of unnatural methods of contraception. The charges were later dismissed.

In 1975 the Minister for Health financed the expenses of nurses and doctors attending seminars on contraception given by the IFPA.

In 1976 the Censorship Board banned the IFPA booklet Family Planning. A year later the High Court declared the banning "null and void".

In 1978 the Minister for Health published the Family Planning (Health) Bill, later the Health (Family Planning) Act 1979. It was the first family planning legislation to be passed in Ireland and makes provision for family planning services and for the availability, importation, manufacture, sale, and advertisement of contraceptives.[2]

A family planning service is defined in the Act as a service for the provision of information, instruction, advice, or consultation in relation to one or more of the following: (a) family planning; (b) contraception; (c) contraceptives. A family planning service as defined does not include within its functions the provision or supply of contraceptives. The Act imposes a duty on the Minister for Health to secure the orderly organisation of family planning services and to provide a comprehensive natural family planning service, that is, one that is concerned with methods of family planning that do not involve the use of contraceptives.

A Health Board is bound by the Act to make available a "Family Planning Service", but a Health Board need make available only a natural family planning service. A Health Board itself does not have to provide the service; it may make such a service available by way of an arrangement with another person or body. A family planning service established by a person other than a Health Board and which gives advice or instruction about contraceptives can only operate with the consent of the Minister for Health and must operate under the "general direction and supervision" of a doctor. A natural family planning service, however, can operate without obtaining such consent. Moreover, there is a statutory obligation imposed on a Health Board or any other person providing a service that gives advice as to the use of contraceptives also to give advice about methods of family planning that do not involve the use of contraceptives. The Act does not, however, prevent a doctor "in his clinical relations with a patient" or a chemist selling contraceptives from giving advice as to their use.

The Act defines a contraceptive as "any appliance, instrument, drug, preparation, or thing, designed, prepared or intended to prevent pregnancy resulting from sexual intercourse between human beings." Under Section 4 of the Act, contraceptives can be supplied only by way of sale, and the only person authorised to sell contraceptives to the general public is a chemist "who keeps open shop for the compounding and dispensing of medical prescriptions in accordance with the provisions of the Pharmacy Acts 1875 to 1977" or his servant or agent. The sale must be made "at the place where he keeps open shop" or in connection with the service provided by the chemist "in keeping such open shop at a place where family planning services are made available."[2]

The sale of contraceptives is restricted to the person named in a doctor's written prescription or authorisation, and prior to issuing any such prescription or authorisation a doctor must be satisfied that the person seeking it requires contraceptives "for the purpose **bona fide**, of family planning, or for adequate medical reasons and in appropriate circumstances." Where a prescription indicates that contraceptives are to be given for the purposes of the Act, the section states "it shall be conclusively presumed" that the person named in it is the person who, in the opinion of the doctor, required contraceptives for the purpose or reasons stated in the Act. A prescription or authorisation can be issued for any period up to one year, but its validity cannot extend beyond one year. Section 4 also permits a licensed importer or manufacturer to sell contraceptives to a chemist, his servant, or agent.[2]

Under Section 5 of the Act a person may import contraceptives if "they are part of his personal luggage accompanying him when he is entering the State, and if their quantity is not such as to indicate they are not solely for his own use". The Act lays down no test for determining whether contraceptives imported are solely for a person's own use. The section also provides for the granting of licenses for the importation of contraceptives by chemists or by persons for sale to chemists. The Act does not permit a person to import contraceptives by post for his own use. Section 6 of the Act provides for the granting of licenses for the manufacture of contraceptives by chemists or by other persons for sale to chemists.

Advertisements concerning contraception or contraceptives may be published or displayed only in relation to family planning services authorized under the Act; in the case of a family planning service provided by a person other than a Health Board, the publication or display must accord with any consent given by the Minister to operate a family planning service that provides information about the use of contraceptives. An advertisement relating to contraception or contraceptives can also be published for the purposes of providing information for:

(i)   Persons providing family planning services in accordance with the Act;
(ii)   Registered medical practitioners;
(iii)   Registered pharmaceutical chemists and registered dispensing chemists and druggists;
(iv)   Persons registered in the Register of Nurses;
(v)   Persons who are in training with a view to becoming members of any of the classes of persons specified in (ii) or (iv).

Publication of advertisements may also be arranged by or on behalf of the Minister for Health.

Section 12 (3) of the Act removes the powers conferred on the Censorship Board by the Censorship of Publications Act, 1946, to ban a book or a periodical publication on the ground that it advocates the unnatural prevention of conception. A book may now be banned only if the Board is of the opinion that it is indecent or obscene or it advocates abortion.

Shatter (1981, p. 109) comments:

The act does not confine the availability of contraceptives to married persons as has been suggested by some commentators. It is clear that any person, single or married, may import contraceptives for his own use in his luggage under the provisions of Section 5 of the Act. It is also clear that a doctor may give a prescription for contraceptives to a single person, if he is satisfied that the contraceptives are required for that purpose, bona fide, of family planning or for adequate medical reasons and in appropriate circumstances. Moreover, it appears that if such a prescription is issued it is not open to a chemist to challenge the doctor's conclusions. A chemist may, however, require proof of identity from the person tendering the prescription.

Doubt must exist as to the constitutional validity of the provisions of the Act concerned with the supply of contraceptives. In the context of married couples it is arguable that the Act is an invasion of the constitutional right to marital privacy first enunciated in the McGee case. It is worth noting that it again renders it unlawful for a spouse to import contraceptives by post for his or her own use.

The decision of the Supreme Court (in the McGee v. The Attorney General case) that it was the constitutional right of Mrs. McGee to import contraceptives by post for her own use, was thus overturned by this Act. The new Act made it unlawful for people to import contraceptives by post, since the family planning clinics were now authorised to supply them on prescription. Shatter (1981) argues that a married couple, wishing to obtain contraceptives without going through their doctor and possibly having to discuss their private sexual relations in order to obtain a prescription, would have good grounds for arguing that the Act is unconstitutional. It could be asserted, he says, that the Act "constitutes an invasion of the right to marital privacy and that it fails to protect, defend, or vindicate the constitutional right of the married couple to determine how many children they wish to have without outside interference" (p. 109).

Abortion

Abortion is prohibited under Section 58 and 59 of the Offences Against the Person Act, 1861. These sections prohibit administering or supplying drugs or instruments to procure abortion. A person involved is guilty of a felony, the maximum penalty being penal servitude for life. Since no legal abortions are available in the State, other than those regarded as therapeutic (and there is no evidence of abuse of this), women seeking abortions have their pregnancies terminated in the United Kingdom, to which there is easy access. Numbers available on abortions obtained by Irish women refer to those having abortions in England and Wales, under the 1967 Abortion Act. These women incur no penalty when they return to Ireland. Numbers of abortions obtained are available only since 1969, during which time there has been a steep rise from 122 in 1969 to 3,700 in 1983. Approximately 15 per cent of Irish women seeking abortions in England and Wales in 1983 were minors but we have no way of knowing whether they obtained parental consent (Dean, 1984).

Walsh (1981) of the Medico-Social Research Board had analysed the then available figures. He summarised the situation thus:

"Irish terminations continue to rise in number, take place almost exclusively in private facilities, pre-dominantly among the single, exceed illegitimate births at all ages after 19 and are still sizeably below rates in England and Wales. Pregnancy termination is now a significant influence in Irish fertility and is the pre-ferred solution to pregnancy in the unmarried after age 19". (p.4)

Family Planning Services

A number of agencies deal with family planning ser-vices in Ireland. The first one we will consider provides a natural family planning service only (FPASNM)[3]. It is a service within the organization the Catholic Marriage Advisory Council (CMAC), which is primarily concerned with marriage and family relationships. It recognises the home as the bedrock of our civilisation, a school of deeper humanity where values and standards are fostered and where faith, hope and love can find their most noble and faithful expression.

The CMAC states its aims as to help people initiate, sustain, and enrich their marriage and family relation-ships. It offers an educational service, designed to help people:

(a) prepare for marriage
(b) mature in their relationships
(c) strengthen the bonds already made by newly married couples
(d) build the confidence of parents to aid them in their task
(e) plan their families, promote fertility awareness, and sometimes come to terms with their own infertility.

At present, the organisation has 47 branches with 1,700 volunteers-counsellors, doctors, nurses, lawyers, and priests. They have been carefully chosen and trained for the task to which they are committed.

The approximately 300 teachers of natural family planning have been selected because they have the motivation and qualities appropriate to help couples with this intimate aspect of their relationship. Each prospective teacher is trained in the methodology and psychology of family planning and in a counselling approach to couples who seek help. Training is given by tutors chosen from existing teachers and given further training to equip them for the role of tutor. There are 40 tutors at present in the service.

The FPASNM service includes discussion of fertility and family planning at pre-marriage courses, public information talks, seminars for concerned professional groups, and personal, confidential instruction and counselling in the natural family method of their choice for couples who seek help in respect to their family planning needs. All services are free.

In 1980, 18,381 people attended pre-marriage courses-approximately 9,000 couples out of 21,723 marriages. This represents more than 40 per cent of all couples marrying in 1980. In addition, 9,164 individuals sought personal instruction at the centres, twice as many as in 1975. The methods taught by CMAC are the temperature method, the cervical mucus method and the symptothermal method. The FPASNM does not offer advice or services to single people, except for engaged couples planning to marry.

The two main family planning agencies providing contraceptives as well as advice and information are the Irish Family Planning Association and Family Planning Service. The IFPA was set up for the purposes of education, advice, and supply of contraceptives, as well as instruction on natural methods, to anyone over 18 years of age. It operates under an annual licence from the Minister for Health. It cannot itself sell contraceptives but operates a franchise with a pharmacist. In order to do this, the IFPA had to overcome the attitude of the Irish Pharmaceutical Union, which gave strict instructions to members that it was "totally contrary to their policy for members to take up employment in family planning clinics" ("Planned Parenthood in Europe", 1981, p. 14).

The organisation's professed objective is to work for the provision of comprehensive family planning services in Ireland. To attain this objective, it provides clinic services and works in a political fashion to campaign for legislative change. It does not receive a State subsidy, although some State assistance is given to organisations promoting only natural family planning methods.

Family Planning Services is an organisation similar to the Irish Family Planning Association, but operating on a smaller scale. It also has an education and information service.

A number of other outlets for the sale of contraceptives circumvent the law. They are not licensed by the Minister for Health and so do not operate within the Health (Family Planning) Act. These agencies do not sell contraceptives as such, but request "donations" from their clients. They do not apply for licences in order to show their rejection of the legislation which they consider repressive. No legal action has been taken against them so far.[4]

The Position of Minors in Ireland

The law regards a person who has not attained the age of 21 years as a person of immature judgement who requires some protection. Such a person, an "infant" or "minor", is subject to a legal incapacity designed to shield and protect him from his own improvidence and from the actions of others. For the purposes of the Children's Acts, 1908 to 1957, a "child" is defined as a person under the age of 15 years and a "young person" as a person 15-17 years old. In Section 2 of the Guardianship of Infants Act, 1964, an "infant" is defined as a person under the age of 21 years.

Legislation in the last decade in Ireland has recognised that young persons mature earlier than hitherto and some of the restrictions on the legal capacity of minors have been removed. The 1964 Guardianship of Infants Act (Section 7 (7)) gave a person under the age of 21 the right to appoint a guardian by will, notwithstanding that the testamentary age was still 21. Since the Succession Act 1965 came into operation on 1 January 1967, the testamentary age is 18, but a valid will may be made by any person of sound disposing mind who is or has been married. Furthermore, Section 19 of the Marriages (I) Act 1844 (as substituted therein by Section 7 of the Marriages Act 1972) allows a widow or widower under the age of 21 to get married without parental or other consent. Section 7 of the 1972 Act came into operation on 1 January 1975.

For unmarried minors, however, statutory protections against the acts of others end at different ages. Thus, unlawful carnal knowledge of a female under 17 years of age is a statutory crime (Criminal Law Amendment Act, 1935). The prohibition against serving alcoholic liquor to a minor ends when the minor reaches the age of 18 (Intoxication Liquor (General) Act, 1924). Sixteen is the minimum age for marriage (Marriages Act, 1972); marriages of persons below 16 need permission of the President of the High Court. A person of 18 may vote (Electoral Amendment Act, 1973), make a will (Succession Act, 1965), and sit on a jury (Juries Act, 1976). There is no Act regarding the right to consent to surgical, medical, or dental treatment without parental consent, but in medical circles a person of 18 years is regarded as medically adult.

The basic legal principle relating to the contracts of minors is that they must be protected in their dealings with other persons. The concept of the emancipation of minors is unknown in Ireland because its legal system is derived from the Common Law. In those legal systems derived from Civil Law (Roman Law) emancipation exists in respect of persons who have not reached the age of majority. The origin of the idea of emancipation is the relief of the minor from parental power and control--a power and control greater in those systems of law that are based on the Civil Law than in those based on the Common Law.

With regard to family planning services, practices differ. The FPASNM provides services only to those minors who are about to marry or are married. The Irish Family Planning Association will not supply or fit contraceptives to unmarried persons under the age of 18 without the written consent of a parent or guardian. If a doctor feels that medical considerations warrant the supply of contraceptives to a minor and parental consent is not obtainable, the doctor will act in the best interests of his/her patient. When lay workers are in doubt about age of callers, they request them to sign forms stating that they are over 18.   About 12.5 per cent of the IFPA's clients were under 19 years in 1980, and another 35 per cent in the 20-24 age group.

Conclusion

The Irish made extreme use of postponed marriage and permanent celibacy, important elements of the Malthusian concept of moral restraint. The impetus was their fear of a repetition of the situation of the mid-19th century. Only in the 1960s did real change begin; the traditional value of permanent celibacy, or at least celibacy until marriage, has been retained to a large extent, particularly in rural areas. From this came the reluctance of politicians to introduce family planning legislation. When they did, it was of a nature regarded by the pro-contraception population as extremely restrictive.

The use of contraceptives presupposes sexual activity. With the moral climate that has prevailed in Ireland until recently, the free availability of contraceptives to adults would hardly be approved of by most people, and their availability to minors would be almost unthinkable.

The rising illegitimacy rate (the concept of illegitimacy is still retained in Ireland)[4], although still low in comparison to rates in other countries, and the startling increase in the numbers of Irish women having abortions in the United Kingdom, testify to a changing climate, despite the attitudes hitherto held by the majority. But the legalisation of abortion is still strongly opposed by a very large majority of the population, by those in favour of more liberal family planning legislation as well as by those opposed to it.

On September 7th, 1983 a Referendum was held to authorise a change in the wording of Article 40, Section 3 of the Constitution. This Section read:

The State guarantees in its laws to respect and, as far as practicable, by its laws to defend and vindicate the personal rights of the citizen.

The Referendum was held in response to pressure from a group calling themselves the Pro-Life Amendment Campaign. They had called for an amendment to the Constitution to specifically mention the rights of the unborn child. A heated debate had taken place between the pro and anti-amendment groups, the latter believing the amendment to be unnecessary since abortion is prohibited by law and protection of the unborn is implied by Article 40, Section 3. However, the Referendum was held and carried, and there is now an addition to Section 3 which reads:

The State acknowledges the right to life of the unborn and, with due regard to the equal right to life of the mother, guarantees in its laws to respect, and, as far as practicable, by its laws to defend and vindicate that right.

In summary, less restrictive laws than heretofore operate for minors in Ireland with regard to such rights as voting and jury service. No specific laws operate for minors in the family planning area. They are entitled to be prescribed contraceptives for the purpose, bona fide, of family planning. The natural family planning clinics will advise on their methods if minors are about to marry. Other clinics will supply contraceptives to minors over 18 years, and to those under 18 with parental consent. Abortion is not legal for any citizen.

Footnotes

1. Because no Catholic (the religion of the majority) could own land in Ireland until the present century, the "inheritance" of the family holding did not necessarily mean owning the land. For Catholics, all that could be inherited was the right to become the tenant farmer who worked a certain piece of land.

2. Although this Act is still the law under which the family planning services operate, an Amendement to it was enacted in March 1985. This Amendment affected a Section - the control and supply of contraceptives - and deals specifically with the expansion of outlets for the sale and supply of contraceptives from the confined outlets permitted by the 1979 Act. When the Amendment becomes law, a doctor may sell contraceptives where he ordinarily carries out his professionals duties. Contraceptives will be available for sale at (a) Health institutions, (b) where a person is the servant or agent of a family planning service under Section (3) of the Health (Family Planning) Act, 1979, and (c) at maternity hospitals or hospitals treating sexually transmitted

diseases. One other change the Amendment will make is that sheaths or spermicides may be sold to any person over the age of eighteen years without a doctor's prescription.

The Amendment will mean that people in rural areas will have greater access to contraceptives, particularly sheaths and spermicides. The implication that people be married before obtaining contraceptives has disappeared.

Although the Amendment has not yet become law, in practice the changes appear to be in operation already.

3. FPASNM is Family Planning Advisory Service Natural Methods.

4. This is no longer the case. These are now selling sheaths and spermicides and no action has been taken against them.

5. The Law Reform Commission published a report in 1982. The report's main recommendations are that the concept of illegitimacy be abolished; that all children born in or out of marriage, have equal succession rights to their parents' estates, and that natural fathers have equal guardianship rights with mothers to their children, regardless of marital status. No legal changes have taken place based upon this report, but the Government decided to make changes in the law relating to the status of children.

A Memorandum was prepared in May, 1985 by the Department of Justice and its purpose is to inform interested persons of the scope and nature of the main changes proposed. A Status of Children Bill to give effect to the changes has been prepared in the Attorney General's Office. The Memorandum states in its Introduction that the Government will be prepared to consider and take account, where appropriate, of any comments or observations that interested parties may wish to address to the Minister for Justice in regard to the matters covered by the proposals. (1985, p.3)

References

Arensberg, Conrad M., and Solon T. Kimball, 1968. **Family and Community in Ireland.** 2nd Edition, Cambridge, Mass.

Harvard University Press.

Connell, K. H, 1955. "Marriage in Ireland After the Famine: The Diffusion of the Match". **Journal of the Statistical and Social Inquiry Society of Ireland**, Vol. 19, pp. 82-103. 1968. "Catholicism and Marriage in the Century following the Famine". **Irish Peasant Society**, Oxford: Clarendon Press.

Dean, Geoffrey, 1984. Termination of Pregnancy, England 1983. **Women from the Republic of Ireland.** Dublin: The Medico-Social Research Board.

Hibernia Review/Irish Marketing Surveys, Ltd., 1974. "Contraception Poll", Dublin: Hibernia.

Humphreys, Alexander J., 1966. **New Dubliners.** London: Routledge and Kegan Paul.

Inglis, Brian, 1965. **The Story of Ireland.** 2nd Edition, London: Faber and Faber.

International Planned Parenthood Federation, 1981. "Planned Parenthood in Europe", 10: 13-15.

Ireland, Department of Justice, 1985. **The Status of Children.** Dublin: The Stationery Office.

Ireland, Department of Justice, 1985. **Eighth Amendment of the Constitution Act, 1983.** Dublin: The Stationery Office.

Kennedy, Robert E., Jr., 1973. **The Irish,** Berkeley: The University of California Press.

Nic Giolla Phadraig, Maire., 1977. "Report on Moral Values" from **Survey of Religious Practice, Attitudes and Beliefs Among Catholics in the Republic of Ireland.** Dublin: Catholic Press and Information Office.

O'Brian, John A., ed., 1954. **The Vanishing Irish.** London: W. H. Allen.

Shatter, Alan., 1981. **Family Law in the Republic of Ireland.** 2nd Edition. Dublin: Wolfhound Press.

Walsh, Brendan, 1980. "Recent Demographic Changes in the Republic of Ireland". **Population Trends,** 21: 4-9.

Walsh, Dermot, 1981. **Pregnancy Termination in England and Wales on Irish Residents.** 1979. Dublin: Medico-Social Research Board.

Wilson-Davis, K., 1975. "Some Results of an Irish Family Planning Survey." **Journal of Biosocial Science.** 7: 435-444.

9

THE RIGHTS OF MINORS, PLANNED PARENTHOOD, AND ABORTION IN ITALY*

Roberto Caterina

Despite a host of obstacles and restrictions, Italian legislation in the past decade has followed up on demands that arose in the late 1960s for a new relationship between the world of adults and the world of adolescents. It has moved beyond the traditional family model, in which authority resided with the father, to take account of the needs and rights of minors gradually to develop independent personalities. An idea that was important in these changes--for adults as well as adolescents--was the possibility of granting individuals greater control over their sexual and reproductive behaviour.

Legislative Changes

The salient features of this legislative process were: the abrogation in 1971 on the part of the Constitutional Court of that passage of the Italian Penal Code that punished the advertisement and "incitement to practices against procreation; "the establishment of 18, rather than 21, as the age of legal maturity (Law 39, 1975); the reform of legislation governing family relations (Law 151, 1975); the establishment of family consultation centers (Law 405, 1975); and the enactment of Law 194 (1978) for maternal welfare and voluntary termination of pregnancy,

----
*Translated from Italian by Ronald Strom.

which preceded the recent reform of the public health
service.

Before examining in detail the passages of these laws
that concern the relationship between adults and minors
in the framework of planned parenthood, it should be
stressed that the legislative situation before the 1970s
was still heavily influenced by institutions and norms that
pre-dated World War II. The Italian National Institute for
Motherhood and Infancy, founded in 1925, played a conservative role in dealing with family problems, until
replaced in 1975 by family consultation centers. The
Juvenile Court was not established until 1934, substantially later than other European countries. And the 1948
Constitution of the Republic of Italy, although open to a
more modern view of the rights of minors, actually made
little difference until the changes of the 1970s.

As Meucci observed (1974, p. 16), children were their
parents' property, a property right sanctioned by Article
315 of the Civil Code which, before the reform of family
law, read: "a child of any age whatsoever must honor and
respect his parents." The state acted, by way of Juvenile
Court or a responsible judge, only to repress a minor's
"deviant" behaviour or to settle specific administrative or
property matters. That an individual was considered fully
responsible before the law at the age of 18 (Art. 98 of the
Penal Code), was legally entitled to contract for his own
employment at 18 (Art. 3 of the Civil Code), could enter
the labor market before the age of 18 (as early as 15) with
the father's permission, and could marry almost at the
moment of pubertal development (age 16 for males and 14
for females, which for serious reasons could be reduced to
14 and 12, respectively, Art. 84 of the Civil Code), did not
accord well with the fact that his "ability to act on" and
enjoy his civil rights was not granted until the age of 21.

It is evident that these norms tended to forbid any
expression of sexuality beyond marriage. Indeed, as Meucci noted (1974, p. 27), the same girl or boy who was
authorized to marry before the age of 16 could not freely
enter into a sexual relationship without the partner being
guilty of corrupting a minor (Art. 530 of the Penal Code).
And the same boy or girl who had a paying job at the age
of 15 or 16 was not allowed to reside outside the family.
(Ossicini's work on runaway children is a classic text,
1963.)

Few spoke of planned parenthood and responsible pro-creation: abortion was a "crime against the integrity and health of the race." This is why the 1971 Constitutional Court decision permitting the advertisement of contra-ceptives was decisively important: It allowed the public advertisement of contraceptive practices, and it did not limit discussion and information to scientific circles but fostered broader diffusion through the mass media. It should be pointed out too that decisions by the Constitu-tional Court that grasped the contradictions between pre-vailing legislation and the spirit of the constitution have fostered the reform of family law as well as the law on voluntary abortion. (Cf. the decision of February 18, 1975, no. 27, which declared part of Article 546 of the Penal Code unconstitutional. That article provided for the punishment of consenting women who aborted in the passage that specifically did not envisage that pregnancy could be legally terminated, except in the case of serious danger to the physical or psychic health of the woman.)

The decision of 1971 and others in the early 1970s influenced public opinion in favor of minors' having proper information about their physical, and particularly, sexual life. It was in those years that the Ministry of Public Education authorized public schools to consider the "advi-sability of providing students with information on sex and sexuality" (Matstroianni, 1979, p. 13).

Changes were taking place, reflecting a need felt by vast sectors of the population. This became even clearer in 1974 when an attempt was made by conservative forces to repeal the law permitting divorce. The conservative position was defeated in a referendum; approximately 60 per cent of the voters supported the existing law.

The reform of family law, which followed soon after the law establishing 18 as the legal age of majority, embodies a view of the minor that is more respectful of his individuality. The modified version of Art. 147 of the Civil Code refers to taking account of "the capabilities, natural inclinations and aspirations of children" in their upbringing, rather than appealing to "principles of morali-ty," as the earlier version did.

Some portions of the revised Civil Code suggest that little has changed in a minor's obligation to accept the tutelage of the family: "The minor is domiciled in the family's place of residence or in that of the guardian"

(Art. 45, C.C.); "a child may not abandon the home of his parents or of the parent that exercises tutelage over him or the lodging they have assigned him" (Art. 318, C.C.). Other portions, however, are less restrictive: "In the case of dispute (between parents and children) on questions of particular importance," the judge is obliged to hear the child "if he is at least 14," and not just the parents, in order to suggest "the decisions he considers most helpful in the interest of the child and the family unit" (Art. 316, C.C.). And, in the event of disagreement that does not involve the child's preferences but the family situation in general, the judge may nevertheless ask the child's opinion "if he has reached the age of 16 and lives with the family" (Art. 145, C.C.). In general, minors who have reached the age of 14 or 16 are given greater responsibility in choices involving the family. Moreover, in the event of conflict, the judge's possibilities of taking action are better organized today than in the past, and his range of action is broader. In several cases it has been possible to provide the minor with a domicile outside the family.[1]

The modifications of articles governing marriage between minors are also important. An attempt has been made to separate the act of marriage from the physical maturity of the people who enter into it. Article 84 of the Civil Code now explicitly says: "Minors may not enter into a marriage contract;" only for "serious reasons," having established the "psycho-physical maturity of the parties," may the court allow "someone who has reached the age of 16" to marry. This appears to be more restrictive than the previous law, but it is only an appearance. The present law does not forbid the minor to have sexual experience, but demands greater responsibility when marriage is involved. In this regard, it is important that the phrase "serious reasons" is referred to the "psycho-physical maturity" of the person and not merely to the fact of pregnancy,[2] as was formerly the case.

Article 90 of the revised Civil Code is also better formulated. It provides for a "special guardian to assist the minor in stipulating the marriage covenant" in the event of conflict between the minor and his parents (or whoever has tutelage). The role of this guardian is different from that envisaged in the old formulation of Article 90, which put greater stress on parental consent.

The standard based on physical maturity and family consent has been replaced in new law by a tendency to foster responsible choice on the part of the minor. All of these observations are important for understanding the spirit behind the legislation that established family consultation centers and, for the first time in Italy, brought family planning into the realm of legislation.

Article 1 of Law 405 of July 29, 1975, the general law, establishes the activities of the consultation centers. The accent is on "responsible motherhood and fatherhood"; to this end centers provide "psychological and social assistence" and "appropriate information for promoting or preventing pregnancy." But they must also provide for "the means that are necessary to achieve what the couple or single party has freely chosen in the matter of responsible procreation," and Article 4 establishes that these means will be provided free of charge. Thus the function of family consultation centers is radically different from that of the Italian National Institute for Motherhood and Infancy, which was responsible only for the care of pregnant mothers and for providing information about contraception. Centers also offer psychological and social assistance and are not intended to be mere distributors of contraceptives.

The law mentions the "problems of minors," but does not make it clear whether a minor may benefit from a consultation center's services without parental authorization. The spirit of the law reflects both the innovations and the limitations of the new family law. Thus, where contraception is concerned, a restrictive interpretation is possible based on family law articles regulating the tutelage of the minor by both parents. But an interpretation based on the concept of responsible choice is equally possible; this would allow minors genuine freedom of choice and an assistance that went beyond the constraints imposed by tutelage (cf. Protetti, 1980, p. 43). Regional legislation varies in its interpretation of the general law. Some regions envisage close collaboration between the Juvenile Court and the consultation centers; others do not. Some regions tend to relegate the centers to a prophylactic role; others are more alert to the problems that family planning involves. For example, there are substantial differences between the law passed in Liguria (Law 26, 1976) and that passed in Basilicata (Law 7, 1977).

The former makes specific provision for "a medical and psychological examination and tests for establishing the appropriate contraceptive method for the interested party." The latter makes broad reference to the general law and then makes specific provision only for tests and examinations for mother and newborn child and for social and psychological assistance for women who wish to abort.

Many of the ambiguities in the law on consultation centers concerning minors' access to their services were clarified subsequently by Law 194, which regulates social care for motherhood and voluntary termination of pregnancy. The last paragraph of Article 2 of this law is quite explicit: "the distribution in health institutions and in the consultation centers of medically prescribed means necessary to achieve freely chosen aims concerning responsible procreation is also permitted for minors." It has been pointed out that this law still does not specify whether a minor is authorized to use a consultation center without parental permission, since Law 194 falls under Article 316 of the Civil Code (Protetti, 1980, p. 44). Nevertheless the aforementioned articles of the reformed family law limiting parental authority and the very spirit of Law 194 ought to tip the balance in favor of a more liberal interpretation, since the norms governing abortion envisage a certain independence of the minor from the legally responsible adult.

According to Article 12 of Law 194, a minor may be authorized to abort even though the request is not backed up by the consent of her parents. Moreover, the same reasons are applicable to a minor as to an adult woman who chooses to abort (fairly broad if the voluntary termination of pregnancy takes place within the first 90 days and much more restrictive after that time).[3] "When there are serious reasons that prevent or discourage consulting the people legally responsible or acting as guardians," it is the judge who gives the minor the required authorization (Art. 12) and in the event of "serious danger to the health of the minor" no consent is required but only a medical certification, as in the case of an adult woman. There is the same parity of law for an adult woman and a minor in the event of voluntary termination of pregnancy after 90 days. Abortion is authorized (Art. 6) only if pregnancy and delivery would involve serious danger for the woman's life" or "when pathological processes have been proven, including those concerning substantial anomalies or malformations of the fetus, that would present serious danger to the physical or psychic health of the woman."

Law 194 does not preclude a woman's recourse to social and health agencies (hospitals and local health and welfare units envisaged by the reform of the health service) or to her family doctor, but it does entrust the problem of voluntary termination of pregnancy to family consultation centers and describes their functions in a way that does not conflict with the wishes of the woman, be she an adult or a minor. This emphasis, assuring maximum respect for the woman's wishes, is at the root of the social service offered by consultation centers. It should foster proceedings that help minors make responsible choices and evaluate in a mature fashion the problems involved in being responsible for one's own body.

Difficulties in Implementing the New Legislation: Contraception and Abortion

The application of Law 194 has been hampered by the very high number of doctors who are conscientious objectors to abortion, often for political or locally contigent reasons. (According to the Minister of Health's Report to Parliament (Relazione del Ministro della Sanità alle Camere, 1980, p. 47) 97 per cent of doctors in Basilicata were objectors, 92 per cent in Trentino, 88.5 per cent in Molise, and 79 per cent in Campania.) The family consultation centers face a myriad of problems, including training and preparation of personnel and the difficulties that often arise from relations with their clients. In addition, social, cultural, and geographic factors lead to enormous differences in the operating conditions of the various centers throughout Italy.

Information recently published by the Ministry of Health highlights this problem. "As of December 31, 1980 (five years after the law was passed), there were 1,029 public consultation centers, but only 130 were in southern Italy and the islands; as of September 30, 1981, there were 1,456 consultation centers, an increase of almost 50 per cent, of which 224 were in southern Italy and the islands; regional differences are enormous, ranging from 303 in Lombardy to 6 in Sicily and 10 in Sardinia" (Ministry of Health, Dati per l'azione donna, 1981). The

Ministry of Health also reports that the average age of clients (almost exclusively women) is between 25 and 35. Although the number of minor clients is increasing, it is still very low. This reflects the fact that Italy, along with Greece and Turkey, trails Europe in terms of the percentage of women who use contraceptives. In 1980 only 4.8 percent of Italian women made use of them.

Overall data concerning the activities of the consultation centers are still fragmentary, but some studies of clients have been made (UICEMP, 1981; Landucci Tosi, Spinelli, Baldini, and Perini, 1981). The data in these studies bear out the general findings of the Ministry of Health, especially the fact that "adolescents are not successfully reached by the consultation centers" (Landucci Tosi et al., 1981, p. 4) and that there is a clear predominance of clients with high-school or university education, especially between the ages of 21 and 25. The aforementioned study also reports that 47 per cent of the clients were referred to the consultation service by a friend, while school and parents were the primary source of information in only 2 per cent of the cases.

But where the consultation centers have been able to operate effectively they have contributed both to a decline in illegal abortion and to more careful choices, especially among minors, among contraceptive methods. Before the consultation centers were established, women between the ages of 16 and 20 rarely used the diaphragm, preferring coitus interruptus, condoms and, to a lesser degree, hormonal methods. Among clients of the consultation centers, 80 per cent in the same age group use the diaphragm or the pill (41 per cent and 39 per cent respectively), 10 per cent use IUDs, and small percentages use coitus interruptus (4 per cent) and the condom (6 per cent) (Landucci Tosi et al., p. 444). The work of the consultation centers in the area of contraception is not regulatory but arises from discussion with clients and is adapted to their different needs, depending on such matters as age and cultural background.

Data concerning voluntary termination of pregnancy, unlike those on contraception, are fairly complete for the years 1978, 1979, and 1980. Thus an objective examination can be made of the application of Law 194 in connection with requests made by minors.

The number of voluntary abortions (for all age groups)

as compared to the number of live births varies greatly among the regions of Italy.   In the first half of 1979, regions like Liguria and Emilia-Romagna registered very high abortion rates, 658.3 (per 1,000 births) and 644.7 respectively. In other areas, including Campania (102.3), Bolzano province (93.1), and Calabria (76.7), recourse to Law 194 was much more circumscribed. The differences among these regions were not reduced in 1980, although there was an overall increase in the number of abortions performed under the criteria of the law.   The substantial increases in the abortion rates in Campania (to 129.1), Bolzano province (to 156.9), and Calabria (to 134.7), was matched by surprising increases in Liguria (to 730.3) and Emilia-Romagna (to 834.1) (Minister of Health's Report to Parliament, 1980, pp. 46-47).

It is legitimate to read these data as favorable, as the Ministry of Health does, since an increase in the number of legal abortions implies a reduction in illegal abortions. But it is hard not to share the view that chiefly in the southern regions (and also in the Bolzano province) illegal abortion persists despite other variables, including "the greater readiness of southern women to accept unwanted pregnancies" (ibid., pp. 46-47).

It is harder to evaluate the data on minors. Here, too, regional differences are substantial. Suffice it to mention two regions with almost the same numbers of residents, Emilia-Romagna and Campania. In 1980 there were 1,565 voluntary abortions on minors in Emilia-Romagna, only 55 in Campania (where, however, the age of the woman was unknown in 73 per cent of the cases). The overall total for minors also rose gradually between 1978 and 1980, but the percentage of abortions performed on minors, as compared with other age groups, went down significantly between the second half of 1978 and 1979, from 4.1 per cent to 3.3 per cent, and then rose to 3.6 per cent in 1980. This decline chiefly involved central Italy (1978: 4.5 per cent; 1979: 2.9 per cent; 1980: 3.4 per cent) and southern Italy (1978: 2.5 per cent; 1979: 1.8 per cent; 1980: 1.9 per cent).   And there was a comparably significant percentage drop in those geographical areas for women who were not married, a group that includes a very high number of minors (central Italy, 1978: 34.1 per cent; 1979: 31.1 per cent; 1980: 30.2 per cent; southern Italy, 1978: 33.7 per cent; 1979: 18 per cent; 1980: 10.3 per cent, although marital status was unknown in 51 per cent of the cases). (The data were provided directly by the regions on behalf of the Ministry of Health.)*

It would be hard not to read these facts with some concern. Even allowing for the brevity of the period examined and for the lack of exhaustive information concerning the age and marital status of the parties, it would seem that minors and women living in the southern regions of the country, where illegal abortions are more frequent and consultation centers fewer, responded less confidently to the aims of Law 194. That the overall abortion rate is higher among minors than among other age groups (ibid., p. 48) is not sufficient in itself to justify optimistic evaluations. For one thing, the percentage of minors that abort is much lower in Italy than in other European and Western countries.

It is interesting to consider the data concerning the consent requirement for minors. Although still incomplete and present only for the northern and central regions, the data provide some useful information. A striking fact emerges from a comparison of Liguria, which has one of the highest voluntary abortion rates in Italy, and Lazio, where the rate is near the national average. In Liguria court consent for abortions went down from 52.8 per cent in 1978 to 11.9 per cent in 1980, while parental consent went up from 44.4 per cent to 77.6 per cent. The opposite happened in Lazio: Court consent went up from 13.3 per cent to 42.5 per cent, while parental consent went down from 75.5 per cent to 35.3 per cent. No attempt will be made to read these figures in terms of the different social and political climates in the two regions, but it does seem worthwhile to emphasize again that the situation in Italy is extremely heterogeneous and that different criteria of judgement are adopted in different geographical areas. Differences in requiring consent are also interesting. In 1979 and 1980, in the Veneto region, there were high percentages of cases (52.1 per cent in 1979, 52 per cent in 1980) in which consent was not required because of the

----

*The author wishes to thank S. Landucci Tosi, M. Grandolfo, and A. Spinelli for making these data and those on consent available before publication.

urgency of the matter. In other regions, except for Lazio in 1980 (20.5 per cent) and Trento in 1979 (20.6 per cent), the percentage of cases not requiring consent was very low and rarely above 10 per cent. Recourse to the judge on the part of minors, then, is far from the exception to the rule, as some have maintained (cf. Protetti, 1980, pp. 44-45). The judge plays an important role, although this role has often been interpreted differently in different regions and in individual cases.

Ministry of Justice reports for 1979 and 1980 include data on authorizations requested from the courts. In 1979, 1,207 were requested and 1,152 approved. Here too, the differences among geographical areas are more interesting than the total figures. The requests in Milan, for example, totaled 452 in 1979 and 516 in 1980, of which 440 and 509 were approved. But in Naples, with a population only slightly lower than that of Milan, there were only 18 requests in 1979 (two rejected) and 22 in 1980 (four rejected). This cannot be ascribed to any unusual local situation in Naples; the ratio of the number of requests made in northern Italy in 1980 to the number made in southern Italy and the islands is the same as that between Milan and Naples.

In Turin, the case was different; only 21 of 37 requests in 1980 were approved. This is not an isolated case, for there were other areas where only a small number of requests were made but the percentage of refusals was very high. In 1980, for example, two of four requests in Cesena were approved; in Catania, 16 of 20; in Siena three of five; in Rapallo, one of three, and in Naples, seven of nine. This results, however, not from differences among geographical areas, but from the different attitudes of individual judges. In recent years, there has been a substantial rupture within the magistracy, and judges now belong to organizations with differing political and social viewpoints.

Article 12 of Law 194 specifies that a judge may authorize an abortion for a minor when "serious reasons" make parental authorization unobtainable or requesting it inadvisable. In evaluating these "serious reasons", more than one conflict has arisen among various judges. The Minister of Justice's Report to Parliament for 1979 (pp. 7-8) and for 1980 (p. 11) show that judges have adopted three different standards. In most cases they have limited themselves to establishing the wishes of the minor to terminate pregnancy. In other cases judges have considered it worthwhile to evaluate young women's levels of maturity, occasionally trying to affect the "decision by trying to dissuade the minor from her intention to abort." In still other cases, they have taken the trouble of gathering medical evidence in order to establish whether "serious danger to the woman's physical and psychic health" existed often acting against the spirit of Article 12 which provides that, in the case of serious danger to a minor's health, a medical certificate is sufficient and supercedes the need for parental or judicial authorization. Many judges, however, have interpreted the minor's right to abort as broadly as possible (Minister of Justice's Report to Parliament, 1980, p. 11) in order to avoid the possibility of an illegal abortion if the request were to be denied.

A careful reading of Law 194 reveals that its central and innovative point is that the final decision about terminating pregnancy rests only with the woman, who should be given the support of the available social services. The question then arises whether a judge, in examining requests submitted by minors, should bear this fact in mind rather than acting as a parental substitute. Greater legislative clarity might be desirable, especially where minors are concerned, in order that the decision not be delegated to health service officers on to a judge. The foregoing data suggest that most judges take this line.

This is a positive sign and suggests that the fundamental problem is actually farther upstream, in the scarcity of public consultation services in vast areas of Italy, the lack of adequate information that still characterizes certain social classes, and the manifest bad faith that sometimes marks the conflict between public and private sector in the medical world. One cannot claim that the problem of illegal abortion, concentrated among the most alienated population of minors, has been resolved by Law 194. Neither, however, can one deny that a major legislative effort has been made, especially since 1975, and that, as a result, there is now much more respect in Italy for the personality and rights of minors.

Two Case Studies

It is important to remember that abortion is not an isolated problem. Often it is only the last manifestation of a long history of maladjustment in which all the other problems of adolescence have played a part. Let me conclude by describing two cases handled by the Juvenile Court in Rome.* They illustrate the complexity of the personal and family history involved, as well as the difficulties, encountered by workers in the field, that obstruct the application of Law 194.

The first case is that of Maria, a 17-year-old with a very troubled family history. Her parents abandoned her in infancy, and she grew up in a foster home believing her foster parents were her natural parents. In adolescence she suffered various disturbances and seemed mentally retarded, although the precise nature of her problems was not known. There were misunderstandings with the foster parents and increasingly serious crises. Finally, the foster parents could no longer tolerate the situation; when Maria was $16\frac{1}{2}$ years old, they told her they were not her real parents and sent her back to her natural father.

In the brief period she spent with her natural father, Maria ran away from home several times and was finally taken in by a religious institution run by nuns. Meanwhile the social service of Juvenile Court was trying to find a way of dealing with Maria's problems, in collaboration with the Mental Hygiene Center. The girl had several psychological problems, and had been raped during one of her flights from her father's home.

Although the religious institution was aware of the rape, it did not provide for a medical examination, when Maria was admitted. When, a few days later, the nuns realized the girl was pregnant and informed the social worker, Maria was almost three months pregnant. Given her situation, there were several reasons for seriously considering abortion and, at least in terms of the law, that was still possible. To this end, the social worker had two separate interviews with Maria and her father.

----

*These cases were handled by Miss Grazia Mineo, a social worker in the municipality of Rome, to whom I express my thanks for having made the material available.

The nuns had not told Maria that she was pregnant, on the grounds that "she wouldn't have understood anyway." The father gave his consent to the abortion. Since he could not keep his daughter with him, he looked on her pregnancy with concern. The conversation with Maria highlighted her extreme fragility and dependency on others. Despite what the nuns had said, she was fully aware of being pregnant. She imagined the delivery would be something monstrous and mutilating, a kind of electro-shock, an experience she would like to avoid if possible. She also consented to an abortion.

At this point the nuns gave the father an ultimatum: If he consented to the abortion, they would no longer look after his daughter.

Because he was unable and unwilling to look after Maria himself, the father gave in. Together with the nuns he persuaded Maria to have the baby. The delivery was extremely traumatic for Maria. She did not keep the baby, nor did she legally recognize him. He was turned over to an institution for adoption.

The second case is very different, at least in its outcome. Seventeen-year-old Anna had problems similar to those of Maria. She too was in conflict with her family, she had run away from home on several occasions, and had had experiences of every kind, including taking drugs and occasional prostitution. She was living in a boarding house for young women. The Juvenile Court's social service had seen Anna because of her conflicts with her family.

Anna got pregnant after a casual encounter and realized it at once. She made contact with the family consultation center through Juvenile Court, a contact facilitated by the fact that she had made an appointment with the center for contraceptives before she became pregnant. Anna discussed her problem with the social worker from Juvenile Court. She experienced pregnancy as something positive, feeling that she too could produce something good. But with a certain degree of awareness she decided to abort, because she had no job and nowhere to live. Moreover, it was a delicate moment in her relations with her family. They had recently been more accepting of her, and she feared that if they learned of her pregnancy they might reject her again.

After a gynaecological examination and an interview with the psychologist at the family consultation center,

Anna completed the formalities required by Article 12 of Law 194 and submitted them to the judge, who authorized an abortion in a hospital. There were no procedural complications in this case. All the steps were completed in a relatively short time (Law 194 had been in effect for only a few months). Anna made her decision in the course of a week, and the various appointments at the consultation center, the interview with the judge, and the hospitalization for the abortion took about 20 days.

There is no question but that the decision to abort must have been traumatic and must have aroused deep conflicts within her, but with the help of the Juvenile Court social service and the consultation center personnel, Anna found the ability within herself to work through the experience with some maturity. Subsequently she was able to organize her life in a more satisfactory fashion, and she found work in another region of Italy.

Whatever one's position concerning abortion, a comparison of these cases demonstrates how important it is to guarantee this type of adolescent a valid consultation service and adequate psychotherapeutic support.   The case of Maria illustrates the sort of difficulties encountered in trying to induce people to show due respect for the personality of the minor.

Footnotes

1. Cf. Protetti, 1980, pp. 123-126.   The text includes extracts from a decision of the Bologna Juvenile Court, October 26, 1973, before the reform of family law. It brings into focus the contrast between the 1942 Civil Code and the rights sanctioned by the Constitution. The sentence authorized a minor to reside outside the family in order to continue his studies. "This Juvenile Court takes note of the minor's wish to settle in Milan in order to continue his studies and to achieve that economic independence he so acutely feels, after the present events, as a necessary defense of his own dignity.   The Court also takes note of the pride with which he asks to be free of any interference on the part of juvenile social service, which he experiences as a lack of trust in him. Yet, while concluding that it would

be an extreme error to mortify him in his self-realization by imposing regulations or forced lodgings, or by forcing him to return home, the Court cannot waive the wardship, albeit simply for purposes of information, of the Juvenile Social Service, which has already been decided by the responsible judge."

2. Regarding the difficulties raised by the new norms governing the marriage of minors, cf. Protetti, 1980, p. 128: "While the new norms have reduced the requests for applications for authorization to marry because of the obstacles raised by the law with the procedure in Article 84 of the Civil Code, it must be pointed out that the evaluation of serious reasons has varied from region to region. The Juvenile Courts of Milan and Turin have accepted about 40 per cent of the requests, while the other regions have authorized them in the range of 90 to 95 per cent, with the result that minors have often given false addresses in order more easily to obtain authorization to marry, authorization that was difficult or extremely difficult to obtain in other regions."

3. It is important to note that when a minor aborts, outside of the cases envisaged by the law, the young woman is not subject to punishment by the law. This is indicated in the third paragraph of Article 19: "When voluntary termination of pregnancy occurs with a woman under the age of 18, or when it is forbidden, outside the cases or failing to meet the requirements envisaged in Articles 12 and 13, the person who performs the abortion is punishable with up to one and one-half times the sentences envisaged in the preceding paragraphs. The woman is not punishable." For an adult woman, sanctions are envisaged, although they are quite modest (a fine of up to 100,000 lire if the abortion takes place within the third month of pregnancy, otherwise confinement for up to six months), if the abortion is not performed according to the provision of the law.

References

Ardigó, A. (Ed.). (1977) **Giustizia Minorile e Famiglia.**

Patron, Bologna.

Finocchiaro, A., & Finocchiaro, M. (1979) **Riforma del diritto di famiglia.** Giuffré: Milan.

Galli, G., Italia, V., Realmonte, F. Spina, M., & Traverso, C.E. (1978) **L'interruzione volontaria della gravidanza.** Giuffré: Milan.

Mastroianni, A. (1979) **L'educazione sessuale in Italia.** Giuffré: Milan.

Meucci, G. (1974) **I figli non sono nostri.** Vallecchi: Florence.

Meucci, G., Gualandri, V., Giarrusso, A., & Amoroso, R. (1979) **La contraccezione nella adolescente.** Longanesi: Milan.

Nicoli, G. (1975) **La riforma del diritto di famiglia.** Gloria: Padua.

Ossicini, A. (1963) **I ragazzi che fuggono.** Giunti Barbera: Florence.

Palmonari, A., Carugati, F., Ricci Bitti, P., & Sarchielli, G. (1979) **Identité imperfette.** il Mulino: Bologna.

Protetti, E., & Protetti, M.T. (1980) **I Consultori familiari.** Cedam: Padua.

Landucci Tosi, S., Spinelli, A., Baldini, A., & Perini, A.C. (1981) "La contraccezione nella popolazione italiana. Studio Campionario nei consultori familiari di sette regioni." **In Contraccezione, Fertilità, Sessualità,** n;5, pp. 425-446.

Relazione sull'attuazione della legge contenente norme per la tutela sociale della maternità e sull'interruzione volontaria della gravidanza. Presentata dol Ministro di Grazia e Giustizia on. Morlino alla Presidenza il 12 Maggio 1980, Camera dei deputati, Doc. LV, n. 1. (Reports of the Minister of Justice to Parliament.)

Relazioni sull'attuazione della legge contenente norme per la tutela sociale della maternità e sull'interrruzione volontaria della gravidanza. Presentate alla Presidenza del Ministro di Grazia e Giustizia, on Sarti il 31 Marzo 1981, e del Ministro della Sanità, on. Aniasi il 21 Aprile 1981, Camera dei Deputati, Doc. LV n. 2. (Reports of Minister of Justice and of Minister of Health to Parliament.)

Ministero della Sanità (1981) **Dati per l'azione donna.** Mimeographed.

Pregnancy and Abortion in Adolescence. Report of WHO Meeting, Technical Report Series 583, World Health

Organization, Geneva, 1975.
UICEMP (Italian Planned Parenthood Federation) (1981) **L'interruzione volontaria della gravidanza.** Nuova Guaraldi, Florence.

10
FAMILY PLANNING AND ABORTION AMONG MINORS: THE SPANISH CASE

Ines Alberdi
Salustiano del Campo

Family planning and abortion among minors in Spain cannot be described very precisely because of changing and ambiguous social norms. Legally, however, the use and distribution of contraceptives are severely restricted, and abortion was, until recently, completely forbidden, regardless of the woman's status or age.

Coming of Age

In 1978, a change in the Constitution established the age of majority as 18 instead of 21 years. Adulthood in civil law means emancipation from parental authority and the end of the parents' economic responsibility for the child. An exception is made for a child who does not have a means of support and continues to live with his parents, or who needs help to continue his studies, or who is physically or emotionally incapacitated. In 1981 important reforms to the Code of Civil Law established greater equality between husband and wife, and a more even distribution of rights between parents and children.

Since the reforms of 1981, parental authority is shared by the father and the mother, who make all decisions which concern their minor child: his education, his job, the administration of his property, his medical treatment, authorization for him to travel and to obtain a passport, etc. Such authority carries with it obligations such as taking care of the child, being with him, and educating and feeding him. The law limits the severity with which parents may "reasonably and moderaterly discipline" their children. The children, in turn, must obey their parents and contribute "equitably" to the family's needs while they live with them. The law cautions parents extensively against the economic abuse of their children.

Between the ages of 16 and 18 a young person who is under parental authority may request emancipation, which will be granted in cases in which the parents separate, divorce, or remarry, or by the judge's decision in view of the circumstances. On the other hand, the minor who lives separately from his parents is considered emancipated for all purposes, provided the parents are not strongly opposed to his emancipation.

Presently children have more rights vis-a-vis their parents than before the reforms of 1981. For example, a minor over 12 years of age must be heard by the judge if his parents separate, in order to determine with whom he will live. On coming of age a young person can make some decisions to nullify those which his parents made for him previously, such as rejecting the acknowledgement of paternity made by the father, in the case of an illegitimate child. Legitimate children can decide to change the order of their last names by placing the mother's last name before the father's.*

In criminal law, the age at which a person becomes legally responsible for his actions is 16. This bears some importance in relation to abortion, because it sets the age at which a woman can be tried for it.

Although some legal experts would like to bring the age of criminal responsibility into alignment with the age of majority in civil law, this change is not being pursued. A proposed amendment to the Code of Criminal Law would identify as crimes against the family a series of acts such as incest, kidnapping a minor, inducing a child to leave his home, and child abandonment--all actions that can affect the situation of adolescents. The courts support the authority of parents over their minor children; this can be ascribed to an increase in the vigilance of the State over the well-being of children and to public sensitivity regar-

----

*In Spain a married woman never loses her own surname and her children's last name is formed by placing the father's last name followed by the mother's.

ding child abandonment and abuse.

Public attitudes are still rather authoritarian. Parents of a certain age seem to be in favour of greater control over their children, even though the majority of children seem to want greater freedom (Foessa Report, 1975). The change in customs has been very drastic within the last 20 years, and parental authority has weakened dramatically, but one must not forget that the change has taken place from a strongly authoritarian family where the children had very few rights vis-a-vis their parents.

A recent report from the Ministry of Culture (Madrid, 1981) stated:

Parent-child relationships seem to be undergoing a progressive and profound change . . . . Social changes at the global level have contributed to the development of a model of greater equality and freedom in parent-child relationships. The fact that this might be a growing tendency does not mean, however, that in Spanish families authoritarianism, repressive education and even violence, lack of mutual understanding or generational conflict have disappeared. According to available data it appears that parent-child relationships are fundamentally conflictive. This is due to generational differences in thinking, which translates into authoritarianism and excessive control on the part of the parents, and a desire for greater freedom and independence by the children.

According to some studies, the majority of the public accepts parental authority and control over children as right and proper: 67.9 percent think parents "should have control over the friendships of their children," 56 percent believe parents should control the money their children earn, and 61 percent "do not think it is right" for children to leave home to live on their own when they finally earn enough to support themselves (Foessa, 1975). Opinions are more liberal in more densely populated areas, and the majority of young people, between 15 and 19 years of age, is strongly in favor of the autonomy of adolescents from their parents.

Contraceptives

Until very recently contraceptives were prohibited in Spain. Article 416 of the Code of Criminal Law, which was abolished in November 1978, set fines of 50,000 to

100,000 pesetas for the use, sale, or dissemination of contraceptives. This did not prevent some methods from being widely used, but it distorted their use. For example, the pill has been used widely since 1965, but in many cases without medical supervision or as a prescription to correct some gynecological disorder. Other methods, such as the intrauterine device, the diaphragm, and sterilization, have been used only by a small minority of women who resorted to private, costly, elite, and clandestine medical facilities.

In November of 1978 the use of contraceptives was declared no longer a crime, and the government undertook to control their distribution as well as to restrict their publicity. But the law was not fully implemented and the situation remains so nebulous that information on contraceptives in books, magazines, and newspapers is still almost nonexistent. The Catholic Church in Spain exerts great influence, and it has consistently pressed for the civil laws to conform to its pastoral doctrines.

Although the sale of contraceptives is no longer a crime, their use continues to be restricted, since most are considered prescriptions and as such their publicity is prohibited. In addition, sterilization, both male and female, was considered a mutilation, falling therefore under Article 418 of the Code of Criminal Law which carried a punishment of six years in prison. Only recently, in May 1983, this article has been abolished.

In spite of all this, the use of contraceptives is much wider than norms would indicate and family planning more widespread than might be thought in view of the obstacles against it. The main problems are the lack of centers to provide information and counseling, and that contraception is not included in Social Security services.

Even before the legalization of contraceptives, there were in some Spanish cities small family planning centers which offered information, counseling, and medical attention at the margin of legality. These first centers were organized by feminist groups. Later some left-wing political groups became interested in the subject as well, and when the Code of Criminal Law was amended some municipal governments controlled by the left organized Health Centers that attend primarily to family planning matters. The number of these centers is small, however, and they cannot meet the demand. As far as we know, the centers do not discriminate on the basis of age or marital status.

Even though Social Security does not formally offer family planning services, many doctors attend to contraception within the context of gynecological consultations. Most frequently it is the doctor who decides, prescribing birth control only in serious cases, such as an already large number of children, or an illness of the woman. The woman herself does not usually influence his decision.

Attitudes of the Public Regarding the Use of Contraceptives

Attitudes toward the use of contraceptives have changed during the last few years from a general position against family planning to obvious acceptance. This has occurred in spite of the fact that contraceptives were outlawed for many years, and that for the majority of women their use still presents many difficulties. In a 1965 study of opinions on religious matters, only 13 percent of the women and 22 percent of the men agreed that "one should be free to have or not to have children." In 1971 in a national survey on birth rate and family planning involving married Spanish women between the ages of 15 and 45, 42 percent favored planning the number of children and when to have them. In both surveys younger people were more in favor of birth control than older people. The first studies on these subjects were always related to opinions on religiosity and respect for the directives of the Church. By 1978, in a national study of attitudes toward the use of contraceptives, 69 percent of people between the ages of 18 and 65, men and women, were in favor of family planning. In the richer and more developed areas of the country, and in large cities, the percentages in favor are even higher.

Opinions about the use of contraceptives among adolescents are influenced by attitudes toward the sexuality of young people. The Foessa Report of 1975 found adult opinions on this subject to be fairly strict. Thirty-two percent responded that "if sweethearts are seriously going together they should be allowed to make love, if they so desire." Forty-nine percent said "it is not important for a youth to be a virgin at marriage," but in the case of a young girl only 20 percent thought the same thing. It must be taken into account that attitudes are strongly correlated with the age of the respondents. For example, in a survey carried out among university students in Barcelona, only 2 percent thought that a woman should be a virgin at marriage. In this same study, 90 percent of the students were in favor of the use of contraceptives (Garcia, 1977).

Knowledge of contraceptives is greater among younger than among older couples. According to the National Survey on Fertility of 1977, 90.7 percent of the women interviewed knew of at least one effective method. Such knowledge was greater among the younger women -- 97.9 percent of married women between the ages of 15 and 24, as opposed to 82 percent of those between the ages of 45 and 49. The contraceptive method most widely used by young women is the pill, which is used by 32.2 percent. Significantly, it is also the method best known by Spanish women, 88.5 percent of whom say they know of it. The method still most widely used is "coitus interruptus," used by 30.7 percent of all women. This points to the traditionalism that still dominates family planning in Spain.

Abortion

Until 1985 abortion has been forbidden in Spain without exception. The Articles in the Code of Criminal Law which condemned and punished it have now been changed. The high rate of clandestine abortions performed in the country, and the opinion campaigns carried out since 1975 primarily by feminist groups, have had a very large impact in liberalizing abortion. Earlier the Code of Criminal Law punished anyone who performed an abortion, with penalties ranging from six months to six years in jail, depending on the degree of consent of the pregnant woman. Medical professionals who performed an abortion were, moreover, barred from their practice, and no exception was made in the case of an abortion performed to save the life of the mother.

The woman who induced an abortion on herself, or who gave her consent for someone else to perform one, would also be sentenced to prison, although the penalty was lessened when the abortion was performed in order to "hide her dishonor." Likewise the penalty was lessened for parents who arranged an abortion for their daughter in order to defend the honor of the family. The manner in which the Spanish Code of Criminal Law regarded abortion reflected   the traditional and sexist view of pregnancy, disregarding present social realities. Medical, ethical, and social circumstances generally accepted as justifications for abortion in many other countries, were not accepted as justifications. Nor were the woman's wishes considered in the matter.

But abortion was and is an undeniable reality in Spain, despite restrictive legislation. The Attorney General of the Supreme Court, in his report for 1973, estimated that there were 300,000 abortions in one year in Spain of which only 10 percent were spontaneous. According to this report, of the 270,000 women who had induced abortions, 40,000 were prostitutes, 20,000 married women, and 210,000 single women and widows. All estimates on the subject agreed in pointing out that, of all women who abort secretly, the majority are single and very young.

The mode of abortion does not seem to vary according to age, since all women encounter the same difficulties, but it does vary greatly according to social class, economic means, and cultural background. Women from the lower social classes abort secretly in remote areas of the country, under conditions lacking in hygiene and safety. Women from the middle class, at least those of a certain cultural level, go to European clinics in countries where abortion is legal, where safer and less painful methods are used. Strict standards do not prevent abortions; they only make them more difficult by placing women at a disadvantage according to social class, place of residence, and education. Urban, educated women have better access to abortion. Whether such differences are reduced, now that the law has been changed, remains to be seen.

The involvement of the parents in the abortion of a minor daughter is not frequent. Most women must obtain abortions secretly and, from the information we have, parents are in most cases unaware of the abortion. Family planning centers report that they receive many consultations on unwanted pregnancies and that the same advice is given to all, irrespective of age or marital status, and without asking for the parents' opinion: they warn of the risks of having an abortion in Spain, and they provide addresses of places in Europe where an abortion can be performed under suitable conditions. Some parents give their daughters financial and moral support during this critical time, but we venture to guess that the majority are not aware of their daughters' experience.

Abortion is a matter which is resolved, as far as information and financial resources go, by the couple itself, or with the help of friends. Each generation has different attitudes toward abortion; while it is relatively well accepted among younger people, the majority of older people reject it as a criminal action. In a national survey taken in 1976, 71 percent of the women interviewed were against the legalization of abortion, considering it an attempt against life. However, in the student poll previously quoted, only 8.3 percent were against abortion. Most of the students, 62 percent, favored the legalization of abortion in cases where "the mother's life is in danger," 50 percent favored it where "there is certainty that the child will be deformed," and 42 percent "when the mother so desires." Five percent of the women in this survey admitted to having had an abortion. Most of them went abroad to have it, and said that their families were not aware of the matter; they had resorted to friends for help in defraying the expenses. The reason they gave for hiding it from their parents was that they would not understand and would be opposed (Garcia, 1977).

It has been especially difficult for young women to obtain abortions because a passport was necessary to leave the country and parental permission was required to obtain one. This situation changed when abortion was legalized in France, because the Spanish border with France can be crossed with a one-day pass. More recently it has become possible to cross all European borders carrying only an identity card. The passport requirement was even more disadvantageous for women of the lower classes than for minors, since they were unable economically and psychologically to afford a trip abroad.

Attitudes of Society toward Abortion

Conservative political parties such as **Alianza Popular** (Popular Alliance) have consistently been opposed to the decriminalization of abortion. The Socialist Party was in favor of revising abortion legislation, and the Communist Party presented an initiative in 1982 that would legalize abortion in certain cases. The parties in the center of the political spectrum, such as the Basque and the Catalan Nationalists, believed that abortion should be legalized, but with stringent controls. Almost all parties agreed that the subject of abortion was politically risky because of Church opposition and no group seemed to be in a great hurry to decide on it.

Public opinion is also divided. According to the liberal newspaper, **El Pais,** abortion is a matter which Spanish society must consider carefully and resolve with fairness. Organizations opposed to abortion have also surfaced. One of them, AVEDIDA, recently made public a statement against abortion signed by 750 university professors. The Madrid daily **Ya,** published by the Catholic Church, has repeatedly criticized all campaigns in favor of legalizing abortion, such as a recent motion by the Municipal Government of Madrid.

There have also been public demonstrations, both for and against abortion. The trial which recently took place in Bilbao against a group of women accused of having abortions has sparked the controversy. In March 1982, after many postponements, this much publicized trial of ten women from one of the poorest districts of Bilbao took place.   All of the women involved were from immigrant families, most of them married, with many children, and in very difficult financial situations. Some were accused of having sought abortions, while others were accused of having performed them in their own kitchens without medical assistance. The case was so dramatic, and the public reaction organized by feminist groups so effective that, for the first time, the judge considered "the state of need" as an extenuating circumstance for the actions of these women. Only two of the women were judged guilty. The judge invoked Article 15 of the Constitution, which states that everyone has the right to life, and interpreted it "as it applies to a person in his own right and not to an embryo or fetus." The judgment states: "intrauterine life is a state which constitutionally deserves protection, but such protection is derived from that extended to the mother as the carrier of life, that life indirectly receiving the protection that results from the fundamental rights of woman: her wholeness as a person, her health, and her personal freedom."

The judgment established an important precedent which might influence similar cases in the future. The following were considered to be extenuating circumstances that influenced the decision: the limited economic means of the women's families; that the abortions were carried out before 1978, when contraceptives were forbidden in Spain; that these women repeatedly asked a doctor for contraceptives to avoid having more children; the scarcity of medical and social institutions in the neighbourhood to help women with children; the social and cultural deprivation of these women and their ignorance that these practices were forbidden; the reality that these practices are legally accepted on the other side of the Spanish border, close to Bilbao; the women's awareness of their family problems and their intention to avoid, with the abortion, bigger troubles for their families and themselves. The General Attorney has appealed the decision in the name of the State and the case will eventually be heard by the Supreme Court. Until then the ten women are free, eight because they were considered innocent and the other two because the punishment was minimal and they had already served their time in prison.

The ambivalence of social attitudes toward abortion is growing because increasingly the problems involved--social, personal, and psychological--are taken into account. Frequently society remains silent about induced abortions; many doctors and hospitals treat women with symptoms of an induced abortion without reporting them to the police. It has become common for women who lack education and economic means to resort to crude methods of inducing abortions, going later to the hospital to be treated for hemorrhage and infection. They know that an abortion hardly can be induced at a hospital, but that they can be treated for the consequences of one. Hospitals and physicians usually report these cases as miscarriages.

The Change with the Socialist Government

The Socialist party won the October 1982 election and they have formed the government in Spain since December 1982. One of the government's first actions was to send to the Parliament a bill to reform the criminal law pertaining to abortion. The new law was to decriminalize abortion in three circumstances: when the life or health of the woman is in danger, when the pregnancy is a consequence of rape, and in cases of malformation of the fetus. Abortion will be forbidden under all other circumstances. The reform is opposed by the Catholic

Church, which calls it a way to "kill innocent lives"; it is also contested by feminist groups that seek a more liberal abortion law.

The most recent polls showed a wide acceptance of the government's projected reform.   In a national survey conducted by the Sociological Research Center in February 1983, 62 percent accept abortion when the physical or mental health of the woman is in danger, 66 percent when the life of the woman is in danger, 62 percent when there are grounds for presuming that the child will be mentally retarded or affected by a serious defect, 56 percent when the pregnancy results from rape, but only 24 percent accept abortion by the free decision of the woman. It is paradoxical but significant that women now appear more restrictive and men more liberal in their position on abortion: 27 percent of the men and only 21 percent of the women accept abortion by petition of the pregnant woman.   Older people are also more opposed to the reform of the abortion law than younger people.

The bill to decriminalize abortion under limited circumstances, passed by Parilament, was challenged by the Popular Alliance on constitutional grounds. The Spanish Constitutional Court, in a close vote, ruled that the bill was unconstitutional. To overcome the Court's barrier, the bill was amended to require a physician to certify that the abortion is necessary to safeguard the life or health of the woman, and to require that abortions take place only in specially licensed facilities. Since the new law has just taken effect, its impact on attitudes and behavior regarding abortion cannot yet be assessed.

References

Campo, Salustiano del. 1982. **La Evolución de la Familia Espanola en el Siglo XX.** Madrid: Alianza Universidad.

Diez Nicolas, Juan. 1973. "Natalidad y Planificación Familiar en Espana, 1971-73". **Revista Espanola de la Opinión Pública** no 31.

García, Anselmo. 1977. **Comportamiento Sexual Universitario,** Barcelona, Edición del autor.

Iglesias de Ussel, Julio. 1979. **El Aborto: un Estudio Sociológico sobre el caso Espanol.** Madrid: Centro de

Investigaciones Sociológicas.
Miguel, Jesús de. 1980. "Sociología de la Población y Control de la Natalidad en Espana." Pag 15-47 en **Revista Espanola de Investigaciones Sociológicas** no 10.
Ministerio de Cultura, Dirección General de Juventud y Promoción Sociocultural: **La Familia espanola en cambio. Elementos preparatorios de un Libro Blanco de la Familia.** Madrid 1981, pag 17.
Pablo, Antonio de. 1975. "La familia espanola en cambio." Pag 345-405 en FOESSA. **Estudios Sociológicos sobre la Situación Social de Espana.** Madrid: Euroamérica.

Polls

1965. Encuesta sobre "Cuestiones Religiosas" **Instituto de la Opinión Pública,** Madrid.
1972. Encuesta sobre "Comportamientos Sociales y Turismo" **Instituto de la Opinión Pública,** Madrid.
1975. Informe FOESSA. **Estudios Sociológicas sobre la situación Social de Espana,** Madrid: Euroamérica.
1977. Encuesta de Fecundidad. **Instituto Nacional de Estadística.** Madrid.
1978. Encuesta sobre "Actitudes ante el Divorcio y la utilización de los Anticonceptivos" **Centro de Investigaciones Sociológicas.** Madrid.
1983. Encuesta de "Actitudes ante el aborto." **Centro de Investigaciones Sociológicas.** Madrid.
1985. Encuesta de "Actitudes ante el aborto". **Centro de Investigaciones Sociológicas.** Madrid.

11
THE FAMILY PLANNING RIGHTS OF MINORS IN SWEDEN

Jan E. Trost

Swedish law requires the person who has custody of a child (normally its parent or parents) to take care of the child, give it a reasonable upbringing in accordance with its background and capabilities, and provide supervision for it. Recently the Swedish Parliament made the child even more central. It is stated that the child has the right to be taken care of, the right to confidence, and the right to a good upbringing. These "rights" translate into "responsibilities" for custodians, and the ancient view of children as the property of their parents seems today to have been turned upside down.

The "age of majority" in Sweden is 18; before that age a child may not marry without parental consent or make independent financial decisions. In other areas of life, the distinction between child and adult is made at earlier ages. For example, at age twelve one has to pay adult fees when travelling by bus or train and at age fifteen one can attend movies on one's own consent.

Fertility and Abortion

In Sweden today, few children are born to minors. The age-specific fertility rates in Table 1 show that the number of children born to teenagers increases, predictably, with age. Since 1959 fertility rates have decreased for all ages, but among teenagers they have decreased more than among adults. Mothers under 16 years of age gave birth to .14 percent of all children born in 1959, .12 percent in 1969, and .08 percent in 1979.

Mothers under 18 years of age gave birth to 2.4 percent of all children born in 1959, 2.1 percent in 1969, and only 1 percent in 1979.

The legal abortion rates have increased considerably until 1975 when the rates started decreasing considerably, cf tabel 2. (These rates refer only to legal abortions. Today there are few if any illegal abortions in Sweden, but the situation was quite different during the 1950s and 1960s.)

Table 1

Children Born per 1,000 Women

Age	1959	1969	1979	1984
13	0.0	0.1	0.1	0.0
14	0.2	0.2	0.1	0.1
15	2.2	2.2	1.1	0.6
16	11.4	10.8	3.6	1.4
17	32.1	29.8	12.8	6.1
18	59.0	53.8	25.4	13.8
19	86.3	75.0	45.9	30.1
20	104.2	91.7	63.5	44.4
21	119.1	106.1	82.8	66.6
22	136.8	121.7	95.1	79.5
23	144.5	129.5	11.6	96.7
24	154.7	135.2	122.5	114.2
25	153.4	138.9	131.6	125.9

Like births, abortion rates increase for teenagers with age (Table 3). In 1979 11 out of 1,000 15-year-old girls had an abortion, while among 19-year-old women there were 34.3 abortions per 1,000 women. The abortion rates have, however, decreased considerably in all age classes during the last ten years.

The abortion law that was in force in Sweden from 1938 until 1975 required that, in general, parental (or custodial) permission be given before a girl under 15 could receive an abortion. Under special circumstances, however, anabortion could be performed upon application of the girl herself, without such permission. During the latter years of this law, parental consent was seldom required, accord-

Table 2

Abortions per 1,000 Women

Age	1959	1969	1979	1984
14	0.8	0.5	3.9	2.3
15-19	1.1	5.3	21.4	17.5

Table 3

Abortions per 1,000 Women in 1979 and 1984

Age	1979	1984	%
15	11.0	7.1	35
16	18.4	12.5	32
17	23.6	17.8	25
18	28.9	22.9	21
19	34.3	25.6	25

ing to some gynecologists. In almost all cases in which the girl did not want to have her parents involved in the abortion decision, the physicians decided that there were special circumstances. This law also required special indications for abortion. In the beginning they were interpreted very strictly, but at the end of the 1960s the interpretation became more permissive; it is not an exaggeration to say that from the beginning of the 1970s, women were perceived as having the right to abortion, although some local variations existed.

The abortion law that came into force in 1975 gives the woman a legal right to an abortion on her own demand before the 13th week of gestation; she has formally to apply for an abortion between the 12th and the 18th week; and from the 18th until the 23th week the National Board of Health decides. It also makes it clear that the physician or social worker taking care of her does not have the right to inform anyone of her choice without her permission. In reality, most physicians and social workers will ask a pregnant minor if she has informed her parents of her decision to have an abortion, but they are by law not allowed to and they will not try to enforce such notification against her will.

Sex and education

Beginning in the mid-1940s sex education was recommended in the Swedish public school system. Since the middle of the 1950s, it has been compulsory. This means that Sweden has officially supported sex education for more than 40 years and has had compulsory sex education for all school grades for almost 30 years.

Learning experiences, like sexual experiences, tend to be quite subjective; this is especially the case when it comes to learning about sex. Thus the actual content and also the degree of sex education vary quite a lot with different teachers. Some like to inform pupils about sex, while others are more resistant. Some are apt at sex education, others are not. There is very little teaching about sex at the teacher's colleges and similar institutions, which means that most teachers have to find out what to present to the pupils by themselves. Some schools, as a complement to the ordinary teachers, invite specialists in gynecology, midwifery, psychology, human sexuality, etc., to give special lessons either to separate classes or to the entire school.

Sex education in Sweden to a very large extent has been and still is education about technical-physical matters such as the reproductive organs and their functions, including information on sexual hygiene and pregnancy prevention, but with little information about sexuality per se. In recent years, however, more and more teachers and instruction books have emphasized the emotional part of sexuality and sensuality rather than the more technical-physical aspects.

The first teachers' handbook in the area of sex education was published in Sweden in 1945. A new handbook, based essentially on its predecessor, was published in 1956. In view of strong criticism of the sexual instruction given and of the 1956 handbook, a state commission was formed at the end of 1964. This commission stressed that personal relationships were to be assigned a prominent place in teaching, together with instruction on sexual matters. In a structurally and ideologically changing society, personal relationships have become increasingly problematic, presenting great difficulties for both individuals and society at large. Therefore the commission recommended that, by means of education in sexual and personal relationships, pupils should acquire a knowledge of anatomy, physiology, psychology, ethics, and social contexts that equip them to experience sexual life as a source of happiness and joy in fellowship with another and to strive for a relationship characterized by responsibility, consideration, and concern.

Pupils should also acquire an objective orientation to different values and philosophies that influence sexual life; fundamental values should be maintained and promoted and controversial values should be treated impartially. They should understand that sexuality is an integral part of life and is connected with the development of personality and relations of "togetherness."

Teaching designed in accordance with these ideas will thus cover three main fields:

1. Sexual anatomy and physiology
2. Sexual life in its various manifestations (intercourse, masturbation, disturbances in the sexual function, methods of birth control, abortion, veneral diseases, etc.)
3. Questions that arise in living together having to do

with emotions, human relations, values, moral standards, and social conditions (SOU, 1974:59).

The commission proposed that sex education should start at the preschool level, when children are three to six years old, and continue through the higher levels. Also, it recommended that there be a collaboration between the home and the school concerning both the content and the methods of presenting material on sexual and personal relationships.

During the second half of the 1970s a new handbook for teaching sexuality and personal relationships was published by the Swedish school authorities. It has not been received by teachers as it was intended to be: many have no idea of its existence. The intended collaboration between the school and the home is very limited in most schools. It is common in Swedish schools for the teacher to invite parents to a meeting once each semester. Seldom, however, do the teacher and the parents touch upon the teaching of sexuality and personal relationships at these parent-teacher meetings.

We can conclude that children in Sweden have the official right to be informed about sexuality and personal relationships, and that the fulfillment of this right is in part a responsibility of the schools. It is not clear, however, whose is the true responsibility to make sure that children receive the information they have a right to receive. The field is open for initiative, but if no initiative is taken . . . .

Marriages

From 1734 until 1915, the age of majority for marriage was 21 years for men and 15 years for women. In 1915 the law was changed so that women could not marry until 18, and between 18 and 21 needed parental permission. Since the end of the 1960s, both men and women have been allowed to marry at 18.

A person younger than 18 who wants to marry may, with parental approval, apply to the county authorities for a dispensation. Until about 20 years ago, such applications were not unusual and were accepted in most cases where the bride-to-be was pregnant. This was almost the only ground for a dispensation. Nowadays very few apply for a dispensation to be married prior to being 18 years old. In 1980, for example, only 20 men and 154 women

married prior to the legal age of majority (Befolkningsför-
ändringar, 1980).

The reason so very few marriages occur between minors
is that between 1965 and 1975 there was a rapid decrease
in the marriage rate and a corresponding increase in the
rate of marriage-like cohabitation (cf. Trost, 1979). Most
of those who marry young are non-Swedish citizens, many
of whom come from countries where it is customary to
marry at a young age. Thus, for instance, of Swedish
citizens aged 15-19, less than 0.1 percent of the men and
0.4 percent of the women were married in 1981, while
among non-Swedish citizens 0.3 percent of the men and
6.5 percent of the women aged 15-19 were married.

Sexual Intercourse

In the Swedish law of 1734 it was forbidden for a man
to have sexual intercourse with a girl younger than 12
years old, upon pain of death. In 1864 this age of minority
for women was changed to 15. Sexual intercourse with a
woman younger than 12 was defined as rape.   The
punishment was either imprisonment or a fine to be given
both to the Church (Sweden had and still has a State
Church) and to the woman. In 1937 the law was modified
so that a man who was younger than 18 at the time of
sexual intercourse with a minor woman could not be
punished, although the act remained a crime.

Today the law forbids sexual intercourse with someone
younger than 15. It is clearly specified that this refers
both to heterosexual and to homosexual acts. Until five
years ago the age of majority for homosexual acts was 18
and for heterosexuality 15; today the law does not differ-
entiate.   There is a further protection for youngsters
between 15 and 18 years old; if the youngster is under the
guardianship of the offender, at a school, institution, or
elsewhere, the offender can be punished by imprisonment
from one month to four years.

The criminal statistics concerning sexual acts with
children younger than 15 show that there was a gradual
increase in the number of cases known to the police
during the latter part of the 1950s; in 1960 they began to
increase considerably.   During the last few years,
however, the number of reported acts has been less than
100 per year.

According to a study done in 1967 (SOU, 1969), the

median age of sexual debut was 17 years and 7 months among an adult population. The study estimated that between 1920 and 1950 the median age of debut decreased one year. Another study (Eliasson, 1971) reported that in Stockholm at the end of the 1960s twelve percent of boys and five percent of girls had had sexual intercourse before the age of 15 and 54 percent of boys and 42 percent of girls had had sexual intercourse before the age of 18.

A more recent study (Lewin, 1980) among a representative sample of 16-year-old boys and girls shows that 39 percent have had sexual intercourse. More than half of those who had had sexual intercourse had their first intercourse with a steady date and 24 percent of them with a friend; more than half had their first intercourse either in their own home or in the home of the partner. Less than half had intercourse frequently (at least once during the last month). At first intercourse, more than half used a condom and about ten percent used pills or an IUD. Lewin also asked the respondents what contraceptive they used at their last intercourse. One third said that they had used a condom, 42 percent had used the pill and 18 percent said that they had used no contraceptive at all. Of all the respondents in the Lewin study less than 20 percent had had their second intercourse with a partner other than the first.

Contraceptives

In 1910 Swedish law prohibited the public sale of contraceptives "intended for immoral use or to prevent the results of sexual intercourse." It was also illegal to provide knowledge about contraceptive techniques. Since 1938, however, there have been no legal restrictions against providing full information about contraceptives or distributing and selling birth control devices.

For several decades condom vending machines have been available almost everywhere - in the streets, at restaurants, at dancing halls, etc. There have also been newspaper advertisements offering mail-order condoms. Packages of condoms are easily available at pharmacies, gas stations, and grocery stores. Posters in public places describe birth control and urge young people to be aware of their responsibility as sexual partners, to prevent both unwanted pregnancies and venereal disease.

In 1933 the Riksförbundet för Sexuell Upplysning

(National Association for Sex Education) was founded. Its basic goals are to provide for harmonious sexual relations, greater knowledge about sex, an openminded and tolerant attitude toward various sexual mores, planned parenthood, etc.   The RFSU is today the largest distributor of condoms, from which it receives most of its income. They have small shops throughout Sweden where contraceptives are sold, as well as a mail-order service. They provide extensive information services and planned parenthood clinics.

In many towns in Sweden there are school gynecological clinics where pupils may obtain information on sexual matters and contraception, prescriptions for pills, and condoms without cost.   These clinics work with total confidentiality and, unless the youngster expresses a wish to the contrary, have no contact with the parents. Most of those visiting these clinics are girls.

Both the clinics and the society at large have a positive attitude toward contraception for minors. It is a common idea that it is better that young girls and boys use efficient contraceptives than that girls become pregnant without the wish to be so. Most Swedes of today look upon adolescent sexual intercourse as non-preferable, although they know that it occurs quite frequently. Sexual intercourse among youngsters occurs independently of prohibitions or negative attitudes in some segments of the population. In general, however, public attitudes toward premarital sex have for a long time been positive and benign.

Literature

Eliasson, Rosmari. 1971. **Könsdifferenser i sexuellt beteende och attityder till sexuallivet,** Lund.
Lewin, Bo. 1980. **Sexual attitudes and sexual experiences among teenagers in a Swedish city,** Uppsala, Sweden, Uppsala University.
SOU. 1969. **Om sexuallivet i Sverige,** Stockholm.
Trost, Jan. 1979. **Unmarried Cohabitation,** International Library, Västerås.

12

SEXUAL INTERCOURSE, CONTRACEPTION, AND ABORTION: MINORS' RIGHTS AND TEENAGERS' BEHAVIOR IN THE UNITED STATES

Hyman Rodman

The issue of children's rights has emerged on the American scene in the wake of the equal rights movement for minority groups and women. Some of the questions raised by child advocates are highly provocative. Do children have the right to pursue sexually pleasurable lives, including sexual intercourse with adults? Do children have the right to "divorce" and to live apart from their parents? (Farson, 1974; Constantine, 1977) Such questions add fuel to the fiery child and family policy debates now endemic to the United States. As Baumrind (1978) notes, the zeal of some child advocates can obscure the fundamental differences between children and adults.

Young children need parental guidance while adults are generally considered competent to make their own decisions. During adolescence, however, as dependent children are growing into independent and autonomous adults, difficult policy judgments have to be made about children's rights. Should minors[1] have the right to work, to marry, to make legal contracts, and to obtain medical care without parental consent? Or should parental consent be required by the state in order to protect minors and to preserve parental authority?[2]

Family Planning

There are clearly many areas in which decisions must be made about the competing legal interests of children and parents. In this chapter we focus our attention upon the family planning[3] area. This topic is of special interest to policymakers because they currently face many questions about minors' contraceptive and abortion rights in Congress, in state legislatures, and in the courts.

The family planning area becomes a critical focus of controversy because of two competing characteristics of American society. First, teenagers are granted a great deal of individual freedom and responsibility in their relationships with members of the opposite sex. They are not physically separated or closely watched by chaperones, as happens in some other societies. This normative dating system encourages independence and aids in a mate selection process that is largely free from parental control (Reiss, 1980). A considerable degree of sexual experimentation occurs. For example, looking at national samples of never-married, metropolitan-area women in 1979, 23 percent had engaged in sexual intercourse by age 15, 38 percent by age 16, and 49 percent by age 17 (Zelnik and Kantner, 1980). As a result, substantial numbers of minors are interested in obtaining medical contraceptive services to prevent pregnancy, and if pregnancy does occur, many are interested in obtaining abortions.

A second characteristic of American society, however, is a legal system with a strong principle of parental authority. This principle is so strong that minors are unable to get a judicial hearing to challenge their parents' decisions or disciplinary actions except under extraordinary circumstances. Parental consent is frequently required for minors to marry, to work, to drive a car, or to obtain medical care. The legal principle of parental control and authority stands in sharp contrast to the social norm of dating freedom. As a result, minors can and often do engage in sexual intercourse without parental knowledge or permission. But if they seek medically prescribed contraceptives to prevent pregnancy, or an abortion to terminate an unwanted pregnancy, the state may try to insist upon some form of parental involvement, such as parental consent or notification.

These two competing characteristics create problems for minors, their parents, and policymakers. For example, minors may have to choose between the risk of incurring parental wrath to obtain medically prescribed contraceptives and the risk of becoming pregnant due to the use of less reliable contraceptive methods.[4] Parents may be torn between the desire to retain knowledge and control of their minor children's family planning activities, and the possibility that such control may increase the risk of premarital pregnancy for their children.

Policymakers also face difficult questions in deciding how to deal with the family planning rights of minors. Are minors who are "mature" enough to engage in sexual intercourse also mature enough to have access to medical contraceptive services and abortion without parental knowledge or consent? Would requirements for some form of parental involvement serve to provide guidance and protection to vulnerable adolescents? Or would such requirements merely inhibit minors from obtaining contraceptive and abortion services, thus increasing the number of unwanted pregnancies and illegitimate births?

Policy questions about family planning rights for minors are not easy to answer. A comprehensive response would require information about adolescent development, maturity, and autonomy; about teenagers' sexual and contraceptive attitudes and behavior; about the nature of parent-child communication regarding sexual and contraceptive questions; and about politics and values. In this chapter the focus is upon teenagers' sexual and contraceptive behavior, and to a lesser extent upon parent-child communication. A more comprehensive treatment of all the above topics and of their relevance for social policy can be found in Rodman, Lewis, and Griffith (1984).

Laws and Policies

Let us briefly review the family planning laws and policies in the United States. In many states, it is illegal for unmarried minors to engage in sexual intercourse because all sexual intercourse between unmarried partners is illegal. Such laws impinge upon minors in particular only because minors below a certain age--the age varying from state to state--require parental consent to marry, and only in marriage is sexual intercourse legal. However, statutes prohibiting premarital sexual intercourse are rarely enforced. Most states also have laws which presume that minors below a certain age are incapable of consenting to sexual intercourse; sex with an unconsenting person constitutes the crime of rape.

Although state statutes are generally silent on minors' access to contraceptive medical services, most states have adopted policies that explicitly permit minors to obtain contraceptive services on their own consent (cf. Chamie et al., 1982). There is also a consensus that decisions of the U.S. Supreme Court on related issues effectively protect minors' access to contraceptive services. Many private physicians and some family planning agencies, however, will not provide medical contraceptive services to minors (especially those under 16 years of age) without the consent of their parents (Torres, Forrest, and Eisman, 1980).

The legal situation regarding abortion is less clear. U.S. Supreme Court decisions prevent states from requiring parental consent to abortion for all minors who wish abortions; it is unlikely that the Court would accept a state statute requiring even the notification of the minor's parents in all instances of abortion (Paul and Pilpel, 1979). But the Court has affirmed a state law requiring parental notification in a case involving an immature and unemancipated minor, at least where there is no concrete evidence that parental notification would be contrary to the minor's best interest. It remains to be seen whether states can place other kinds of limits on minors' access to abortions.

The direction of policy, thus far, is toward granting minors many of the rights of adults in the reproductive health area, while recognizing the special situation of minors. But policies are still being worked out; there will be many more legislative and judicial decisions on minors' rights before their approximation to, or divergence from, adult rights is fixed.

Sexual Intercourse

Minors do not require the consent of their parents to engage in sexual intercourse, except indirectly through the requirement of parental consent for marriage. Many of the minors who engage in premarital sexual intercourse do so in their homes, and occasionally this involves the tacit consent of their parents. Frequently, however, it indicates no more than that the parents are away from the home, so that minors have the opportunity and privacy for sexual intercourse at home or at their partner's home. Twenty-three percent of never-married women between 15 and 19 who have engaged in sexual intercourse report that their most recent act of sexual intercourse took place in their own home, and 51 percent that it took place in their partner's home (Zelnik and Kantner, 1977). For adults, sexual intercourse has become largely a matter of mutual consent, since the remaining state laws against fornication are rarely enforced. The same is generally true for minors, though the state sometimes intervenes in cases where one partner is a minor and the other an adult.

To what extent do minors engage in premarital sexual intercourse? In 1974 an estimated 11 million 15- to 19-year-olds had engaged in sexual intercourse; in 1978, approximately 12 million (Alan Guttmacher Institute, 1976; 1981). The average age of first sexual intercourse is 16.2 for young women and 15.7 for young men (Zelnik and Shah, 1983). A 1976 national probability sample indicated that 35 percent of never-married women aged 15 to 19 had engaged in sexual intercourse. Since we are interested in minors we will concentrate on those who were under 18 in the 1976 study. Of those aged 15, 18 percent had experienced sexual intercourse; of those aged 16, 25 percent; of those aged 17, 41 percent (Zelnik and Kantner, 1977). There is evidence that such rates have been rising since about 1967 (Chilman, 1978, pp. 113-117). If we focus on national samples of never-married metropolitan-area teenagers, we can see sizeable changes from 1971 to 1979 (Table 1). For example, the percentage of 17-year-old women who have experienced sexual intercourse rises from 26 in 1971 to 43 in 1976 to 49 in 1979. Although the

Table 1

Percentage of Metropolitan-Area Never-Married Women
with Premarital Sexual Experience:
1971, 1976, and 1979

Age	1971	1976	1979
15	14.4	18.6	22.5
16	20.9	28.9	37.8
17	26.1	42.9	48.5

Source: Zelnik and Kantner (1980)

percentages for teenagers from metropolitan areas are higher than those for teenagers from nonmetropolitan areas, the percentages for both groups are rising. In another estimate of sexual activity, for 1978, Zelnik, Kantner, and Ford (1981) report the following percentages for unmarried females (and males): age 13, 2 (12); age 14, 11 (24); age 15, 20 (35); age 16, 32 (45); and age 17, 45 (56).

What is the frequency of intercourse by sexually experienced women aged 15 to 17? In the 1976 study, 20 percent of those who had engaged in sexual intercourse reported only one such experience. In the four weeks prior to their interviews, 51 percent reported no sexual intercourse, 30 percent reported one or two sexual experiences, 10 percent reported three to five sexual experiences, and nine percent reported six or more experiences. Further, since beginning their sexually active lives, 54 percent had confined themselves to one partner, 32 percent had had two or three, and 14 percent four or more (Zelnik and Kantner, 1977).

Whether we react to such information about the sexual activities of female minors with alarm or aplomb, it is clear that a sizeable and growing number are at risk of becoming pregnant. Are they aware of the nature of that risk? Do they know when during the menstrual cycle they are at greatest risk? As Zelnik (1979, p. 356) points out, "Knowledge of the period of greatest risk is an important topic. A major reason given by sexually active teenagers for nonuse of contraception is that intercourse took place at a time of the month when they thought they could not become pregnant." Zelnik and Kantner asked women when, during the menstrual cycle, they were at greatest risk of pregnancy. The percentages with correct answers were quite low (Table 2). Less than half of the white or black adolescents in each age group (see "total" columns in Table 2) answered correctly. White minors were more knowledgeable than blacks. Whites were also more likely to answer correctly with increased age and experience, while blacks were not.

What factors determine whether adolescent girls engage in premarital sexual intercourse? Clearly, as the Zelnik and Kantner study shows, age is one: older girls are likelier to have had sexual intercourse than younger girls. In addition, as several studies show, blacks are more likely to have had sexual intercourse than whites. Among those who are sexually active, however, whites engage in sexual intercourse more frequently than blacks (Zelnik, Kantner, and Ford, 1981). Sexual intercourse is also likelier to occur "for those who date frequently, who go steady, or who consider themselves in love" (Chilman, 1978, p. 123). Finally, those daughters who have better communication and more affectionate ties with their mothers are more likely to postpone sexual intercourse (Inazu and Fox, 1980; Walters and Walters, 1980). More recent evidence, however, suggests that parent-child communication may not have much effect on adolescent sexual behavior (Newcomer and Udry, 1985).

Table 2

Perecentage of Never-Married Women with Correct
Knowledge of Pregnancy Risk: 1976

Age	15	16	17
All	29.5	33.5	47.0
Sexually experienced	33.5	42.8	51.7
Not sexually experienced	28.6	30.3	43.7
White	30.5	39.8	48.0
Sexually experienced	40.5	50.8	51.0
Not sexually experienced	28.9	36.6	46.2
Black	22.7	18.0	26.6
Sexually experienced	17.6	17.4	28.4
Not sexually experienced	25.9	18.8	22.7

Source: Zelnik and Kantner (1977, p. 58).

Use of Contraceptives

Over the past two decades it has become easier for minors, as well as adults, to gain access to both non-prescription and prescription contraceptives. The situation for minors, however, is somewhat precarious. Only a few state legislatures have tried to enact a statute requiring parental consent in order for minors to have access to contraceptive medical services. Common law, however, requires parental consent for medical treatment of minors (with exceptions for emergencies and for emancipated or mature minors) and "physicians often hesitate to serve young people without first obtaining parental consent because they fear possible civil liability" (Paul, 1977, p. 4). Yet we know of no case of a lawsuit being won against a physician who provided contraceptive services to a minor (Paul and Scofield, 1979).

Unlike physicians and other health-care providers in private practice, family planning clinic practitioners have much experience in serving minors and, consequently, familiarity with their needs and legal rights. As a result, family planning clinics provide excellent access to teenagers. In a survey of 1,676 family planning agencies, Torres et al. (1980) report that a very large majority serve minors without requiring parental consent. Twenty percent of the agencies have parental consent or notification requirements for patients 15 and younger; only ten percent have such requirements for 16- and 17-year-olds. The requirements are, however, frequently waived at the discretion of a physician or for a variety of other reasons (Torres et al., 1980). It should be noted that many clinics encourage minors to consult with their parents, although they do not make it mandatory. Adolescents themselves stress that confidentiality is the most important reason in their selection of a family planning clinic (Zabin and Clark, 1983).

Do minors who are sexually active make use of contraceptives? Surveys conducted by faculty members of the Johns Hopkins University give detailed answers to this question. In 1976 and 1979 Zelnik and Kantner (1980) collected information by means of which they were able to divide all sexually active women (aged 15 to 19) in their samples into three groups: those who always used contraceptives; those who sometimes did; and those who never did. The percentage in the always group rose from

29 in 1976 to 34 in 1979, in the sometimes group from 36 to 39. The 1976 survey found that 38 percent, the 1979 survey that 49 percent, practice contraception at their first experience with sexual intercourse. These figures indicate some improvement in the consistency of contraceptive use between 1976 and 1979.

The contraceptive methods used by women aged 15 to 19, in 1971, 1976, and 1979, are shown in Table 3. Although the samples and the data provided are not fully comparable, as indicated in the footnotes to the table, we can nevertheless get an approximate idea of the changes that have occurred. Use of the pill increased sharply from 1971 to 1976 and then declined, probably because of publicity about the dangers of oral contraceptives (Jones, Beniger, and Westoff, 1980). Use of the condom declined from 1971 to 1976, and then increased very slightly. Use of the withdrawal method dropped sharply from 1971 to 1976, and then increased somewhat. In summary, major changes took place from 1971 to 1976, relatively minor changes from 1976 to 1979.

Zelnik and Kantner (1979), in their 1976 national survey, obtained information on why young women did not use contraceptives. They were asked to select one reason, from among the reasons listed on a card, to explain their last instance of nonuse. Among women aged 15 to 19, who had experienced premarital intercourse more than once, 20 percent reported that they "didn't expect to have intercourse." Twenty-three percent reported that they "had intercourse at (a) time of month when (they) couldn't become pregnant." An additional 28 percent selected a variety of other reasons to explain why they thought they couldn't become pregnant -- e.g., they were "too young to become pregnant" or they "had intercourse too infrequently to become pregnant" (p.292).

Lack of motivation to avoid pregnancy (or unconscious motivation to have a baby) has often been suggested as a factor contributing to teenagers' failure to use contraceptives, but we still have only very limited information in this area (cf. Furstenberg, 1976; Freeman and Rickels, 1979; Rosen, 1982). From 1945 to 1965 the prevailing clinical myth that substituted for knowledge held that unmarried women who became pregnant unconsciously desired pregnancy, and that for young women it served as a means of protest against adult authority. A classic book with this thesis is Leontine Young's (1954) Out of Wedlock. The myth could not be refuted by evidence, since women who insisted that they did not want to become pregnant were said to be unaware of their unconscious desires. The myth went hand-in-glove with state policies that severely limited access to contraceptives, especially to unmarried minors. After all, if sexually active teenagers unconsciously want to become pregnant, access to contraceptives is a moot point. Regardless of the availability of contraceptives, their unconscious

Table 3

Contraceptive Method Used Most Recently by Women Aged 15 to 19

	1971[1]	1976[1]	1976[2]	1979[2]
Pill	23.8	47.3	47.8	40.6
IUD	1.5	3.4	3.2	2.0
Diaphragm	*	*	0.9	3.5
Condom	32.1	20.9	22.9	23.3
Foam	*	*	3.8	3.9
Douche	5.8	3.5	2.8	2.1
Withdrawal	30.7	16.9	14.6	18.8
Rhythm	*	*	3.8	5.8
Other	6.1	8.0	0.2	–
Total	100.0	100.0	100.0	100.0

[1]Never-married women (includes metropolitan and non-metropolitan areas).
[2]Metropolitan-area women (includes ever-married and never-married).
*Breakdown not given.

Source: Zelnik and Kantner (1977); Zelnik and Kantner (1980).

desires will lead them to pregnancy. Moreover, from the moral viewpoint of the time, it was reasonable to present unmarried women with a clear choice: abstinence, or sexual activity followed by deserved punishment (pregnancy).

Even the limited information now available on reasons for contraceptive use or nonuse by teenagers indicates how provincial and shortsighted the clinical myth was. Presser (1974) reports that one of the reasons the women in her sample did not use contraceptives, even though they were not trying to become pregnant, was that they did not mind becoming pregnant. The 39 percent of her sample who gave this reason probably includes women who might be identified by a clinician as "unconsciously" desiring pregnancy. But it also includes women who, according to Luker (1975), are willing to risk pregnancy for a variety of reasons that could be considered rational. For example, they may see pregnancy as a test of their partner's commitment and they know that abortion is ultimately available. Other studies have pointed out that some women are too embarrassed to obtain contraceptives (Herold, 1981) or are afraid to use the pill because of possible side effects on their health (DeLamater and MacCorquodale, 1979).

Chilman (1978, 1980) and Freeman and Rickels (1979) review several studies of the psychological and motivational factors involved in the use or nonuse of contraceptives. The evidence generally suggests that these factors only partially explain contraceptive use. Social factors such as social class, religious commitment, and the sexual attitudes of friends also affect contraceptive choices. Finally, from a policy perspective, the availability, efficacy, and safety of contraceptives are important considerations. Before the early 1970s, when effective contraceptives first became readily available to minors, the most commonly reported contraceptive techniques were use of condoms and withdrawal (see Table 3). These were primarily under the control of men, who were less motivated to use contraceptives (Finkel and Finkel, 1978), and who were culturally conditioned to equate contraception with diminished pleasure. Use of condoms and withdrawal are also methods that involve precautionary activity with each act of intercourse. When effective and intercourse-independent methods under women's control, such as the pill and the IUD, became more readily available in the 1970s, many women--including teen-agers--were quick to take advantage of them. This suggests that attributing deficient motivation to women was incorrect, and that the deficiencies were primarily in contraceptive technology and the system of distribution.

But we must not allow the pendulum to swing from the clinical myth of unconscious desire to a new myth of deficient technology and insufficient access (cf. Zelnik, Kantner, and Ford, 1981). Among the reasons given for some women's--especially teenage women's--not using contraceptives is one that has to do with self-image rather than with access. It is the belief that being contraceptively ready implies that one expects to be sexually active. This threatens the self-image of women who hold conservative sexual values. By not using the pill, by not wearing an intrauterine contraceptive device, by not having a fitted diaphragm and spermicide, a teenager preserves her "good girl" image. Sexual intercourse, if it does occur, is then a spontaneous and unpredicted act. But she then risks an unwanted pregnancy, a new threat to her image (Rains, 1971; Shah, Zelnik, and Kantner, 1975; Fox, 1977; MacIntyre, 1977; Reisman, 1980). As Reiss (1980, p. 197) puts it, "acceptance of oneself as a sexual being with the right to sexual choice is one crucial determinant" of contraceptive use. Several studies also identify lack of knowledge about the menstrual cycle as a reason for using contraceptives (Kisker, 1985).

Should state policy require parents' involvement in their minor children's contraception and abortion decisions? Since this is a highly controversial issue, we shall examine the extent of consultation and discussion about contra-ception that voluntarily takes place between parents and children (cf. Furstenberg et al., 1982). Several studies suggest that the extent is considerable. Fox and Inazu (1980b) separately interviewed mothers and daughters on their communications about sex, and on most issues the aggregate figures are very similar. Seventy-five percent of the mothers and 70 percent of the daughters reported that they had talked about birth control at least once; 30 percent of the mothers and 33 percent of the daughters reported talking about birth control five or more times in the last six months. Both mothers and daughters reported a median age for daughters of 14 as the time birth control was first discussed, and 57 percent of each group reported that it was the mother who usually initiated the discussion. The largest difference is in how comfortable they felt in discussing the topic: 76 percent of the mothers felt "very comfortable" in contrast to 38 percent of the daughters. But the significance of this difference is somewhat lessened by the 20 percent of mothers and 49 percent of daughters who were "fairly comfortable."

In a study by Torres et al. (1980) information was gathered from 1,241 unmarried minors receiving contraceptives at 53 family planning clinics throughout the United States. They were asked whether their parents knew they were visiting the clinics. Fifty-four percent reported that their parents knew, 41 percent that their parents did not know, and five percent were uncertain. Those teenagers who reported that their parents knew were asked how their parents found out; 56 percent said they had told their parents voluntarily, 39 percent that their parents suggested the visit, 4 percent that their parents found out from relatives or friends, and 2 percent that the clinic required them to inform their parents. The percentage of parents who knew their minor daughters were attending family planning clinics, 54 percent, is very similar to that reported in an earlier study by Torres (1978),55 percent. In the earlier study, 65 percent of parents of girls under age 15 knew, 59 percent of parents of girls at age 15, 58 percent of parents of girls at age 16, and 50 percent of parents of girls at age 17.

What difference do birth control discussions with parents make in the sexual and contraceptive behavior of adolescent girls? When both mother and daughter agree on whether birth control has been discussed, Furstenberg (1976) reports that 52 percent of daughters whose mothers discussed birth control with them used contraceptives at some time; only 23 percent of daughters used birth control if the topic was not discussed. In a later study, however, Furstenberg et al. (1984) report that family communication has little influence upon adolescent use of contraceptives.

Fox and Inazu (1980a), having studied 449 girls (aged 14 to 16) from the Detroit public schools, indicate that the more frequently daughters have discussed sexual intercourse and birth control with their mothers, the more likely they are to reply to questions in a way that signifies knowledge about and capacity to employ contraceptives. Daughters whose mothers have discussed birth control with them by age 11 or 12 postpone sexual intercourse longer than daughters whose mothers have not discussed the topic. Fox and Inazu (1980a, p. 26) suggest "that mothers can play at least two roles in communicating about sexuality with their daughters -- the roles of protector and (of) guide." Initially, as protectors, mothers provide information on such topics as menstruation, conception, dating, and morality. Subsequently, as guides, some mothers are able to anticipate or respond to their daughters' sexual activity, and to discuss intercourse and birth control with them.

The research evidence suggests that family discussions may have a deterrent or delaying influence on girls initiation of sexual intercourse and may also increase the use of contraception once sexual intercourse begins. It must be emphasized, however, that these are voluntary discusssions; it must also be emphasized that the evidence is limited, and that there are also contradictory findings.

Unwanted Pregnancy

How effective are present policies and programs in preventing unwanted pregnancies. Continence would certainly prevent pregnancy, but the Reagan administration's effort to encourage continence has not been in existence long enough, and has been too fragmented, to permit evaluation. Among sexually active couples, unwanted pregnancies are experienced primarily by those who never use contraceptives, do not practice contraception consistently, or use the less effective methods of contraception. The question that must be asked about policies and programs is clear enough: How successful are they in promoting consistent and effective contraceptive practices, and in thus preventing unwanted pregnancies? We have examined selected data on contraceptive use; let us now look at the incidence of unwanted pregnancy among minors.

"11 Million Teenagers", published in 1976 by the Alan Guttmacher Institute, was a well timed and well presented publication of the problems associated with teenage pregnancy. Its subtitle, "What Can Be Done About the Epidemic of Adolescent Pregnancies in the United States," sets a dramatic tone that is borne out by statistics like the following:

Each year, more than one million 15-19-year-olds become pregnant, one-tenth of all women in this age group. (Two-thirds of these pregnancies are conceived out of wedlock.) In addition, some 30,000 girls younger than 15 get pregnant annually. (p. 10)

In a more comprehensive follow-up report, the Institute (1981) says that in 1978, 12 million of the 29 million teenagers in the country were sexually active (7 million men and 5 million women), and adolescent pregnancies increased to 1.1 million. By 1981, teenage pregnancies increased to 1.3 million (Henshaw et al., 1985).

The media have focused upon the problem, federal programs have until recently given increased attention to it, and social scientists are gathering information about its causes and results. Green and Poteteiger begin an article (1978) on teenage pregnancy by saying, "Teenage pregnancy has reached epidemic proportions in the United States." But there is not universal agreement about the magnitude of the problems and there is even less agreement about how to deal with it. Some have suggested that it is being exaggerated and that organizations like Planned Parenthood and Zero Population Growth have a vested interest in sounding the alarm because the "ultimate goals of the population control lobby" involve major expansions of contraception, sterilization, and abortion services for all segments of the population (Kasun, 1978, p. 15).

Leaving aside the clash of values that underlies the debate, let us look at some of the statistics on teenage pregnancy. Zelnik and Kantner's (1980) analysis of data on metropolitan-area teenagers again provides an opportunity to examine the changes that have taken place between 1971 and 1979 (Table 4). Among all women aged 15 to 19, including both those who did and those who did not have premarital intercourse, there is an increase in ever experienced premarital pregnancy from 9 percent in 1971 to 13 percent in 1976 to 16 percent (almost one in six) in 1979. For whites the percentages rise substantially through the years, for blacks they rise slightly. The percentages for blacks are nevertheless considerably higher than are those for whites. Among those women aged 15 to 19 who had premarital intercourse, the percentages who ever experienced premarital pregnancy rise very slightly from 1971 to 1976 to 1979: from approximately 28 to 30 to 33 percent (one in three). Overall, it is clear that the rise in premarital pregnancy is due, not to increases in contraceptive nonuse or failure among those who are sexually active, but to the much higher percentages of teenagers who are sexually active (see Table 1).

The figures in Table 4 refer to metropolitan-area women aged 15 to 19. Metropolitan-area women generally have higher rates of sexual activity and premarital pregnancy; this means that the percentages for all women aged 15 to 19 in the United States are likely to be lower, but it does not affect the upward trend. Since we are interested in minors, however, aggregate figures for women aged 15 to 19 are misleading. We therefore turn to a study in which percentages are given for each age.

What percentage of all women in a particular age have

Table 4

Percentage of Premaritally Pregnant Women Aged
15 to 19, by Race, for 1971, 1976, and 1979

	All	Those with pre- marital intercourse
1971		
All	8.5	28.1
White	5.6	21.4
Black	25.3	47.2
1976		
All	13.0	30.0
White	10.0	26.1
Black	26.5	40.1
1979		
All	16.2	32.5
White	13.5	29.0
Black	30.5	45.5

Source: Zelnik and Kantner (1980).

experienced a premarital pregnancy? Estimated percentages for young women between the ages of 12 and 19 are provided by Zelnik, Kim, and Kantner (1979) for 1971 and 1976. They are based on information collected from women who were between 15 and 19 years old at the time of the interview. The percentages at age 14 are very low: 0.3 in 1971 and 0.1 in 1976. The percentages by age 15 are 1.0 in 1971 and 1.5 in 1976, by age 16, 3.4 and 4.2, by age 17, 7.0 and 8.5. In other words, approximately 8.5 percent of all young women interviewed in 1976 had become premaritally pregnant by age 17. The percentage of teenage women engaging in sexual intercourse has been increasing since 1976, but their effectiveness as contraceptors has not; as a result the percentages premaritally pregnant at specific ages are undoubtedly higher today than in 1976 (cf. Koenig and Zelnik, 1982). Of course, if we were to focus only on those women who are sexually active, the percentages experiencing pregnancy would be considerably higher. For example, in 1976, the percentage by age 17 would be 25.8 rather than 8.5 percent.

A premarital pregnancy is not ipso facto an unwanted pregnancy. In 1979, for example, 18 percent of metropolitan-area teenagers who had been premaritally pregnant, and who did not "resolve" the problem through marriage, had wanted to become pregnant. In 1976, 25 percent, and in 1971, 24 percent reported that they had wanted the pregnancy (Zelnik and Kantner, 1980). In 1976, among all premaritally pregnant teenagers, not just those from metropolitan areas, 23 percent said that they had wanted the pregnancy (Zelnik and Kantner, 1978). Clearly, a substantial number of premarital pregnancies are wanted, for a variety of reasons (Luker, 1975). Nevertheless, a very large majority of the premarital pregnancies was unwanted.

Teenagers experience anxiety and fear when faced with an unwanted pregnancy and with the decision of whether to inform their parents. Although some parents strongly condemn their pregnant daughters, most parents react with more sympathy than their daughters expected (MacIntyre, 1977; Rains, 1971).

A minor's discussion of a premarital pregnancy with her parents is generally carried out in the context of deciding what to do about the pregnancy. Having and keeping the child is one possibility; adoption is another; abortion is a third. We have more to say about parent-adolescent communication in the following section on abortion.

Abortion

Since the early 1900s, abortion was illegal throughout the United States, and for the most part therapeutic abortions were only available when the woman's life was threatened by the pregnancy. Between 1966 and 1972, 13 states reformed their abortion laws to permit therapeutic abortions on such grounds as preserving the woman's health, fetal deformity, and pregnancy due to rape or incest. In 1970, four states (Alaska, Hawaii, New York, and Washington) repealed their anti-abortion laws, permitting a woman to request and a physician to perform an abortion without having to rely upon limited legal grounds to justify the abortion. Although abortion remains controversial in the United States, its legal and constitutional status was strongly affected by the U.S. Supreme Court's decisions of 1973 (Sarvis and Rodman, 1974). As a result of those decisions, abortion became legal throughout the United States, a woman's right to have an abortion was granted constitutional protection, and abortion became increasingly available, especially in the larger cities.

The availability of abortion to minors was not at issue in the 1973 abortion decisions (the two cases involved adults), and the Court deliberately avoided taking a position on the constitutionality of parental consent requirements. At that time, ten states required parental consent for a minor's abortion, and several states added such requirements subsequently. After 1973, the requirements were successfully challenged in most states that had such laws, and in 1976 (Planned Parenthood of Central Missouri vs. Danforth) and again in 1979 (Bellotti vs. Baird) the Supreme Court ruled that states may not arbitrarily prohibit all minors from obtaining abortions without parental consent. As a result of the liberalization of abortion statutes in about one-third of the states between 1966 and 1972, the 1973 abortion decisions, Danforth in 1976, and Bellotti in 1979, legal abortions were becoming increasingly available to minors throughout most of the 1970s.

Several obstacles to abortion also emerged in the 1970s. One obstacle, for example, is that several states enacted

laws denying Medicaid funding for nontherapeutic abortions, and in 1977 the U.S. Supreme Court upheld these
restrictive statutes. Second, the Hyde amendment barred
the use of federal funds for virtually all abortions, including therapeutic abortions. Heatedly debated and challenged as discriminating against poor women who had to
rely on Medicaid, the amendment was nevertheless passed
each year beginning in 1976, and upheld by the U.S.
Supreme Court in 1980 (Harris vs. McRae) despite a
constitutional challenge. Third, groups organized to picket
abortion clinics, to publicize the anti-abortion message,
and to support a variety of anti-abortion bills at the local,
state, and federal levels. Although some of these bills
were passed, most of them have not passed, or if passed
have been declared unconstitutional. But the zeal of the
"pro-life" movement, by the late 1970s, had nevertheless
offset the favorable publicity on abortion in the early
1970s (Sarvis and Rodman, 1974). Fourth, the U.S.
Supreme Court's decision in H. L. vs. Matheson (1981)
upheld Utah's law requiring physicians to "(n)otify, if
possible, the parents or guardian of the woman upon whom
the abortion is to be performed, if she is a minor . . . ."
Although the decision pertains only to unemancipated
minors who have made no showing of maturity (and who
have not shown the abortion to be in their best interests),
it nevertheless arrests the notion, encourged by earlier
decisions, that a minor's right to an abortion is virtually
equivalent to an adult's, and that states could not insist on
any form of parental involvement. Several states have
therefore recently enacted statutes requiring parental
consent or notification (Bush, 1983). Finally, the Reagan
administration's hostility to abortion poses a threat of
unknown magnitude to its availability, especially for
minors.

The annual number of induced abortions throughout the
1970s reflects the increased availability of abortion. For
all women in the United States the number of reported
abortions rose from approximately 193,000 in 1970 to
855,000 in 1975 to 1,300,000 in 1980; the abortion ratio
(abortions per 1,000 live births) rose from 52 to 272 to 362
(Centers for Disease Control, 1983). If we use figures that
more completely cover abortions by private physicians,
the rise is from 1,034,000 in 1975 to 1,574,000 in 1982
(Henshaw et al., 1984). For minors--17 years or younger--

the estimated number of legal abortions rose from 127,000 in 1973 to 167,000 in 1975 to 199,000 in 1980 (Dryfoos and Bourque-Scholl, 1981, p. 26; Henshaw and O'Reilly, 1983, p. 6).

Another perspective on the use of abortion by teenagers (aged 15 to 19) is the percentage who end a first premarital pregnancy by induced abortion. Among whites who did not marry in response to their first premarital pregnancy, and who were not pregnant at the time of the interview, 39 percent had induced abortions in 1971 and 51 percent in 1976; among blacks there was an undercount (Zelnik and Kantner, 1978). Restricting the comparison on teenager abortions over time to young women (black and white) living in metropolitan areas, Zelnik and Kantner (1980) report that 23 percent had induced abortions in 1971, 33 percent in 1976, and 37 percent in 1979 (Zelnik and Kantner, 1980). The percentage of pregnancies ending in abortion was increasing, the percentage of marriages (and live births) was decreasing. By combining figures on those marrying and those adopting other resolutions, we arrive at the following distribution of responses to premarital pregnancy in 1979: marriage (typically followed by live birth), 16 percent; stillbirth or miscarriage, 12 percent; live birth without (or prior to)marriage, 42 percent; induced abortion, 31 percent.

For 1976, the percentages of young white women whose first premarital pregnancy ended in induced abortion (or miscarriage) are available by age: age 14 or younger, 29 percent; age 15, 33 percent; age 16, 39 percent; and age 17 to 19, 56 percent (Zelnik, Kantner, and Ford, 1981, p. 151).

As mentioned earlier, many minors tell their parents that they are attending family planning clinics, even though they are usually not required to do so in order to get medical contraceptive services. Do minors also consult their parents about how to deal with unwanted pregancies; in particular, do they consult them about abortion? The question is critical, for two reasons. First, unlike other resolutions of a problem pregnancy, such as childbirth, it is relatively easy to have an abortion without one's parents' knowledge or consent. Second, this is the area pertaining to the reproductive rights of minors about which there is the greatest controversy, the least consensus, and the largest number of unresolved policy issues.

There is, unfortunately, very little information about the extent to which parents are involved in abortion decisions (or, more generally, in decisions about dealing with unwanted pregnancies). One study reports that 55 percent of the parents of unmarried minors who sought abortions knew their daughters were doing so. (The study was based on a survey of 1,170 unmarried minors who attended 52 abortion clinics across the country (Torres et al.,1980).) The younger the patient, the more likely she was to tell her parents: 75 percent of minors aged 15 or less did so, 52 percent of 16-year-olds, and 46 percent of 17-year-olds. Fifty-four percent of all minors reported that they had discussed the abortion decision with their parents; i.e., in virtually all cases where the parents knew, the decisions had been discussed.

In another study, Rosen (1980) collected information from 432 minor women throughout Michigan who were unmarried and faced unwanted pregnancies. When they first thought they might be pregnant, 14 percent sought advice from their parents (in contrast to 33 percent who sought advice from their male partners and 33 percent who turned to girlfriends). When seeking pregnancy tests, 23 percent consulted their parents. After confirming their pregnancies, 57 percent consulted their parents about what to do. Confronting premarital pregnancy is a process in which the percentage of women who seek advice from their parents increases substantially at each successively more critical stage. Moreover, regardless of whether they chose abortion, adoption, or keeping their children, more than 50 percent in each category reported that their mothers had had some influence on their decisions.

These findings suggest that the process of informal and voluntary communication between minor women and their parents works reasonably well, although they do not provide a definitive answer to the policy question of whether parental involvement should be legally required.

Attitudes and Values

Our focus thus far has been on the family planning behavior of teenagers--sexual intercourse, contraceptive use, unwanted pregnancy, and abortion. These are items that can be readily counted: How many teenagers have engaged in sexual intercourse? How frequently? How many have used contraceptives? How consistently? In order to understand the current situation in the United States, it is essential to provide this kind of information. But it is also essential to recognize that these behavioral items are part of a much larger system of sexuality and social relationships. What do children learn from parents and others about values and attitudes toward themselves generally and toward themselves as sexual beings? What do they learn from the informal and nonverbal behavior of their parents, as well as from their parents' explicit communication about sexual matters? What do they learn about gender roles? What do they learn about the part that sexual behavior plays within life in general? Are they learning that sexuality is a circumscribed phenomenon having to do with sexual intercourse, physical positions, and erotic techniques, or that it permeates all relationships to a greater or lesser degree?

In order to provide a broader base of understanding, we shall summarize the available data on values and attitudes toward various aspects of sexuality. Not all of these data are focused on teenagers, and this represents a serious limitation. Nevertheless, since teenagers grow up within the larger society, and learn their values within the society, the information is relevant. Children are socialized by their parents, their peers, the media, teachers, ministers, and others. The values and attitudes that they learn influence their behavior and, conversely, their behavior may influence their attitudes and values.

In a probing summary of information on changes in behavior and attitudes regarding premarital sexual intercourse, Reiss (1980) suggests that "from 1880-1980 one can see an almost constant increase in the acceptance of sexuality, both within and outside of marriage" (p. 168). According to Reiss, major changes took place between 1915-1925 and between 1965-1975, with intermediate periods of consolidation. In 1963, approximately 80 percent of a representative national sample of adults believed that premarital intercourse was always wrong; in 1975 only 30 percent believed this. Reiss points to several other major changes in 1915-1925 and in 1965-1975--war (World War I and Vietnam), rising numbers of women in the labor force, and rising divorce rates. It is possible that gender role changes, including greater independence on the part of women, fueled the changes in behavior and attitudes on sexuality. Reiss' major point is that these were decades marked by social change in several areas, and that all of these changes had some influence on each other.

A national sample of teenagers (aged 13 to 18) by the Gallup Youth Survey, carried out in 1978, reported that 30 percent thought premarital sex was wrong, 59 percent thought it was not wrong, and 11 percent had no opinion. Younger teens are somewhat more conservative: among 13- to 15-year-olds, 32 percent judged premarital sex wrong and 54 percent not wrong; among 16- to 18-year-olds, 28 percent said wrong and 64 percent not wrong. Girls were more conservative than boys. Twenty-two percent of the boys thought premarital sex was wrong, compared to 38 percent of the girls; 66 percent of the boys thought it not wrong, compared to 52 percent of the girls.

Despite an historical trend toward acceptance of a variety of forms of sexual behavior (cf. Clayton and Bokemier, 1980), there is today certainly no unanimity on sexual standards. For example, despite the sweeping changes of the last 20 years, substantial numbers of adults and teenagers still believe that premarital sexual behavior is wrong. In order to portray value differences, Reiss formulated a model of four basic views of premarital sexual behavior:

1. Abstinence: Premarital intercourse is considered wrong for both men and women, regardless of circumstances;
2. Double standard: Premarital intercourse is more acceptable for men than for women;
3. Permissiveness with affection: Premarital intercourse is considered right for both men and women when a stable relationship with love or strong affection is present;
4. Permissiveness with or without affection: Premarital intercourse is considered right for both men and women if they are so inclined, regardless of the amount of stability or affection present. (Reiss, 1980, p. 177)

Clearly there are adherents to each of the four standards. In focusing on change, Reiss necessarily emphasizes the extent to which adherence to abstinence (and to the double standard) has decreased while adherence to permissiveness with affection has increased. But these findings pertain to the acceptance of premarital intercourse in general; it is far from certain that adults (or teenagers) would reject abstinence and accept permissiveness to the same extent if they were considering only the behavior of teenagers.

One clue to parents' values regarding their younger children is found in a report on the American family commissioned by General Mills (1977) and based on a national probability sample of 1,230 households with children under 13. Many of the parents surveyed were trying to teach their children traditional values, even when they did not hold these values themselves. With regard to one traditional value, that "having sex outside of marriage is morally wrong," 47 percent of the parents believed it and wanted their children to believe, 25 percent had doubts but still wanted to teach it to their children, and 28 percent did not believe it and did not want to teach it to their children (General Mills, 1977, p. 82).

A study that points to relatively conservative attitudes about one's own sexual behavior is reported by Fox (1979). In her Detroit study of young women aged 14 to 16, she asked about the personal acceptability of sexual intercourse when they were in love. Only 39 percent found it acceptable; and only 10 percent of the mothers found it acceptable for their daughters.

Having young children in the family makes parents more traditional in their values, particularly in those values that they consciously want to pass on to their children (Reiss and Miller, 1979). It is, however, very difficult for parents to teach values they do not believe in. Moreover, our society increasingly accepts permissiveness with affection, and this influences the attitudes and behavior of teenagers. It is not likely, from a policy perspective, that it would be feasible to promote different values for people of different ages, with minors encouraged to adopt abstinence as a value. We were not successful for long in maintaining the informal rule, "No tea or coffee until you're twenty," and sex is more stimulating than caffeine. Changes in sexual behavior in the last 20 years cannot leave anyone of conservative bent too sanguine.

The attitudes and behavior of Americans with respect

to contraceptives -- the birth control pill, intrauterine devices, condoms, diaphragms, and spermicides -- now reflect almost total acceptance by virtually all segments of the population. Reiss (1980, p. 361) says, "the general evidence indicates that in the last two decades we have undergone a contraceptive revolution" (cf. Westoff and Ryder, 1977). Despite the formal teachings of the Roman Catholic Church against the use of artificial contraceptives, the contraceptive practices of Roman Catholics in the United States are virtually identical to the practices of Protestants. On the question of whether "birth control devices should be made available to teenagers," a substantial majority of Americans is favorable, but public opinion is far from unanimous--67 percent agree, 28 percent disagree, and five percent have no opinion (ABC News/Washington Post, 1981).

What about the attitudes and values of Americans regarding abortion? People who hold "pro-choice" views believe that women should be able to control their bodies and their decisions about childbearing, and therefore have the right to choose (or to reject) abortion. People who hold "pro-life" views object to all abortions except those undertaken to save pregnant women's lives, because they believe that abortion is the killing of an "unborn child." The United States Supreme Court, in a series of decisions since 1973, has leaned strongly in the direction of a "pro-choice" position, drawing the ire of "pro-life" partisans. As a result, we continue to see intense controversy, at the state and federal levels, about legislative and regulatory efforts by "pro-life" supporters to restrict abortions as much as possible, within the constitutional guidelines of the court. In addition, legislation and constitutional amendments that would prohibit abortions are under consideration by Congress.

Partisan views of abortion give rise to intense emotions; on the "pro-life" side they occasionally lead to violence against abortion clinics. But the sharp contrast between "pro-choice" and "pro-life" positions, while real and bitter for small groups of partisans, oversimplifies the range of values and the ambivalence (Silber, 1980; Blake and Del Pinal, 1981) that people feel about abortion. The National Opinion Research Center has carried out many surveys of attitudes toward abortion since the early 1960s. The findings of five of the surveys are presented in

Table 5, with the exact wording of the questions included in the table. The major increase in favorable attitudes toward abortion shows up between 1965 and 1972, with a further moderate increase in 1976 and a slight decrease thereafter. For example, when serious danger to a woman's health is the reason, the percentages approving legal abortion rise from 73 percent in 1965 to 87 percent in 1972 and to 91 percent in 1976; subsequently, there is a decline to 89 percent in 1985.

Summary and Conclusion

It is noteworthy that some of the major changes in attitude and behavior in the United States occurred between 1965 and 1975. This is the case for abortion attitudes and behavior as well as for changes in attitudes and behavior regarding premarital sexual intercourse.

In short, the behavior and the values of Americans have been changing in tandem, and this includes the behavior and values of teenagers. The change has been toward greater acceptance of previously unacceptable forms of behavior, such as premarital sexual intercourse and abortion. Some applaud it as a movement in the direction of greater choice and freedom. Others lament it as a movement toward permissiveness, immorality, and irresponsibility. These sharply different social and moral philosophies are now very much part of the political process in the United States, and reflect underlying divisiveness and controversy about potential changes in law and policy.

At present, largely as a result of changes since 1965, minors' access to contraceptives and to medical services for contraception are generally good throughout the United States, especially in the major metropolitan areas. Access to abortion services is more limited, but minors are certainly not prohibited from having abortions. An oversimplified summary of the legal situation is that minors in most states can make their own decision about whether or not to have an abortion, but some states are insisting upon parental involvement in the abortion decision. The U.S. Supreme Court has ruled that it is unconstitutional for a state to require all minors to have parental consent in order to have a legal abortion. States may, however, require minors who do not want to involve their parents to convince a judge that they are mature

Table 5

Percentage of U.S. Adults Who Approve of
Legal Abortion, 1965-1985*

	1965	1972	1976	1980	1985

"Please tell me whether you think it should be possible
for a pregnant woman to obtain a legal abortion:

	1965	1972	1976	1980	1985
(1) If the woman's health is seriously endangered by the pregnancy	73	87	91	90	89
(2) If she became pregnant as a result of rape	59	79	84	83	81
(3) If there is a strong chance of a serious defect in the baby	57	79	84	83	79
(4) If the family has a very low income and cannot afford any more children	22	49	53	52	44
(5) If she is not married and does not want to marry the man	18	43	50	48	41
(6) If she is married and does not want any more children	16	40	46	47	40

*Percentages are based on respondents who answered yes
or no. Respondents who gave other answers are excluded.

Source: National Opinion Research Center surveys, as
reported in Granberg and Granberg (1980); Tom W. Smith,
NORC, personal communication, June 25, 1985.

enough to give informed consent on their own or, if they are not mature, to convince a judge that the abortion is in their best interest (Donovan, 1981, 1982).

The Reagan administration is attempting to limit minors' family planning rights, but it has not had much success thus far. The rule requiring federally funded family planning clinics to notify parents of contraceptive services provided to minors has been overturned by the courts. Several efforts to pass legislation or a Constitutional amendment that would prohibit abortion to all women, or that would give each state the authority to legislate on abortion, are also stalled. Although their chances for passage are not very good, the current tide toward conservatism makes it possible that some form of restrictive legislation may be passed. Finally, with the possibility that President Reagan may make further appointments to the U.S. Supreme Court, it is also possible that the Court may eventually back away from its strong support of the reproductive health rights of women and take a more restrictive position.

Footnotes

1. Children, adolescents, teenagers, and minors are sometimes used interchangeably in this chapter. In legal terms a child is a minor--someone who has not yet reached the age of adulthood or majority. In practical terms, the children or minors that this chapter is primarily concerned with are adolescents or teenagers.
2. For discussions of the competing legal interests of children, parents, and the state in the United States, see Mnookin (1978), Rodman, Lewis, and Griffith (1984), and Besharov (1985).
3. Family planning is often used conventionally and euphemistically to refer to sexual activity, contraceptive use, and abortion (cf. Roberts, 1981). From the context of our focus upon unmarried minors who are sexually active, it should be clear that the "family planning" rights at issue are contraceptive and abortion rights.
4. At present contraceptive services for minors are generally available without parental consent or notifica-

tion. The proposed 1982 regulation of the Department of Health and Human Services requiring parental notification for minors served by government subsidized clinics drew many objections, including objections from more than three-quarters of the states. The media referred to the regulation as the "squeal rule." It was blocked by the courts.

References

ABC News/Washington Post Poll, 1981. Survey if No is not available simply omit 0034, June 8.

Alan Guttmacher Institute, 1976. **11 Million Teenagers.** New York.

Alan Guttmacher Institute, 1981. **Teenage Pregnancy: The Problem That Hasn't Gone Away.** New York.

Baumrind, D., 1978. Reciprocal rights and responsibilities in parent-child relations. **Journal of Social Issues** 34:179-196.

Bellotti vs. Baird, 433 US 662 (1979).

Besharov, D.J. (1985). "Doing something" about child abuse: The need to narrow the grounds for state intervention. **Harvard Journal of Law and Public Policy** 8:539-589.

Blake, J. and J.H. Del Pinal. 1981. Negativism, equivocation, and wobbly assent: Public "support" for the prochoice platform on abortion. **Demography** 18:309-320.

Bush, D.. 1983. Fertility-related state laws passed in 1982. **Family Planning Perspectives** 15:111-116.

Chamie, M., S. Eisman, J.D. Forrest, M.T. Orr, and A. Torres. 1982. Factors affecting adolescents' use of family planning clinics. **Family Planning Perspectives** 14:126-139.

Centers for Disease Control. 1983. **Abortion Surveillance 1979-1980.** Public Health Service.

Chilman, C.S., 1978. **Adolescent Sexuality in a Changing American Society.** U.S. Department of Health, Education, and Welfare, Public Health Service, DHEW Publication No. (NIH) 79-1426.

----------. 1980. Social and psychological research concerning adolescent childbearing: 1970-1980. **Journal of Marriage and the Family** 42:793-805.

Clayton, R.R. and J.L. Bokemeier. 1980. Premarital sex in

the seventies. **Journal of Marriage and the Family** 42:759-775.

Constantine, L.L., 1977. Open family: A lifestyle for kids and other people. **Family Coordinator** 26:113-121.

DeLamater, J. and P. MacCorquodale. 1979. **Premarital Sexuality.** Madison: University of Wisconsin Press.

Donovan, P., 1981. Your parents or the judge: Massachusetts' new abortion consent law. **Family Planning Perspectives** 12:224-228.

----------. 1982. Fertility-related state laws enacted in 1981. **Family Planning Perspectives** 14:63-67.

Dryfoos, J.G. and N. Bourque-Scholl. 1981. **Factbook on Teenage Pregnancy.** New York: Alan Guttmacher Institute.

Farson, R., 1974. **Birthrights.** New York: MacMillan.

Finkel, M.L. and D.J. Finkel. 1978. Male adolescent contraceptive utilization. **Adolescence** 13:443-451.

Fox, G.L., 1977. "Nice girl": Social control of women through a value construct. **Signs** 2:805-817.

----------. 1979. Mothers and Their Teenage Daughters: A Report to the Participants in the Mother-Daughter Communication Project. Mimeographed.

Fox, G.L. and J.K. Inazu. 1980a. Patterns and outcomes of mother-daughter communication about sexuality. **Journal of Social Issues** 36:7-29.

----------. 1980b. Mother-daughter communication about sex. **Family Relations** 29:347-352.

Freeman, E.W. and K. Rickels. 1979. Adolescent contraceptive use: Current status of practice and research. **Obstetrics and Gynecology** 53:388-394.

Furstenberg, F.F., Jr. 1976. **Unplanned Parenthood: The Social Consequences of Teenage Childbearing.** New York: Free Press.

Furstenberg, F.F., Jr., R. Herceg-Baron, D. Mann, and J. Shea. 1982. Parental involvement: Selling family planning clinics short. **Family Planning Perspectives** 14:140-144.

Furstenberg, F.F., Jr., R. Herceg-Baron, J. Shea, and D. Webb. 1984. Family communication and teenagers' contraceptive use. **Family Planning Perspectives** 16:163-170.

Gallup Youth Survey. 1978. Associated Press Release, October 11, 1978.

General Mills. 1977. **The General Mills American Family Report.** Conducted by Yankelovich, Skelly, and White,

Inc., Minneapolis: General Mills, Inc.

Granberg, D. and B.W. Granberg. 1980. Abortion attitudes, 1965-1980: Trends and determinants. **Family Planning Perspectives** 12:250-261.

Green, C.P. and K. Poteteiger. 1978. Teenage pregnancy: A major problem for minors. **Society** 15:8-13.

H.L. vs Matheson. 450 US 398 (1981).

Harris vs McRae 448 US 297 (1980).

Henshaw, S.K., N.J. Brinkin, E. Blaine, and J.C. Smith, 1985. A portrait of American women who obtain abortions. **Family Planning Perspectives 17:**90-96

Henshaw, S.K., J.D. Forrest, and E. Blaine. 1984. Abortion services in the United States 1981 and 1982. **Family Planning Perspectives** 16:119-127.

Henshaw, S. and K. O'Reilly. 1983. Characteristics of abortion patients in the United States, 1979 and 1980. **Family Planning Perspectives** 15:15-16.

Herold, E.S., 1981. Contraceptive embarrassment and contraceptive behavior among young single women. **Journal of Youth and Adolescence** 10:233-242.

Inazu, J.K. and G.L. Fox. 1980. Maternal influences on the sexual behavior of teenage daughters. **Journal of Family Issues** 1:81-102.

Jones, E.F., J.R. Beniger, and C.F. Westoff. 1980. Pill and IUD discontinuation in the United States, 1970-1975: The influence of the media. **Family Planning Perspectives** 11:293-300.

Kasun, J.R., 1978. Teenage pregnancy: A reply to zero population growth. **Society** 15:9-15.

Kisker, E.E., 1985. Teenagers talk about sex, pregnancy and contraception. **Family Planning Perspectives** 17:83-90

Koenig, M.A. and M. Zelnik. 1982. The risk of premarital first pregnancy among metropolitan-area teenagers: 1976 and 1979. **Family Planning Perspectives** 14:239-247.

Luker, K., 1975. **Taking Chances: Abortion and the Decision Not to Contracept.** Berkeley: University of California Press.

MacIntyre, S., 1977. **Single and Pregnant.** London: Croom Helm.

Newcomer, S.F. and J.R. Udry. 1985. Parent-child communication and adolescent sexual behavior. **Family Planning Perspectives** 17:169-174.

Mnookin, R.H., **Child, Family, and State.** Boston: Little, Brown.

Paul, E.W., 1977. Danforth and Bellotti: A breakthrough for adolescents. **Family Planning/Population Reporter** 6:3-5.

Paul, E.W. and H.F. Pilpel. 1979. Teenagers and pregnancy: The law in 1979. **Family Planning Perspectives** 11:297-302.

Paul, E.W. and G. Scofield. 1979. Informed consent for fertility control services. **Family Planning Perspectives** 11:159-168.

Planned Parenthood of Central Missouri vs Danforth, 428 U.S. 52 (1976).

Presser, H.B., 1974. Early motherhood: Ignorance or bliss? **Family Planning Perspectives** 6:8-14.

Rains, P., 1971. **Becoming an Unwed Mother.** Chicago: Aldine-Atherton.

Reisman, J., 1980. Nice girl imagery and teenagers' decision to abort: A study of middle-class teenagers' reaction to pregnancy. Paper presented at American Sociological Association annual meeting. August 28, 1980, New York.

Reiss, I.L., 1980. **Family Systems in America.** 3rd ed. New York: Holt, Rinehart, and Winston.

Reiss, I.L. and B.C. Miller. 1979. Heterosexual permissiveness: A theoretical analysis. In W.R. Burr, R. Hill, F.I. Nye, and I.L. Reiss, eds., **Contemporary Theories About the Family,** pp. 57-100. New York: Free Press.

Rodman, H., S.H. Lewis, and S.B. Griffith. **The Sexual Rights of Adolescents: Competence, Vulnerability, and Parental Control.** New York: Columbia University Press, 1984.

Rosen, R.H., 1980. Adolescent pregnancy decision-making: Are parents important? **Adolescence** 15:43-54.

----------. 1982. Pregnancy resolution decisions: A review and appraisal of research. In G.L. Fox, ed., **The Childbearing Decision: Fertility Attitudes and Behavior,** pp. 247-266. Beverly Hills, Calif.: Sage.

Sarvis, B. and H. Rodman. 1974. **The Abortion Controversy.** 2nd ed. New York: Columbia University Press.

Shah, F., M. Zelnik, and J.F. Kantner. 1975. Unprotected intercourse among unwed teenagers. **Family Planning Perspectives** 7:39-44.

Silber, T.J., 1980. Values relating to abortion as expressed by the inner city adolescent girl: Report of a physician's experience. **Adolescence** 15:183-189.

Torres, A., 1978. Does your mother know...? **Family Planning Perspectives** 10:280-282.

Torres, A., J.D. Forrest, and S. Eisman. 1980. Telling parents: Clinic policies and adolescents' use of family planning and abortion services. **Family Planning Perspectives** 12:284-292.

Walters, J. and L.H. Walters. 1980. Parent-child relationships: A review, 1970-1979. **Journal of Marriage and the Family** 42:807-822.

Westoff, C.F. and N.B. Ryder. 1977. **The Contraceptive Revolution.** Princeton, NJ: Princeton University Press.

Young, L.R., 1954. **Out of Wedlock.** New York: McGraw-Hill.

Zabin, L.S. and S.D. Clark, Jr. 1983. Institutional factors affecting teenagers' choice and reasons for delay in attending a family planning clinic. **Family Planning Perspectives** 15:25-29.

Zelnik, M., 1979. Sex education and knowledge of pregnancy risk among U.S. teenage women. **Family Planning Perspectives** 11:355-357.

Zelnik, M. and J.F. Kantner. 1977. Sexual and contraceptive experience of young unmarried women in the United States, 1976 and 1971. **Family Planning Perspectives** 9:55-71.

----------. 1978. First pregnancies to women aged 15-19: 1976 and 1971. **Family Planning Perspectives** 10:11-20.

----------. 1979. Reasons for nonuse of contraception by sexually active women aged 15-19. **Family Planning Perspectives** 11:289-296.

----------. 1980. Sexual activity, contraceptive use and pregnancy among metropolitan-area teenagers: 1971-1979. **Family Planning Perspectives** 12:230-237.

Zelnik, M., J.K. Kantner, and K. Ford. 1981. **Sex and Pregnancy in Adolescence,** Beverly Hills, CA: Sage.

Zelnik, M., Y.J. Kim, and J.F. Kantner. 1979. Probabilities of intercourse and conception among U.S. teenage women, 1971 and 1976. **Family Planning Perspectives** 11:177-183.

Zelnik, M. and F.K. Shah. 1983. First intercourse among young Americans. **Family Planning Perspectives** 15:64-70.

13
FAMILY PLANNING AND SEX EDUCATION FOR YOUNG PEOPLE

Bo Lewin

Introduction

During 1981-1982 the Family Planning Unit of the World Health Organization, Regional Office for Europe, conducted a study, Family Planning and Sex Education of Young People. This study was initiated by the Regional Officer for Family Planning, Ms. Wadad Haddad, and was conducted by Dr. Bo Lewin, Department of Sociology Uppsala University, and Consultant to the World Health Organization.

This article presents a short overview of the rationale for special services for young people in the areas of sex education and family planning in addition to the summary of findings of the study. The conclusions are those of the author, not necessarily those of the World Health Organization, and are based on this study only. The policy of the World Health Organization is derived from a complex array of data and consultations with the Member States.

Family Planning and Sex Education for Young People

Human sexuality depends not only on biological and physiological factors, but also on psychological and social factors. Since it is in the interest of every society that its members be secure, have self-respect, and take a responsible attitude toward their sexual lives, it logically follows that young people should be prepared for sexuality.

There are many different cultural traditions within the

199

WHO European Region, and there can be no one right way to prepare young people for sexual life. The diversity of cultures and the complexity of the task, however, must not be used as an excuse for neglecting to provide adequate education and family planning services for this segment of the population.

During adolescence the individual goes through rapid physical development and reaches reproductive maturity. Sexual change, however, begins in early childhood, and includes the development of gender identity and the beginning of sex roles. With the onset of puberty comes the development of secondary sex characteristics, including growth of the reproductive organs, body hair, and adult male/female body configurations, and a rapid increase in sexual interest and sexual behaviour. Biological and physical changes are accompanied by cognitive and psychological development, but often not at the same rate, thereby creating tension within an individual.

It is common for younger children to explore their own bodies and to masturbate, and this behaviour increases during puberty. Masturbation is natural and healthy, and should not be regarded as a form of regression unless it replaces all other forms of sexual behaviour.

Typically, in early adolescence, teenagers develop close relationships with individuals of the same sex, and it is normal that such relationships should occasionally include explicit homosexual behaviour. The persistence of such behaviour to the exclusion of subsequent heterosexuality is poorly understood, but it is important that the occurrence of homosexuality be recognized and accepted.

In most instances, however, puberty means the rapid development of heterosexual preferences and behaviours which have biological roots, but which are profoundly influenced by the values and standards of the family and society. Courting behaviour varies widely among the cultures and subcultures of the European Region, but usually progresses from group social interaction involving both sexes to social interaction involving one couple. The debut of sexual intercourse appears to be occurring earlier and earlier. In many if not most areas of the Region the majority of both sexes has experienced sexual intercourse before their nineteenth birthday (WHO 1979).

The process of socialization into the adult world implies the learning of social roles and skills as well as the internalization of cherished values of one's society, its norms, and its perceptions of the world. This complex task takes place during the childhood and teenage years, although individual and cultural differences may account for variations in the process.

During adolescence the individual often leaves school and enters the labour force. In static preindustrial societies social differentiation was relatively limited, and the geographical and social closeness between home and work made adult tasks well known and comprehensible. What was expected of an individual was in many respects self evident, and the social setting usually offered several adults who could serve as role models.

With industrialization and urbanization the transition into adulthood becomes increasingly complex. A far wider variety of work opportunities is formally available, although prolonged education for increasing numbers of young people means longer economic dependence on parents and problems in the labour market often make entry into the labour force uncertain.

The value of previous generations as models for future behaviour is often reduced. Parents may work outside the home in pursuits not easily understood by a child. They may be stunned by recent changes in the surrounding society, while adolescents experiencing internal changes in themselves and in the world about them may tend to exaggerate the inappropriateness of parents as role models.

It is more important than ever before to provide whatever services may be required to enable the young to understand the changes going on in their bodies and the social significance of these changes, and to facilitate their maturing into responsible citizens.

Sex education can be given many names and implemented in many different ways. Educational programmes may be called "health and sex education," "sex and family living," "study on sex and living together," "preparation for parenthood," "humanization of the relations between the sexes," to mention some known terms. The term used for this kind of education is of interest in itself, since it probably reflects some cherished values of a country. More interesting, however, is the content and organization of the education. It has been suggested that sex education in Europe can be classified into four markedly different types (Kozakiewicz, 1981).

Type 1 - Population Education: strikingly anti-natalistic, it advocates moral responsibility for the demographic explosion. Human reproduction is discouraged; strong emphasis is placed on contraceptive use.

Type 2 - Sex Education: based on a traditional Swedish pattern (mid 1960s), its focus is on preparation for sexual life, apart from marriage and the family. Its primary aim is to teach effective forms of achieving sexual satisfaction. Great emphasis is placed on contraception, and importance is attached to any physiological or psycho-sexual problems which might occur in sexual life.

Type 3 - Education for Inter-human Relationships and Communication: a more human version of traditional "sex education," linking basic sexual information with personal attitudes towards the opposite sex (E.g., Denmark, Finland, Sweden since mid 1970s, and Yugoslavia).

Type 4 - Preparation for Marriage and Family Life: sex education is connected with preparation for future marital and parental life, and is regarded as only one component in the preparation for adult life in general. Marital and family life is seen as far more than the sexual cohabitation of two persons, and must be understood in the context of the total society. Parenthood is considered to be a value, the aim of every human being (E.g., some socialist countries and some European Latin culture countries).

Several arguments have been marshalled against this typology. For example, it is unclear whether it is based on a single dimension or on several dimensions. Moreover, the distinctions are not altogether clear and the types are not mutually exclusive: adherents to one type of sex education are likely to accept many aspects of the other types. Nevertheless, the typology does point to divergent kinds of sex education in Europe.

Not only does the content of sex education vary among the countries of Europe, wide variations also exist among the populations to whom such education is offered. In some countries sex education is offered in one form or another to pre-school children, while in other countries it is provided, if at all, only to older secondary school adolescents in biology courses.

There is, of course, no one single way to prepare young people for future sexual life. A recent WHO Conference on the Child and the Adolescent in Society (WHO 1979, p. 40), however, made the following recommendations, which were considered essential to the success of sex education programmes: "First, sex education should be broadened to family life education and should provide information concerning sex roles, parental roles, child care and family interaction with the aim of forming a complete and socially active personality, prepared for a happy life with a partner and a sound family. The emphasis of these programmes, which in the past has been negative (prevention of pregnancy, prevention of sexually transmitted diseases), should be on the positive aspect of sexuality: planning for wanted children and the achievement of rewarding, loving human relationships."

The recommendations also included that these education programmes in sexuality should begin early, be age-specific, and be a continuous health promotional activity throughout the school years. They should start in the family with a pre-school child and be linked to the school.

The term "family planning" is ambiguous, applying in some countries only to clinical-medical services, and in others to various counselling and advisory services. Even within one country the services offered might vary considerably from one family planning unit to another, and in some countries different family planning organizations have differing opinions regarding what constitutes family planning. In one country of the Region a well-informed observer summarized a study of two agencies by stating that, if a couple went to Agency A with a contraceptive problem, they came out with a relational problem, whereas if a couple went to Agency B with a relational problem, they came out with a condom.

Family planning was defined and described by a WHO committee in 1970:

Family planning refers to practices that help individuals or couples to attain certain objectives; to avoid unwanted births; to bring about wanted births; to regulate the intervals between pregnancies; to control the time at which births occur in relation to the ages of the parents; and to determine the number of children in the family. Services that make these practices possible include education and counselling on family planning; the provision of contraceptives; the management of infertility; education about sex and parenthood; and organizationally related activities, such as genetic and marriage counselling, screening for malignancy, and adoption services (WHO 1971, p. 8).

According to this definition, family planning should include not only the negative aspect of avoiding unwanted births, but also the full services needed to make it possible for a couple or an individual to plan when to have children.

Societal reactions to the increase in sexual activity among adolescents have varied. In some countries the special needs of adolescents have been anticipated, and special family planning services have been provided. In other countries this has not yet happened. There ought to be, however, universal recognition of the need for such services, since adolescent sexual activity is increasing, and adolescents in general are a particularly vulnerable group.

Not only are there increased medical health risks involved with pregnancy in younger adolescents, but there are also serious social effects of unplanned pregnancies. Educational plans are often ruined by too early child-bearing, and often neither the adolescent father nor mother is in a position, socially or economically, to support a child. Through numerous studies it is known that contraceptive use is considerably lower among adolescents than among adults. Sometimes the reason for this is lack of adequate knowledge, not only about contraceptives, but also about the very basic facts of reproduction. The remedy is, of course, education and still more education. Contraceptive use is low, however, even when there has been education concerning reproduction and contraception. Knowledge of family planning has to be transformed into active use of family planning. Not only is it necessary that the adolescent know how and where to get contraceptive supplies and information, it is also necessary that he or she accept and trust the service providers. Many young people abstain from the use of family planning and related services because they fear, justly or unjustly, that they will be morally condemned or that their sexual activity will be made known to parents or other people in their immediate social surrounding.

The Study

The purpose of this study was to assess the status of education for sexuality, family living, and family planning as well as to describe some family planning services for young people in the European Region of the World Health Organization, which extends from the Scandinavian countries in the north to Morocco and Algeria in the south, and from the Atlantic islands in the west to the Soviet Union, including Asian parts, in the east.

In this study, sex education is understood to be education that centers on human sexuality, human sexual behaviour, family planning, and social aspects of human sexuality. Young people are here regarded as children and adolescents below the age when people in a given country of the study usually marry or start to cohabit under marriage-like conditions.

Information for the study was obtained by the following means: (1) The literature on previous studies of family planning and sex education for young people was surveyed, and a short bibliography was compiled. (2) A short questionnaire was sent to Ministries of Health in the countries of the Region in order to determine the extent to which sex education is compulsory or otherwise implemented in the school system, and which aspects of sex education and family planning for young people are regarded as urgent by various government agencies. (3) In order to be able to compare official views with social reality a number of educational and/or family planning projects aimed at young people were studied in more detail by means of an extensive questionnaire sent to these projects in advance of site visits by the researcher. In all, 16 projects in 9 countries were included in this part of the study. During the country visits discussions also were held and information gathered from numerous institutions and government agencies in the respective countries. Projects were selected because they were known to have programmes aimed at young people. This part of the study is not meant to convey a representative picture of family planning or educational projects but to identify a selection of working approaches.

The first part of this report is based on information obtained through the initial questionnaires sent to the Ministries of Health in the countries of the Region. At the time of this writing completed questionnaires have been received from Algeria, Czechoslovakia (Slovak Republic), Denmark, Finland, France, Federal Republic of Germany, Greece, Hungary, Iceland, Luxembourg, Monaco, Norway, Spain, Switzerland, United Kingdom, and Yugoslavia.

The person who received the initial questionnaire was asked to answer it in order to help us to identify the official policy for her/his country. The respondents were asked not to give their personal opinions but to quote the official opinion. It was pointed out that "in some instances interpretations of official documents and policies may be necessary so that the official policy can be clearly stated. We are, however, convinced that you are in a position to make such interpretations of the official policy. Since you are the only person in your country to whom these questions are put, your cooperation is essential for the success of the study. Although we ask you to answer, you are of course free to consult others if you are uncertain about some matters." It was also pointed out that some questions might seem very awkward, in that the same questionnaire was being sent to all countries of the WHO European Region.

Sex Education for Young People

Sex education is claimed to be a compulsory topic in the schools of twelve countries, whereas five countries report that it is not regulated by law. It must be realized, however, that sex education can mean different things in different countries, and even when mandatory, it does not follow that a comprehensive programme of sex education is given to all children, or even to a majority. In France, for instance, a basic knowledge of physiology and anatomy is compulsory, while supplementary sex education is recommended but not systematically implemented.

There are, however, no direct legal obstacles to sex education in any of the countries; in no country is sex education prohibited. The absence of direct prohibition is of course only the first prerequisite for implementing sex education. Other barriers -- such as informal objections to sex education -- may also need to be overcome.

One final complication should also be noted. Some countries are federations, and laws concerning education might vary markedly from one part of the country to another. Such is the case in Switzerland, where the question was answered, "depending on cantons." Switzerland was therefore counted twice in the study, once as not regulated by law and once as mandatory, since both alternatives were checked.

In connection with this discussion of the legal status of sex education, another report of WHO's Family Planning Unit ought to be mentioned: Swartz, Barbara, Family Planning Legislation, Euro Reports and Studies 85, World Health Organization, Regional Office for Europe, 1983. This report presents a detailed study not only of formal legislation but also of cultural backgrounds and traditions governing legal practices in Greece, Italy, Morocco, Portugal, Spain, Tunisia, and Turkey. A special section in this well documented report is also devoted to teenagers and family planning.

The twelve countries that claimed sex education to be compuslory were asked to indicate which institutions formally provided this education. Three mentioned pre-school; nine, primary school; eleven, secondary school; and six, "other," usually meaning University or special occupational school (Appendix 1). Four countries also mentioned the army, and eight countries mentioned other organizations or institutions. In some countries sex education is compuslory in several of the above institutions, whereas in other countries only one or two institutions teach sex education. That secondary school followed by primary school are the most popular institutions for providing sex education is hardly surprising.

In some countries, and not only in the federations, local self-administration is important. Of the countries that claimed sex education to be compulsory, three indicated that programmes were implemented at the discretion of local governments, while eight claimed that no such local discretion was possible.

Among countries in which sex education is compuslory four indicated that the curriculum content is determined by national boards or general directorates of education/health, three indicated local government control, and four indicated curriculum decisions by joint effort involving national government agencies, local government, and/or the local school. That sex education is compulsory by law does not necessarily mean that a broad education on the subject is always given. Support at the national level is important for creating formal possibilities for sex education, but the actual implementation and content of a programme is dependent on the interest and goodwill of people active in the local community, particularly local administrators, who are in closer contact with the potential recipients of sex education.

Some possible settings are clearly underutilized. The army could be utilized for sex education much more than it is at present. Several countries in the Region have defense systems which require that all young men be enrolled for a period of time. Because of their ages and the deprivation of contacts with women, sex and male-female relations are important topics of conversation, making this an opportune time for sex education. Special programmes have been developed for the army in the Federal Republic of Germany and in Poland.

Among the government agencies responding to the questionnaire adolescent boys and girls were the most frequently mentioned target groups for sex education (see Table 1). This emphasizes the widespread importance attached to preparing young people for their future sexual life.

Respondents from Finland, Hungary, and Yugoslavia added comments to the effect that sex education should not be aimed at only one group, but should include all of the population. This is eminently reasonable; it would be most unfortunate, however, if that idea prevented countries from developing special programmes for young people.

While not all governments responded, estimates of the proportion of young people who had received any formal sex education in school ranged from 5 to 100 percent (cf. Table 2).

Government agencies were asked to rate the importance of each of several sex education topics for young people, and to indicate whether any of these were compulsory or considered unfit topics. In Table 3 we see that four topics are most often considered important:

Human sexual anatomy, reproductive biology, contraceptives, and parenthood. The emphasis of the government agencies in the Region seems to be on the biological basis of sexuality/reproduction and subsequent parenthood. Topics most often given low priority are pornography and petting. Most controversial -- in the sense that almost equal numbers of respondents consider them important and unimportant -- are: religious views of marriage and the family, petting, masturbation, sterilization, and sexual dysfunctions.

Table 1. Governments' Rating of Target Groups for Sex Education.

Question: "Which of the following groups are considered by the government (or other responsible institution handling these matters, such as the National Board of health education or general directorate of health/education) to be important target groups for sex education?"

1 = not important at all
5 = very important

Number of countries indicating respective importance

	1	2	3	4	5
Preschool children	4	2	2	0	2
Children in primary school	1	0	5	1	5
Children in secondary school	0	0	0	3	10
Adolescent girls	0	0	0	1	12
Adolescent boys	0	0	0	1	12
Girls just below usual age of marriage	0	0	4	0	6
Boys just below usual age of marriage	0	0	3	0	6
Newly-married women	1	2	2	1	4
Newly-married men	1	2	2	1	4
Women with many children	1	2	0	1	6
Men with many children	1	2	1	0	6

The number of responses varies since several of the 16 countries which returned completed questionnaires had abstained from rating one ore more possible target groups.

Homosexuality is the only topic that is not reported to be compulsory in at least one country. Attitudes toward homosexuality are often ambiguous and a compulsory teaching programme would presumably be difficult to institutionalize since there is no general agreement on how to deal with it from a moral standpoint. Homosexuality is also the only topic not considered "very important" by any respondent. In contrast, both parenthood and venereal disease are considered important and are often compulsory; the former presumably is given a distinct positive moral value and the latter a negative moral value, and hence they are easier to handle in an educational setting.

It is regrettable that homosexuality does not receive more attention, since it is well known that individuals with a predominantly or exclusively homosexual orientation exist in all cultures. It is also well known that young people often pass through a period of identification and occasional acts that might be called homosexual. Adolescents uninformed in these matters may be subject to unnecessary strain and anxiety.

Pornography is the only topic which at least two countries find unfit for young people, according to the official view. It is interesting to note that, among the nine countries that rated pornography's importance, seven find it unimportant and two consider it important; one country finds it important enough to make it a compulsory

Table 2. Governments' Estimates of Proportion of Adolescents Receving Sex Education and Having Easy Access to Family Planning Services.

Proportion receiving sex education

	0-33	34-36	67-	NA
no of countries	2	1	8	5

Proportion with easy access to family planning

	0-33	34-36	67-	NA
no of countries	1	1	7	7

topic in the sex education of young people.

Table 3. Governments' Rating of the Importance of Sex Education Topics.

QUESTION: Which of the following themes are considered by the government (or other responsible instution handling these matters, such as the National Board of health education or general directorate of health/education) to be important in the sex education of young people? Are any of these themes compulsory and part of all curricula and are there any that, on the other hand, are considered not at all suitable for the education of young people?

1 = not important at all
5 = very important
* = compulsory
** = not fit

	Number of countries importance					*	**
	1	2	3	4	5		
Sexual anatomy of humans	0	0	1	1	10	7	0
Sex roles	0	2	1	3	5	4	0
Parenthood	0	0	0	2	9	5	0
Reproductive biology	0	0	0	1	10	6	0
Love	1	0	0	4	5	4	0
Psychology of puberty	0	2	1	3	4	2	0
Religious view of marriage and the family	4	1	1	0	4	2	1
Pornography	5	2	0	1	1	1	2
Intercourse	1	1	1	2	5	3	0
Petting	3	3	1	1	3	1	1
Masturbation	3	1	1	2	3	3	0
Homosexuality	2	1	3	2	0	0	1
Contrceptives	0	0	0	2	9	4	0
Venereal diseases	0	0	1	3	6	4	1
Sterilization	2	1	3	1	3	1	1
Abortion	2	0	0	2	6	1	1
Sexual dysfunctions (e.g. impotence)	2	3	2	0	3	1	1

Sex education for young people is offered by a variety of different institutions, as is seen in Table 4. In 14 of the 16 responding countries some kind of sex education is offered in the secondary schools. As indicated earlier, the process of developing and implementing sex education programmes in the schools is a difficult one. It therefore cannot be assumed that these 14 countries offer appropriate sex education programmes, but they have certainly made a start.

One note of caution is appropriate about the figures in Table 4. The government agency responding to the questionnaire is more likely to be aware of the sex educa-

Table 4. Institusions Offering Formal Sex Education (compulsory as well as voluntary) to Young People: Government Responses.

QUESTION: Which institutions/organizations offer formal sex education to young people and is the education specially directed towards young people?

	special program	welcome to join program
Preschool	5	0
Primary school	10	0
Secondary school	14	1*
The army	5	1*
Family planning association	5	4
Student organization	7	2
Church	3	4
Women's movement	4	4
Other government institutions	5	4
Other volutary organizations	4	2

*These cases are reported as having sex education for adults to which young people are welcome. The meaning of this is unclear, however, since it would ordinarily be assumed that education arranged by these intitutions was targeted primarily at young people.

tion efforts of other government agencies than of voluntary agencies.

Family Planning for Young People

Family planning, not to be confused with population control, is seen primarily as services offered and measures taken to allow people to have the number of children they choose and at the times they choose. It focuses on the individuals' ability to control their own health and social well-being by the spacing of births, rather than on societal control of birth rates in terms of some perceived optimum population density.

In most instances birth control is used to avoid rather than facilitate births. The attitude of a government toward that country's birth rate might thus be relevant to the availability of family planning services. Only one country indicated that its birth rate was too high, three countries considered it acceptable, and five countries found it too low. One country gave two responses -- too low and acceptable. In some countries, such as the United Kingdom, it was reported that the government holds no official view on the magnitude of the birth-rate. Yugoslavia indicated that family planning is a constitutional right, implying that an official government policy on the birth rate would be unconstitutional (See Appendix 1 for responses from individual countries).

There are three important prerequisites for the successful use of family planning: knowledge, availability, and acceptance. Our focus here is upon availability. The requirements for medical prescriptions and other regulations on the sale of contraceptives are an important aspect of availability. Government agency responses to our questionnaire suggest that there are only minor differences among the countries of the Region regarding the availability of contraceptives for young people. Actually, however, the differences between countries are greater than the official answers would indicate, at least so far as the pill is concerned. In some countries prescriptions are required for most contraceptives, but pills can usually be bought without prescription at a pharmacy, despite legal requirements (Swartz, 1983).

Hormonal contraceptives of long duration (injectables) are available in thirteen countries only when prescribed by medical personnel. In one country they are not available to young people, and in one country they are not available at all. Fifteen countries indicated the availability of both oral contraceptives and IUD's by medical prescription, and one, that they are available in pharmacies without prescription. Diaphragms are available in pharmacies without prescription in eight countries, and not available at all in one country. Spermicides are available in pharmacies without prescription in eight countries, in one country with prescription, and in one country in shops or other public places without prescription. Condoms are easily available in shops or other public places in eight countries, and in pharmacies only (without prescription) in eight countries.

Major differences in sales regulations are reported only for diaphragms and condoms. Since the diaphragm requires fitting, its availability with or without prescription is of little importance. The availability of condoms, whether in shops or only in pharmacies, may be of greater importance to young people. Since adolescent sexual encounters tend not to be premeditated, the slightest obstacle to access to this particular type of birth control may be decisive. Considering the irregularity of many adolescent sexual encounters, condoms are in many ways the preferred contraceptive for young people. To facilitate the availability of condoms would seem to provide a simple way of increasing the likelihood of contraceptive use among young people, especially when they are adequately informed and when the social climate is one of acceptance.

The most frequently mentioned target group for family planning activities among respondents in the study is women with many children. It is interesting to note that young boys and young girls are seen as important target groups equally often, whereas the same is not true of women with many children and men with many children.

Although most contraceptives are to be used by females, the successful implementation of family planning depends on the acceptance and participation of males. Their motivation is essential, since in many countries their social status and influence make male acceptance of family planning crucial for its effective use. Use of the condom, which has been pointed out above is particularly suitable for youth who do not regularly have sexual intercourse, makes the cooperation of males even more essential among young people. Educating and motivating boys to assume a responsible attitude toward family planning will also pay off at a later date, when they enter into more stable relationships.

In addition to the target groups listed in Table 5, Algeria mentioned single mothers; Finland listed abortion patients and patients with inheritable diseases; and France listed women with a deprived socio-economic background, rural women, and immigrant women as important target groups. Hungary commented that in the

Table 5. Governments' Rating of Important Target Groups for Family Planning Services.

QUESTION: Which of the following groups are considered by the government (or other responsible institution handling these matters, such as the National Board of health education or general directorate of health/education) to be important target groups for family planning/counselling services?

1 = not important at all
5 = very important
   Number of countries indicating respective importance

	1	2	3	4	5
Women with many children	0	1	1	1	10
Men with many children	0	2	1	1	7
Married women	0	2	5	1	3
Married men	0	2	4	1	3
All adult women	1	0	5	1	5
All adult men	1	0	5	1	4
Newly-married women	0	0	4	1	5
Newly married men	0	0	3	1	6
Girls just below usual age of marriage	0	0	2	3	6
Boys just below usual age of marriage	0	0	2	3	6
Young girls as soon as possible after menarche	1	1	1	2	8
Young boys as soon as possible after first emission of semen	1	1	1	1	8

official view all groups are of equal importance.

If health for all is the ultimate goal, it is important to make family planning services equally available to all. In order to achieve this goal, however, special efforts may be necessary to reach certain groups. The lack of variation in the relative importance assigned to the various target groups (see Table 5) may reflect conflict between the goal of making family planning services available to all and the means required to achieve this goal.

In thirteen countries there are no legal obstacles to dissemination of information about contraception, although the United Kingdom and Yugoslavia report some regulations against advertising commercial products. In the United Kingdom, for example, branded contraceptives cannot be advertised on television. Minor regulations of this kind probably exist in other countries as well. One country reported a general ban on information or advertising about contraceptives, and another country reported a ban against directing such information at young people. No country has indicated that the sale of contraceptives is illegal, although the pill and the IUD are often available only through prescriptions by medical personnel.

The availability of family planning services to young people is a somewhat more complicated issue. Nine countries have indicated without qualification that there are no obstacles to the use of family planning services by young people (Appendix 1). Denmark indicated that there are no legal obstacles, but added "legal if more than 15 years." Yugoslavia also reported no legal obstacles, but signified a restriction by checking the pre-coded response, "Medical staff ... must if the client is a minor take special steps (like informing parents or the client's physician)." Two other countries checked this pre-coded response and did not claim that there were no legal restrictions. The United Kingdom reported that only under exceptional circumstances may contraceptive services be provided to patients under 16 without parental consent; the U.K. nevertheless indicated that there were no legal obstacles to the use of family planning services by young people. Since details were not requested, it is reasonable to believe that there may be other countries reporting "no legal obstacles" that permit minors to consent to their own medical treatment at some age (e.g. 15 or 16) below age of majority, but that require parental consent below that age.

Availability of family planning services to young people is contingent upon their acceptance by adolescents, who must recognize and trust the advisory role of the service provider. In many cases young people probably abstain from the use of family planning and related services, which are formally available to them, because they feel, justly or unjustly, that they will be morally condemned or patronized, or that their sexual activity will be made known to parents or others.

In almost all countries special programmes or clinics for family planning and counselling are operated by a large number of institutions, and are available to young

Table 6. Institutions Offering Family Planning to Young People: Government Responses

QUESTION: Which institutions/organizations are offering family planning/counselling services and are there any special programmes or clinics for young people?

	special program	welcome to join program
School	7	0
Student organization	6	1
Family planning association	7	6
Government hospitals	7	10
Private hospitals	5	5
Women's movement	3	5
Church	2	2
Other government institutions	4	5
Other voluntary organizations	3	2

Note: In some countries there are counselling services which have been included here although these agencies do not prescribe contraceptives but only advise on them (cf. Appendix 1).

people. As a rule, however, they are not available nation-wide, and in some countries they offer only counselling services. Seven countries indicated special programmes organized by schools. These programmes deal primarily with counselling, but in some instances, such as in War-saw, reciprocal arrangements are made with other institu-tions that offer family planning services. Such working arrangements are seldom codified, and are often unknown to the authorities. We became aware of them through our site visits.

The cost of family planning services may be the decid-ing factor as to whether or not they will be used by young people. There are two aspects of costs: (1) the extent to which the government provides financial support for either government or non-government programmes, and (2) what the client has to pay for the services.

The survey indicated that family planning services for young people are available in eight countries through government hospitals (Appendix 1). Five countries report other government services which include the existence of special family planning services for young people. In four countries there are no family planning services for young people available through the government. Ten countries indicated that local governments operate family planning services for young people, with no direct authority or control coming from the national government. In four countries there are no such services operated by local governments.

Government subsidies for family planning services vary from one country to another. In three countries family planning services for young people are free of charge, whereas most medical treatment in the country is not free. Family planning services are free of charge, as well as most other medical treatment, in nine countries. One country subsidizes the cost of family planning services for young people, so that the cost is lower than for most medical treatment. In two countries family planning services cost young people about as much as most medical consultations.

Eight governments subsidize non-government efforts in family planning/counselling and sex education, while se-ven governments do not. In many countries voluntary organizations like planned parenthood associations are totally dependent on government subsidies, since they

offer their services to the general public, or to adolescents in particular, at far below cost.   Even small
subsidies can have significant symbolic benefits.   In
Morocco, for instance, in addition to the small economic
subsidy the Family Planning Association receives, there is
a recommendation by the responsible minister to all
government institutions that they should facilitate its
activities whenever possible, and share facilities.   Such
support is difficult to translate into monetary terms but it
is nonetheless extremely important.

A Summary of Ratings made by the Selected Projects

The information for this section of the report was
obtained from 20 selected projects in nine countries: the
Netherlands, Belgium, Portugal, Morocco, Federal Republic of Germany, Poland, Yugoslavia, Italy, and Sweden.
A detailed questionnaire was sent to the selected projects
in advance of an on-site study visit.   In a few instances
administrative or language difficulties restricted the information available to that which could be collected
during the study visit.   Tables are therefore based on the
16 projects that returned the questionnaire. Due to the
very different structures and aims of the projects not all
questions were relevant to all of them. Each summary
table indicates the number of projects upon which it is
based.   In the full report (Lewin, 1984) each project, its
aims, strategies and perceptions of obstacles are presented and discussed.

The obstacles to effective sex education and family
planning, as listed by the 14 projects to which this
question was relevant, are presented in Table 7.   The
obstacles most frequently mentioned are: (1) that parents
of potential clients object to family planning for young
people; (2) that it is not socially recognized that young
people have intercourse; and (3) the constant risk of the
project being forced to close due to lack of money.   The
first two obstacles are part of the cultural values of
society, and can only be expected to change gradually.
The lack of funding, however, usually results from the
lack of systematic support by the government, a situation
that both could and should be remedied by appropriate
measures.   The adverse effects of too early pregnancies
and the benefits of sex education and family planning to
both individuals and society are too great to be ignored.

Moreover, in comparison with other government expenditures for health, the cost of sex education and family planning services for young people is indeed minor.

The sex education topics most often considered important or very important by the projects, in descending order, are: contraceptives, sex roles, love, intercourse, and abortion (see Table 8). Answers from the government agencies (see Table 3) indicate that the following topics are considered to be most important: sexual anatomy, reproductive biology, parenthood, and contraceptives. The projects seem to favour a sex education centered on the individual and her/his relations with other individuals (e.g. love, sex roles, and intercourse). Their emphasis on contraception is not surprising since they are primarily service-oriented projects. The governments, on the other hand, seem to prefer a sex education with less emphasis on the individual and interpersonal relations and more on the biological foundations of sexuality and its social consequences.

Table 7. Projects' Rating   of Obstacles (Based on responses from 14 projects).

QUESTION: There are many possible obstacles to the success of a program/project for family planning and/or sex education of young people. Some possible obstacles are listed below. We would like you to indicate for each of the obstacles mentioned whether it could be said to be an obstscle to the success of your project or not.

1 = no problem whatsoever
5 = severe problem

NUMBER OF PROJECTS INDICATING RESPECTIVE IMPORTANCE OF OBSTACLES

	1	2	3	4	5
Potential clients have too vague an idea about family planning	1	1	8	3	0
Potential clients hostile to family planning	8	4	2	0	0

Potential clients hostile to sex education	9	1	0	2	0
Parents of potential clients object to family planning for young people	1	2	4	5	1
Parents of potential clients object to sex education for young people	3	3	6	2	0
General traditional values in society	1	4	4	2	2
Illiteracy	6	3	2	2	0
The uncooperative attitude of the boy-friends	4	1	6	2	0
That it is not socially recognized that young people have intercourse	3	4	1	2	3
The geographical location of the programme/project centre makes it difficult to reach	7	3	2	0	0
Bussiness hours of the programme/project may make it difficult for potential clients to get in touch	8	3	0	1	0
Other organizations/institutions do not tell potential clients about project	7	2	2	2	0
Constant risk of being forced to close due to lack of money	5	0	3	3	2
Constant risk of being forced to closed due to lack of political support	8	2	2	0	1
Lack of specialist personnel	7	1	3	2	0
Lack of voluntary workers	9	1	1	1	0
Lack of continued traning of personnel	4	1	6	1	1
Problems of cooperation among staff	8	5	0	0	0
Lack of clearly-understood objective	5	2	4	0	0
Lack of clearly-defined target group	5	4	4	0	0
Lack of equipment	3	4	4	1	1

The projects are in agreement with the governments on

Table 8. Projects' Rating of the Importence of Sex Education Topics (Based on responses from 16 projects)

QUESTION: Which of the following themes are considered to be important in the sexual education of young people according to the point of view of the programme/project?

We would also like you to indicate whether any of these themes are compulsory in sex education or, on the other hand, considered totally unsuitable for young people according to official (government) policy.

VIEW ACCORDING TO PROGRAMME/PROJECT
PROJECTS PERCEPTION OF GOVERNMENT POLICY
1 = not important at all
5 = very important
* = compulsory
** = not fit for young people

	Importance						
	1	2	3	4	5	*	**
Sexual anatomy of humans	0	1	5	0	9	8	0
Sex roles	1	0	1	0	13	4	1
Parenthood	1	1	2	2	9	7	0
Reproductive biology	0	1	4	2	8	8	0
Love	0	0	1	2	12	2	1
Psychology of puberty	0	2	2	1	10	3	1
Religious view of marriage and the family	7	1	4	1	2	4	2
Pornography	2	3	5	2	2	1	4
Intercourse	0	1	2	6	6	1	1
Petting	1	2	0	3	8	1	1
Masturbation	1	1	2	3	8	1	1
Homosexuality	0	2	3	6	4	1	1
Contraceptives	0	0	0	3	12	3	1
Veneral diseases	0	1	2	4	8	4	1
Sterelization	6	0	7	1	1	1	1
Abortion	0	0	3	2	10	2	1
Sexual dysfunctions (e.g. impotence)	0	2	3	5	5	1	1

the importance of adolescent boys, adolescent girls, and children in secondary schools as primary targets for sex education (cf. Tables 1 and 9).

When comparing the ratings of target groups for family planning, we find that the projects discriminate between groups to an even lesser extent than do governments (see Table 5 and 10). All groups are considered important by most projects and governments. Table 10 also reports the number that view the various groups as targets. Young people are targets more often than other groups; this is not surprising since projects were initially selected because of the services they provided to young people.

Table 9. Projects' Rating of Target Groups for Sex Education (Based on responses from 16 projects)

QUESTION: Which of the following groups is it important to reach with sex education according to the point of view of the project, and which groups (if any) are included in the present target for the activities of the programme/project?

1 = not important at all
5 = very important

	Importance					Included
	1	2	3	4	5	
Preschool children	1	2	3	1	6	1
Children in primary school	1	2	1	2	8	3
Children in seconndary school	0	1	0	3	12	7
Adolescent girls	0	0	0	0	15	12
Adolescent boys	1	0	0	0	14	11
Girls just below usual age of marriage	1	0	1	0	11	8
Boys just below usual age of marriage	1	1	1	0	10	7
Newly-married women	3	1	1	0	8	3
Women with many children	5	1	0	0	7	3
Men with many children	6	1	0	0	6	3

Conclusions

Sex education is not forbidden by law in any of the countries that responded to the questionnaire. In several countries the legal situation is unclear due to the absence of explicit statutes or policies concerning sex education. In all countries, whatever the legal status of sex education may be, its implementation is dependent on local initiatives and the cooperation and interest of local authorities, such as school boards and/or head masters.

Table 10. Projects' of Target Groups for Family Planning Services (Based on responses from 13 projects)

QUESTION: Which of the following groups is important to reach with family planning/counselling services according to the point of view of the programme/ project, and which groups (if any) are included in the present target group for the activites of the programme/project?

1 = not important at all
5 = very important

| | Importance | | | | | Included |
	1	2	3	4	5	
Women with many children	3	0	1	2	7	3
Men with many children	4	0	1	1	7	2
Married women	3	0	1	3	6	3
Married men	4	0	1	2	6	2
All adult women	3	0	2	3	5	2
All adult men	4	0	1	3	5	2
Newly married women	3	0	2	2	6	3
Newly married men	4	0	1	1	7	3
Girls just below usual age of marriage	1	0	1	2	9	7
Boys just below usual age of marriage	2	0	1	1	9	7
Young girls as soon as possible after menarche	0	2	2	1	8	9
Young boys as soon as possible after first emission of semen	1	1	2	1	8	9

An interesting difference was found between the views of government agencies and those of projects. At the government level priority was placed on a demographic-technical approach to sex education, emphasizing the biological foundations of sexuality, parenthood, and contraception. The projects, by contrast, were individual-relational centered, with emphasis placed on contraceptives, love, sex roles, intercourse, and abortion. This was confirmed during study visit discussions with project personnel.

Almost all project personnel interviewed considered the sex education their clients had received prior to their initial contact with the project to be inadequate. This was true even in countries where sex education is compulsory. That some kind of sex education is compulsory in no way ensures that it is adequate, that it is available everywhere, or that pupils will be receptive to it.

The projects studied represent very different approaches and work under very different conditions. Some receive continuous funding through various government ministries and are able to plan their activities on a long-term basis. Others work under the severe handicap of insufficient funding and lack of support.

A classification scheme, consisting of three categories, is suggested in order to facilitate understanding of how the projects operate, how difficulties are dealt with, and how they relate to their clients. Some of the projects studied fit very well into one of the categories, while others share characteristics of more than one category. It is hoped that the classification scheme might not only aid in understanding individual projects but might also provide clues on how to strengthen certain projects. No category is generally considered better than another; all three types are potentially important, and local conditions would have a strong influence on the type of project to be found.

(1) The enthusiasts are the true amateurs; they love their task and are willing to suffer considerable hardship in order to further the good cause they advocate. For them there is little difference between their work with the project and the rest of their lives. While they are often competent professionals in their field -- physicians, social workers, etc, -- they may lack training in the provision of services. Most important of all, they do not

have institutional contacts or government support. The Aimer Jeunes in Brussels and the APF (Associacao Para o Planedmento da Familia) in Lisbon are examples of this category.

This group is probably necessary in order to have any services at all under very unfavourable circumstances, and in order to raise public awareness of the need for services. They run great risk, however, of ending in unproductive frustration because of the many difficulties they encounter, not the least of which is their lack of political influence and support.

(2) The professionals are characterized by their expertise, their professional identity, and their desire to help others. Unlike the enthusiasts, they are not crusaders, but are "simply" doing their professional duty. In their relationship to the client it is quite clear who is the provider and who is the receiver of services. They may be found in projects that are underfunded, such as Planning Josaphat in Brussels, as well as in stable and well funded projects, such as the Rutgershuis in the Hague, although this clinic also has some characteristics of the third category.

The professionals run the risk of becoming isolated in their professional roles, thereby diminishing their ability to adapt to the changing needs of their clients. If they become overly impressed with their own expertise, they may lose the ability to cooperate with others in serving clients.

(3) The institutionalized project is typically part of a larger bureaucratic organization which dispenses funds and exerts some control over project activities. Unlike the first two categories, the label in this case does not refer to the persons working with the project, but to the project itself. Being an institution and much less dependent on individual personalities, vacancies can, in principle, be filled with any formally competent applicant. Examples of such institutional projects are the Adolescent Clinic of the Stockholm schools and the TRR (Towarzystwo Roswoju Rodziny) clinic in Warsaw.

The institutionalized project would become totally impotent if the bureaucratic organization to which it belongs adopted an unfavourable attitude towards family planning for young people. Such projects also run the risk of its individual staff members becoming institutionalized and losing their efficiency under the weight of bureaucratic regulations. In short, staff members may become more civil servants than service providers.

Recommendations

Based on the information obtained in this study, four recommendations on sex education and seven recommendations on family planning services are presented for countries to consider. It should be noted that sexual intercourse among adolescents has become more common in recent decades, regardless of whether it is socially acceptable. Policies and programmes need to deal with what is actually taking place. In particular, educational and service programmes are needed to minimize early and unwanted pregnancies, sexually transmissible diseases, forced marriages, abortion (legal or illegal), ruined educational plans, and immature parents. Such occurrences are in no one's interest, and the recommendations are made to prevent, or at least to minimize, these occurrences.

Education

(1) To provide a legal basis for compulsory education on sexual matters in all countries.

(2) To develop school curricula in all countries, not only for sex education in a narrow sense, but also in a number of subjects taught in schools by various professions, so that sexuality, sexually related matters and relations between the sexes are given due consideration wherever appropriate.

(3) To ensure in all countries, while developing curricula, that the education given will not only be comprehensive and comprehendable for the pupils, but also felt by the pupils to be relevant to them. When dealing with this task it ought to be considered that the projects/programmes studied, of which most have experiences from directly being confronted with young people and their problems, tend to advocate an individual-relational sex education centering not only on contraception, but also on love, sex roles and sexual acts as opposed to the more technical-demographical sex education, which seems to be preferred by the governments.

(4) To support in all countries local initiatives and to seriously undertake motivational programmes aiming at the motivation of local officials, head-masters and

teachers since appropriate motivation of these groups is a necessary prerequisite for a successful implementation of any education on sexual matters.

Services

(1) To establish, in all countries, special family planning clinics for young people providing necessary contraceptive as well as counselling services.

(2) To develop on a regional and on a national level programmes for continued training of service providers, where the less experienced can learn from the more experienced, and where the more experienced through contacts with developing projects and services will be able to learn about recent developments in approaches and organizations of services.

(3) To develop on a national level a network of contacts between the service providers to facilitate an exchange of information, which is now almost totally lacking.

(4) To develop on a regional level through courses, seminars and working groups, international contacts between the service providers. Such contacts are important to all service providers but particularly to those who work in countries where the development of services is still in the initial phases.

(5) To strengthen the contacts between the international organizations and projects/programmes working under unfavourable circumstances since the lack of local support makes monitoring and development of the project/programme extremely difficult.

(6) To develop on the national level systems of financing under which the government takes an increasing responsibility for the services provided to their young citizens and enable projects/programmes to plan for longer periods of time. The present situation with often unclear and uncertain funding does in many cases lead to misuse and waste of professional resources.

(7) To develop on a regional and on a national level new projects/programmes and to strengthen already existing ones which offer special services to particularly vulnerable groups such as migrant adolescents.

References:

Kozakiewicz, Mikolaj, **Sex Education and Adolescense in Europe: Sexuality, Marriage and the Family,** London, International Planned Parenthood Federation, 1981.

Lewin, Bo, **Sex and Family Planning: How We Teach the Young,** Copenhagen, WHO Publich Health in Europe 23, World Health Organization Regional Office for Europe, 1984.

Swartz, Barbara, **Family Planning Legislation,** Copenhagen, EURO Reports and Studies 85, World Health Organization Regional Ofdfice for Europe, 1983.

WHO, **Family Planning in Health Services,** Geneva, World Health Organization Technical Report Series 476, 1971.

WHO, **The Child and the Adolescent in Society: Report on a WHO Conference,** Copenhagen, EURO Reports and Studies 3, World Health Organization Regional Office for Europe, 1979.

Appendix 1

COUNTRY	Legal status of sex education of young people Q1			Institutions to convey mandatory sex education Q5							Information on Family Planning for young people Q10			Family Planning for young people Q12				Cost of Family Planning for young people Q18					National Family Planning for young people Q19					Local/Munici-pal Family Planning for young people Q20		Economic Support to non-government Sex Education Q21		Economic Support to non-government Family Planning Q22		Government position to birth-rate Q27			Prop. young people with easy access Sex Ed. Q28 PCT	Prop. young people with easy access to Family Pl. Q29 PCT
	Prohibited	No law	Mandatory	Preschool	Primary School	Secondary School	School	The army	Other School	Other org. or inst.	Not legal	Not legal to young people	No legal	Not legal	Special restrictions	No legal obstacles		Free unlike most treat.	Free like most treat.	Not free but especially subsidised	Cost like most medical treatm.	No	Through Government hospitals	Special Government Family Planning	Family Planning Services	Other	No	Yes	No	Yes	No	Yes	Too low	Acceptable	Too high	PCT	PCT
ALBANIA																																					
ALGERIA	X																																			missing	missing
AUSTRIA																																	X				
BELGIUM																																					
BULGARIA																																				100	100
CZECHOSLOVAKIA			X		X	X	X					MISSING	MISSING		MISSING		MISSING	X	X	X		X							X		X					100	100
DENMARK			X		MISSING	MISSING	X	X			MISSING		X		X		X	X				X		X			X		X		X			X		90	100
FINLAND			X		X	X	X					X	X	X								X		X	X		X		X		X			missing	missing	missing	missing
FRANCE			X	X	X	X	X			X			X	X				X				X		X	X		X		X			missing		missing		missing	missing	missing
GDR																																					
GREECE																																					
HUNGARY			X		X	X	X		X	X			X	X			X	X				X		X			X		X		X			missing		missing	100	100
ICELAND	X				X					X			X	X								X				X		X		X		X			missing		missing	100	100
IRELAND	X												X	X								X					X		X		X		X			missing	missing
ITALY																																					
LUXEMBOURG																																					
MALTA	X				X		X						X	X			X					missing	missing				missing		missing		missing		X			missing	missing
MONACO												MISSING		MISSING			MISSING					missing					missing		missing		missing					missing	missing
MOROCCO	X				X								X	X								X		X			X		X		X		X			25	15
NETHERLANDS																																					
NORWAY			X		X		X			X			X	X				X				X		X			X		X		X			X		100	100
POLAND																																					
PORTUGAL																																					
ROMANIA																																					
SAN MARINO																																					
SPAIN		X						X					X	X			X					X					X		X		X			missing		5	15
SWEDEN			X		X		X		X				X	X				X				X		X			X		X		X			X		50	50
SWITZERLAND		X																																			
TURKEY		X			X		X					X					X					X			X		X		X	X			missing		missing	(75)	100
USSR																																	missing			100	
UNITED KINGDOM			X	X	X	X	X		X	X			X	X			X	X				X		X		X	X		X		X		X		missing			
YUGOSLAVIA																																					

	Sex Education Q1			Institutions to convey mandatory sex education Q5	Information on Family Planning for young people Q10	Family Planning for young people Q12	Cost of Family Planning for young people Q18	National Family Planning for young people Q19	Local/Munici-pal Family Planning for young people Q20	Economic Support to non-government sex Education Q21	Economic Support to non-government Family Plan. Q22	Government position to birth-rate Q27	Prop. young people wit easy acce to Famil Pl. Q29	Prop. young people wit easy acce to Famil... C??
	Prohibited	No law	Mandatory										PCT	PCT

14

A COMPARATIVE PERSPECTIVE

Hyman Rodman and Jan Trost

The adolescent dilemma faced by societies is clearly visible in the family planning area. Should family planning decisions be turned over to adolescents at a relatively early age, while they may still be vulnerable to hurtful influences? Or should family planning decisions be subject to parental control until a relatively late age, risking conflict between parent and child? Or should adults other than parents provide the guidance that may be needed by adolescents?

Family planning (or reproductive health) issues are of critical concern to all individuals and all societies. Being able to engage in sexual intercourse, to use contraceptives, to obtain abortions, to marry or cohabit, to bear children, to release a child for adoption or to maintain responsibility for a child, are issues of extreme importance. Until what age should parents guide and control their children's reproductive behavior? Until what age should parents exercise veto power over children's access to contraceptive and abortion services? At what age are adolescents competent--socially and psychologically--to take responsibility for their own behavior? Or should some criterion other than age be used to decide when children might legally have access to contraception and abortion without parental involvement: perhaps marriage? perhaps some test of competence?

There are no easy answers to the questions raised by the adolescent dilemma. The research evidence on the development of adolescent competence, and on parent-child relations, as reviewed by Rodman, Lewis, and Griffith (1984), provides some guidance to policymakers. But these authors are frank to acknowledge that research knowledge is limited and that one must resort to values to bridge the gap between what we know and what we do. Their policy recommendations for easier access to contraceptive and abortion services in the USA are partly based on the research evidence and partly based on their proclivity to value individual choice and freedom in reproductive decision making. Others, starting with a different set of values, may read the research evidence differently and may come to very different conclusions. As Lewin* says, "There are many different cultural traditions within the WHO European Region, and there can be no one right way to prepare young people for sexual life."

Legal and Social Changes: A Trend Toward Liberalization

The detailed accounts by the contributors to this book confirm the existence of a pronounced trend toward liberalization in the family planning area. Over the past two decades there has been a trend toward more permissive attitudes and behavior about sexuality and family planning and toward more permissive legislation. The trend toward liberalization involves adults as well as minors, abortion as well as contraception, and sex education in the schools as well as counseling centers for family planning. Sweden seems to be most advanced in these areas, but there are changes in most countries. Lewin, for example, refers to an earlier age of sexual intercourse generally within the countries of the WHO European region. O'Higgins documents a change in the 1970s toward more favorable attitudes regarding contraception, even in conservative and Catholic Ireland. And Rodman documents more favorable attitudes toward premarital sexual intercourse and a greater incidence of premarital sexual intercourse by adolescents in the United States.

One significant example of the greater social recognition of the competence of adolescents and of the greater freedom and responsibility being granted them is the widespread lowering of the age of majority. The term

* References to chapters in this book are not made explicitly.

"age of majority" is somewhat complicated. One meaning is the age at which the individual is allowed to vote. Another meaning is the age at which the child is generally considered to be an adult: parents no longer have formal obligations and the child no longer has formal rights to be taken care of by the parents. Sometimes, however, the term denotes a partial right or responsibility of the child, e.g. the age at which a person is legally allowed to obtain a driver's license or to buy alcoholic beverages. Occasionally it denotes the age at which the child is treated like an adult for a particular purpose, such as the age at which the child has to pay adult fees to attend the movies or to ride the bus. Mostly, however, the term denotes the age when the child and its parents no longer have formal responsibilities/rights visà-vis each other; that is the way we use the term, if not otherwise indicated. The age of majority in Ontario, Canada, was lowered from 21 to 18 in 1971. In the USA the voting age was lowered from 21 to 18 in 1971, and many states then lowered the age of majority from 21 to 18. In 1972 the age of majority was lowered from 20 to 18 in Denmark. And it was lowered from space 21 to 18 in France in 1974, in Italy in 1975, and in Spain in 1978.

Programs for the dissemination of information and understanding about sexuality, intimacy, and contraception have become more common. Czechoslovakia, Denmark, and Sweden have had such programs for a long time; they include required sex education in the schools as well as counseling agencies associated with the schools and directed toward adolescents. At the other end of the continuum, without any--or with very limited--adolescent programs for sex education or sexual counseling, we find Ireland and the USA.

Changes bringing about easier access to medically prescribed contraceptives also took place in many countries during the 1970s. Access became easier informally, at least for some groups in the population, regardless of restrictive legislation. In addition, legislation to remove restrictions was widespread. In 1973 legislation was passed in Belgium making access to contraceptives more readily available, and legalizing the display, transport, and sale of contraceptives. In France access to contraceptives was legally made available to all women in 1967, but minors' privacy was generally not respected by physicians or pharmacists. In 1974 new legislation made it possible for minors to obtain contraceptives at no cost and without the requirement of parental consent. In Sweden, minors have had access to contraceptive counseling and to contraceptives, at no cost and without parental consent, since 1975; in Denmark, since 1976. The use of contraceptives was decriminalized in Spain in 1978 and in Ireland in 1980.

The same trend toward more permissive legislation regarding abortion can also be discerned. In Hungary permissive legislation was first approved in 1956, and in Czechoslovakia in 1957. In Denmark, limited access to abortion was first introduced in 1937, with several changes involving further liberalization since then. Since 1973 abortion has been available to all women at no cost; minors generally require parental consent. In France, abortion was legalized in 1975 for a trial period of five years; in 1980 the law was again passed, this time without any time limitation. In France, too, minors generally require parental consent. In Sweden abortion has been legal since 1938, but certain medical or social justifications had to be provided, and minors under 15 generally required parental consent. In 1975 the law was changed to make abortion available on the woman's request, at no cost to her, and abortion became available to minors without any requirement for parental consent. In Italy abortion was legalized in 1978, and unmarried minors are generally required to obtain either parental consent or judical permission. Access to abortion services, however, is seriously hampered by the large number of doctors who conscientiously refuse to perform abortions, (cf. Tosi et al., 1985).

Although the liberalization trend is clear, it is important to note that in most countries it is only of one or two decades' duration, and that the trend can be stopped or even reversed. In Ontario, Canada, for example, a recommendation to lower the age of consent for health care services to age 16 was not passed because of strong opposition. In Belgium, the 1973 law which liberalized access to contraceptives made it possible for family counseling centers to dispense contraceptives; the medical establishment strongly opposed this provision, and it was reversed in 1975. In Hungary, concerns about low birth rates and high abortion ratios led to incentives to increase the birth rate and also to restrictions on access to abortion. In France, as in other countries, minors' access to birth control services is a threat to traditional family values, and there are strong movements that oppose the liberal legislation and that seek to have it reversed. In the United States, abortion was legalized throughout the country in 1973 as a result of a decision by the United States Supreme Court. Since that time there has been a great deal of controversy about abortion. Although abortion remains legal, legislation to prohibit spending federal funds to support abortion services has been passed by Congress and upheld by the courts. Many states have passed restrictive legislation; for the most part these statutes have been declared unconstitutional by the courts. Conservative groups continue to pressure Congress to find a way, either through legislation or through a Constitutional amendment, to reverse the decision of the U.S. Supreme Court. The greatest threat of all, however, stems from the Reagan administration's opposition to abortion. Should any of the justices of an aging Court retire or die, President Reagan's further appointments may lead to a Court that would effectively reverse its earlier decision or, less drastically, that would approve new restrictions on access to abortion.

Women's Status, Women's Risks

While family planning and population control are issues of general relevance to the social and industrial development of a country, they are issues of special relevance to women. Women bear children, and for the most part women rear children; they typically care for children born to them when they are single, and spend much more time caring for their children even when they are married and have a husband present. In cases of separation and divorce, women typically get custody of the children. As a result, questions of fertility and birth control are of prime importance to women.

It is well known that the number and spacing of a woman's children have a strong bearing upon her health, her educational opportunities, her occupation and income, and her social activities (Cook, 1975; European Parliament, 1981; International Labour Organisation, 1982). Adolescents are especially vulnerable (Rodman, Lewis, & Griffith, 1984). Giving birth to a child can cut short a young woman's education, can limit her occupational opportunities, and can reduce her involvement in social and recreational activities. It is therefore critical that all women, including minors, have appropriate access to family planning and birth control services. While political and cultural realities in some countries may place restrictions upon the availability of family planning services, it is important to provide as many services as possible within the context of these restrictions. (It may also be important to raise questions about restrictions that have negative consequences for women's lives and that increase the social, economic, and health risks that women face.)

It is clear, from the chapters in this book, that women generally, and minors particularly, face many problems in the sphere of family planning. Even when access to contraceptive and abortion services is legal, women may face special administrative requirements that are not necessary for other forms of medical treatment. France has a one-week waiting period for an abortion. In Canada and Czechoslovakia specially constituted abortion committees must approve each abortion, and the abortion must be justified on legislative grounds. In countries where access to abortion is illegal, women with sufficient knowledge, contacts, social status, and financial resources are able to obtain illegal abortions safely, or to have their condition diagnosed to fit the legal requirements for an abortion. Moreover, these advantaged women are able to travel to other countries for a legal abortion. For example, women travel from Belgium to the Netherlands or to England; from Ireland to England or Wales; from Spain to France and to other European countries.

Access to abortions is an open secret in many European countries with restrictive laws, but such access is not equally available to all segments of society. As Guyatt says about Canada, there are "sharp disparities in the distribution and accessibility of therapeutic abortion services," and many women go to the USA for an abortion (cf. Badgley, 1977; Rodman, 1981). In France, minors from the lower social classes experience more difficulty in obtaining an abortion because they lack financial resources and because communication about sexual matters is more difficult with their parents. In Italy there are large regional differences in the availability of contraception and abortion services; Southern Italy is more conservative and fewer services are available there. In some areas very high percentages of physicians (over 75 percent) conscientiously object to performing abortions. In the United States, despite legal access to contraception and abortion, rural areas tend to be more conservative and to be underserved, and rural women seeking services often must travel to the larger urban centers.

To summarize, access to family planning services is not equally available to all women within a country, regardless of whether these services are legal or illegal. Women who come from more conservative regions or rural areas, who are of lower educational or social status, who have fewer financial resources, and who are minors, face the greatest difficulties. As Sai (1981, p. 44) has said, the major challenge faced by family planners throughout the world "is how to make family planning information, advice and services available and accessible geographically, socially and economically to all the millions who need them wherever they are. Among groups having the most difficulty with family planning and contraception are the young and the adolescent."

Value Differences

There are sharp value differences within each country on the issue of abortion. In the political battles to liberalize abortion laws in many countries during the 1970s, partisans opposed and fought each other with deeply felt arguments that permitted few compromises (Sarvis and Rodman, 1974). The abortion controversy and the political battles (to make the laws more permissive or more restrictive) continue unabated in many countries precisely because the issues are so strongly held by opposing factions. The continuing battles are especially visible in the United States, where the opposing camps are strongly organized, where they make extensive use of the mass media, and where any victory for one side is met by further resolve by the other. The controversy in the United States is also visible because it is being played out in 50 separate states as well as in the federal Congress, and because state courts and federal courts become involved.

There are also value differences within each country regarding contraception and sex education. Koeppel points out that, in France, there is more tolerance of adolescents' use of contraception by those who are younger, urban, middle class, and not practicing Catholics. Paludan points out that sex education is required in Denmark, but that value differences about the appropriate content create a problem, and that the extent and content of sex education is often left to individual school principals or individual teachers. Lewin's summary for the WHO European Region is that no country responding to his questionnaire prohibits sex education by law, but that there are large differences between countries in terms of how they deal with sex education; in addition, the implementation of sex education or family life education programs varies within each country, depending on the initiative and interest of local officials.

There are, of course, substantial differences between countries in their policies regarding contraception and abortion for minors. It is possible to categorize countries, albeit roughly, in terms of whether they are liberal, moderate, or conservative on family planning issues; since there is less controversy and less differentiation on contraception, it is helpful to refer to abortion policies in classifying countries. Among those countries individually covered in this book we would classify Czechoslovakia, Denmark, Hungary, Sweden, and the USA as liberal, which is to say that abortions are legal and are available either on the adolescent woman's request or on broad social and medical grounds. In the moderate category we would place Canada, France, and Italy, countries in which abortion is legal but which have substantial administrative restrictions (as well as large regional variations) in actual access. The conservative countries, in which abortion is illegal (or has been illegal at least until 1985), are Belgium and Ireland; Spain, also conservative, legalized abortion in 1984 under limited conditions.

In general, the countries with liberal abortion laws and practices are the Eastern European and Nordic countries. The conservative countries are those with large Roman Catholic populations and with strong Church influence. Those in the moderate category are countries in which the Roman Catholic Church is not as influential, but where it is strong enough (along with other conservative elements in the population) to maintain restrictions upon the availability of abortion.

Some readers will, no doubt, want to challenge our

classification of certain countries.   Belgium arguably belongs in the moderate category because of the informal availability of abortions despite the legal prohibition (cf. Lohlé-Tart, 1974). Since abortions are more readily available in Canada than in Italy, some might contend that Canada belongs in the liberal camp. The USA might be classified as moderate because of restrictions in some states and because of actual and threatened restrictions at the federal level. Some Eastern European countries, because of their desire to raise birth rates, have placed restrictions on access to abortion, and arguably belong in the moderate category: "The upsurge in teenage fertility in the socialist countries of eastern Europe is probably... explained by the pronatalist policies promulgated by their governments, which encourage earlier marriage and have tightened access to legal abortion (Westoff, Calot, & Foster, 1983:110). We expect, however, that most readers will agree with our classification (as of 1985) of most, if not all, of the countries.

The differences in abortion legislation among the nine countries of the European Community (Belgium, Denmark, France, Germany, Ireland, Italy, Luxembourg, the Nether-lands, and the United Kingdom) have been discussed in the Commission of the European Communities and in the European Parliament. Questions have been raised as to "whether the nine member states should not harmonise legislation in the form most conducive to women's liber-ties in order to solve the problem created by the growing number of women who travel to member states with liberal abortion laws to have their pregnancies termina-ted." The response to such questions has been that abortion "is not a matter within the responsibility of the European Community" (Euroforum, 1979). In a similar vein, the Chinese delegate to the UN Economic Commis-sion for Asia and the Far East, Chi Lung, stated that "population policy is the internal affair" of a country; an internal group can usefully exchange information but "we cannot seek a forcibly uniform policy on population" (quoted in Okedij, 1978:626). Family planning issues clearly remain highly sensitive, both within countries and between countries.

Family planning policies can be part of a government's population policies. If a government is concerned about high fertility rates and the drain this represents upon limited resources and economic development, it may adopt antinatalist policies. Conversely, low fertility rates may lead to pronatalist policies. We shall comment briefly on the ethical questions raised by government policies and programs to reduce or increase population growth.

First, it is generally agreed that governments have a right to adopt population policies, just as they adopt policies in other areas. Second, that governments ought to use the least coercive methods possible to achieve their goals. Third, that the severity of the population problem would influence the type of policies adopted. And fourth, that certain policies--in particular those that drastically reduce individual choices--are ethically impermissible except under exceptional circumstances. For the most part, population policies adopted throughout the world have been in keeping with these principles. Many developing countries, for example, have adopted educational campaigns and voluntary family planning services to reduce fertility. Only in a few cases have questions been raised about the ethical propriety of policies, and this is with regard to countries that have faced the most serious population problems--China, India, and Indonesia (Berelson & Lieberson, 1979; Mosher, 1983).

The developed countries covered in this book are likelier to face problems with low rather than high fertility rates. The secular trend toward reduced fertility rates poses a potential problem for the countries of Europe and North America, and some of these countries have introduced policies to increase the fertility rate (Westoff, 1978). None of the policies in the countries we have covered appears to be overly coercive or to raise questions of ethical acceptability. It is possible, however, that a continuing decline in fertility rates might lead to negative rates of population growth and to more drastic pronatalist measures than those adopted thus far. Thus, although we acknowledge cultural and political differences, it is worth noting the existence of an ethical hierarchy that may usefully guide government population policy in any society. Least problematic are educational programs and voluntary family planning services. Then, in order of increasing ethical concern, are programs of positive incentives, negative incentives, organized peer pressure, and prohibitions of certain forms of contraceptive behavior. In general terms, the more coercive the policy (the less choice the individual has), the greater the ethical concern and the greater the burden of deliberation and justification faced by a government (Berelson and Lieberson, 1979; Callahan, 1972). These are not merely abstract questions; population problems and policies have been and continue to be on the political agenda of many countries. But they are certainly very difficult questions, and they become all the more difficult where they intersect with the adolescent dilemma and involve policies for minors.

An abortion policy to regulate population size builds upon a false assumption; it can be argued that pregnancies ending in childbirth and those ending in induced abortion do not belong to the same "population" of pregnancies (cf. Trost 1984). The opposite belief--that abortion policy can regulate fertility--might not only be classified as un-ethical and inhumane, but may also lead to unintended negative consequences. An example: Policy makers in Rumania, in the early 1960s, considered the fertility rate to be too low. In 1966 the abortion law became very restrictive. The legal abortion rate decreased, of course, and the fertility rate increased to some extent for a two-year period, after which it went back to about the same level as before. What is more important, however, is that the abortion related death rate increased tremendously--from 15 to 95 per 1,000,000 women aged 15-44 (Tietze, 1981); the increase was due to illegal abortions. As Ketting and van Praag (1983:484) conclude, ". . .das Geburtenniveau gegenwärtig primär durch die Anzahl gewollter Schwangerschaften..."

Summary and Conclusions

The last two decades have seen a considerable degree of liberalization in the family planning policies of many countries. Policies have been liberalized for minors as well as for adults, but the inherent problems posed by the adolescent dilemma--whether adolescents need control or freedom in their decision making--often lead to ambiguous or restrictive policies for minors. We have also seen that change is not a one-way street: the United States, Hungary, and Czechoslovakia, countries with the most liberal abortion policies, have become more conservative in recent years. In the United States, the Reagan administration is morally opposed to abortion, and several

restrictions have been implemented. In the centrally planned governments of Eastern Europe, very low fertility
rates have generated pronatalist policies, including the
imposition of tighter controls over access to abortion. It
is an open question as to whether the trend toward
liberalization will continue or whether it will be reversed.
Since each country makes its own decisions, and since
there are strong national concerns about optimal population size and growth, we are certain to see considerable
variation, with changes both toward more liberal and
toward more conservative family planning policies.

Many countries have recognized the earlier maturity
and competence of adolescents and have lowered the age
of responsibility for certain actions or increased minors'
involvement in certain decisions that affect them. In the
United Kingdom, 16 is the age of consent for medical
services. In Italy, Canada, Spain, and France the courts
are paying more attention to the preferences of children
in questions of custody. In Czechoslovakia and Denmark,
although the legal age for marriage is 18, the courts may
approve marriage at age 16. In Hungary, at age 16, an
adolescent may work without parental consent and may
leave home with the permission of a state agency. In
Ireland, O'Higgins reports, the legislature "has recognised
that young people mature earlier than hitherto and some
of the restrictions on the legal capacity of minors have
been removed." Moreover, the voting age (or the age of
majority) has lowered to 18 in many countries.

Regarding contraception, the legal restrictions have for
the most part been removed. Sex education, in some
form, is common. Nevertheless, strongly held conservative values by significant proportions of the population
still impede the teaching of sex education and the use
(especially by minors) of contraceptives. As a result,
access to contraceptives and exposure to sex education
varies considerably, even within the same country. In the
United States, with comparatively less openness about
sexuality and less tolerance of teenage sexual behavior,
teenage fertility and abortion rates are comparatiavely
high (Jones et al., 1985).

There is widespread concern about the limited use that
sexually active teenagers make of contraceptives, and a
great deal of speculation about the reasons for such
limited use. Among the reasons offered are lack of

information by teenagers, lack of motivation, lack of access, and lack of contraceptive preparedness (because teenagers do not perceive themselves as sexually active and find it easier to have sexual intercourse "spontaneously" and "unexpectedly".) There is no easy way to resolve these varying views of the problem; the relevance of the different factors depends upon the particular teenage population being discussed. Interestingly, even in countries with liberal family planning policies and with low teenage fertility rates, such as Denmark, strong concerns continue to be expressed about the inadequate use of contraceptives by adolescents.

The liberalization of abortion policies in many countries has been accompanied by even more controversy than that which surrounds contraception and sex education. Although the abortion controversy remains bitter, and is bound to continue for many years because of the uncompromising positions of the opposing partisans, there is a hint of a policy compromise on the horizon (cf. Rodman, 1981). This consists of a tendency for countries to adopt more liberal policies regarding indications for abortion (permitting abortion for a broad array of social, economic, and medical reasons, or permitting abortion on the woman's request); but these liberal policies apply only to abortions in the early weeks of pregnancy. Czechoslovakia, Hungary, and Denmark, for example, all have liberal policies for adolescents' abortions performed during the first twelve weeks of pregnancy, but more stringent requirements after the twelfth week. In Italy the dividing line is 90 days. There are also developments in both Canada and the United States that are harbingers of the compromise (Rodman, 1981).

Finally, we have seen that access to family planning services varies within each country. Poor women, rural women, and minors usually have greater difficulty in gaining access to family planning services in their own country or in other countries. From a policy standpoint, what seems to be most needed are concerted efforts to improve access to all segments of society, and in particular to improve access to poor women, rural women, and minors.

The adolescent dilemma suggests that access for minors is not a simple matter, and involves the state, minors, and minors' parents. Minors may not be competent to make good decisions on their own; parents may have a vested interest in their children's decisions; the state may find it difficult to establish policies that meet all competing interests. In the final analysis, however, the special importance that family planning decisions and their con-sequences have for adolescents, and the difficulties often experienced by parents and adolescents in discussing issues pertaining to sexuality, contraception and abortion, suggest that policies generally should enable adolescents to make reproductive health and family planning decisions on their own consent (cf. Bogue, 1977). Consultation with parents, other adults, or professional counselors should be available on a voluntary basis. In addition, the situation suggests that greater efforts are generally needed to improve sex education for children of all ages and to deliver family planning services to adolescents.

References

Badgley Report. 1977. **Report of the Committee on the Operation of the Abortion Law.** Robin F. Badgley, Chairman. Ottawa, Canada: Minister of Supply and Services.
Berelson, Bernard, and Jonathan Lieberson. 1979. "Government Efforts to Influence Fertility." **Population and Development Review** 5:581-613.
Bogue, Donald J., editor. 1977. **Adolescent Fertility: The Proceedings of an International Conference.** Community and Family Study Center, University of Chicago.
Callahan, Daniel. 1972. "Ethics and Population Limita-tion." **Science** 175:487-494.
Cook, Alice H. 1975. **The Working Mother: A Survey of Problems in Nine Countries.** New York State School of Industrial and Labor Relations, Cornell University.
Euroforum, 7-12-79.
European Parliament Working Documents, 1980-1981. 29 January 1981. Document 1-829/80, Part II. Report of the Ad Hoc Committee on Women's Rights on the position of women in the European Community.
International Labour Organisation, **Population Develop-ment,** 4th edition, Geneva.
Jones, Elise F., Jacqueline Darroch Forrest, Noreen

Goldman, Stanley K. Henshaw, Richard Lincoln, Jeannie I. Rosoff, Charles F. Westoff, and Deirdre Wulf, 1985. "Teenage Pregnancy in Developed countries: Determinants and Policy Implications." **Family Planning Perspectives** 17:53-63.

Ketting, Evert and Philip van Praag. 1983. "Schwangerschaftsabbruch, Gesetz und Praxis," Stimezo Nederland.

Lohlé-Tart, Louis. 1974. "Belgium." Pp. 193-224 in **Population Policy in Developed Countries,** edited by Bernard Berelson. New York: McGraw-Hill.

Mosher, Steven W. 1983. "Why Are Baby Girls Being Killed in China?" **Wall Street Journal,** July 25.

Okediji, F.O. 1978. "The Limitations of Family Planning Programmes in the Developing Nations." Pp. 617-639 in **Marriage, Fertility and Parenthood in West Africa,** edited by C. Oppong, G. Adaba, M. Bekombo-Priso, and J. Mogey. Canberra: Australian National University.

Rodman, Hyman. 1981. "Future Directions for Abortion Morality and Policy." Pp. 229-237 in P. Sachdev, ed., **Abortion: Readings and Research.** Toronto: Butterworths.

Rodman, Hyman, Susan H. Lewis, and Saralyn B. Griffith. 1984. **The Sexual Rights of Adolescents: Competence, Vulnerability, and Parental Consent.** New York: Columbia University Press.

Sai, Fred T. 1981. "Keynote Speech: Family Planning in the 1980's," in **Family Planning in the 1980's: Challenges and Opportunities,** International Conference on Family Planning in the 1980's, Jakarta, Indonesia.

Tietze, Christopher. 1981. **Induced Abortion: A World Review 1981,** The Population Council, New York.

Tosi, Simonetta Landucci, Michele E. Grandolfo, Angela Spinelli, Kevin R. O'Reilly, and Carol J.R. Hogue. 1985. "Legal Abortion in Italy: 1980-1981." **Family Planning Perspectives** 17:19-23.

Trost, Jan. 1984. **"Divorces, Children, and the Public,"** Key-paper presented at the XXth International Seminar of the Committee on Family Research, Melbourne, August 19-24, 1984.

Westoff, Charles F. 1978. "Marriage and Fertility in the Developed Countries." **Scientific American,** 239:51-57.

Westoff, Charles F., Gerard Calot, and Andrew D. Foster. 1983. "Teenage Fertility in Developed Nations: 1971-1980." **Family Planning Perspectives** 15:105-110.

ABOUT THE AUTHORS

INES ALBERDI, born in Sevilla in 1948, Ph.D. in Sociology and Political Science (Madrid University, 1978) is currently Assistant Professor at the Department of Social Structure of the University of Madrid teaching courses on Education and Family. She has been Visiting Scholar at the Sociology Department at Georgetown University, Washington D.C., (1979-80) and Technical Adviser at the Justice Department for the preparation and elaboration of the New Civil Code on Family and Divorce (September 1980-September 1981). She has published two books, El fin de la familia? 1978 and Historia y Sociología del divorcio en Espana 1979, and has currently in print a book of readings on Women's Education. She has published several articles on Family, Divorce and Women's Status and is an elected member, since June 1983, of the Sociology and Political Science Professional Association Board in Spain.

SALUSTIANO DEL CAMPO, born in 1931, is Professor of Sociology and Head of the Department of Social Structure at the University of Madrid. In 1979 he was elected as a member of the Royal Academy of Moral and Political Sciences of Spain and since 1976 he is a member of the Board of Directors of the European Coordination Center for Research and Documentation in Social Sciences (Vienna Centre). He has been Director of the National Opinion Research Centre of Madrid and Dean of the Faculty of Political Science and Sociology at the University of Madrid. His books include Para una Sociología de la familia espanola (in collaboration with E.G. Arboleya, 1959), La familia espanola en transición (1960), Cambios sociales y formas de vida (1968), Análisis de la población de Espana (1972), La política demográfica de Espana (1974), El ciclo vital de la familia espanola (1980) and Análisis sociolgico de la familia espanola (in collaboration with Manuel Navarro, 1982).

ROBERTO CATERINA is a clinical psychologist and volunteer researcher at the University of Salerno. He attended the Child Psychotherapy courses organised by the Tavistock Clinic in London and in Rome. He has published several articles and a book on separation anxiety in young children and has just completed, under the direction of Prof. Pina Cavallo Boggi, a research project entitled: "The Construction of the Self and Gender Roles in Two

Communities in Southern Italy."

WILFRIED DUMON, born in Maldegem in Belgium in 1933, dr. rer. Pol. Soc., University of Leuven, 1963. He was Dr. h.c. at the University of Uppsala, 1983 and is Prof. ord. at the University of Leuven since 1969. Head, Centre for Sociology of Family and Population, University of Leuven. He is a member of the Executive Committee of the International Sociological Association. He has published many books and articles on family sociology; is associate editor of different international sociological reviews; and is editor of International Migration.

DORIS E. GUYATT, D.S.W., is a senior policy adviser with the Ministry of Community and Social Services, Government of Ontario. Her current area of responsibility is family policy and income maintenance. She has a long-standing research interest in family planning, adolescent pregnancy and one parent families and is the author of several articles and reports on these subjects. She was recently an adviser to a legislative committee on wife battering.

PETÉR JÓZAN, is Chief of Population Statistics Section of the Hungarian Central Statistical Office and Senior Lecturer in Community Medicine and Epidemiology at the Postgraduate Medical School in Budapest. He graduated from medicine at the Debrecen University Medical School in 1961. Between 1961-64 he worked in the Department of Pathology of the County Hospital of Hajdu-Bihar in Debrecen. In 1964 he joined the Hungarian Central Statistical Office. He received his M. Sc. degree in Medical Demography at the London School of Hygiene and Tropcial Medicine in England in 1975. Among other scientific societies he is a member of the International Union for the Scientific Study of Population, the International Epidemiological Association and the Demographic Committee of the Hungarian Academy of Sciences. In the second half of 1960's he was on the Editorial Board of the XVIII. Section of the Excerpta Medica /Publica Health, Social Medicine and Hygiene/. He edited with others "Population and Population Policy in Hungary" published by the Publishing House of the Hungarian Academy of Sciences. He has often been invited by the WHO to serve as temporary adviser in issues of mortality, family life and aging. He wrote papers on mortality, fertility, family planning, birth control, family life cycle and aging.

BEATRICE KOEPPEL, psychologist, worked for youth courts in Paris and Hauts-de Seine 1965-73. During her work at Centre de Formation et de Recherche de l'Education Surveillée, she has published a number of articles about young women at legal institutions. Among her publications are On m'a placée un peu partout, La parole de jeunes femmes en Institution en la Femme et la criminalité, del la Pénitence à la Sexologie. She is presently at Centre de Recherche de Vaucresson (CRIV).

BO LEWIN, Ph.D., is a sociologist who has worked mainly with sociology of the family and sexology and published works on unmarried cohabitation and various aspects of adolescent sexuality. He is presently responsible for a research project on Handicap and Sexuality at Uppsala University. He has on several occasions worked with the World Health Organization and was during 1982 a Consultant to the WHO. In 1984 he was a Fulbright Visiting Professor at Kalamazoo College and a Research Associate at the Kinsey Institute.

ERIK MANNICHE, born 1927, since 1961 with University of Copenhagen Institute of Sociology. Member of Board, Institute for Longitudinal Studies, Copenhagen; studying Metropolitan male cohort (Nc. 10.000) born 1953, from birth to death. Editor of Sociological Microjournal, with Kaare Svalastoga. Editor of Micro Publications: Social Science Series, with Erik Hoegh and Preben Wolf.

ZDENEK MATEJCEK, Ph.D., is associate professor of psychology at Charles University and on the staff of the Paediatric Department of the Postgraduate Medical Institute in Prague, Czechoslovakia. He is co-author of "Psychological Deprivation in Childhood" which appeared in Czech, English, German and Russian editions. He has directed the methodology of the Prague Study of Children Born from Unwanted Pregnancies and of several other studies of child development under unfavourable emotional and social conditions.

MIEKE VAN NULAND, born 1949, studied law at the Katholieke Universiteit Leuven. She is working at the B.G.J.G. (Gond van Grote en van Jonge Gezinnen) a Flemisch Family Organisation where she is leading the study department.

KATHLEEN O'HIGGINS, M.Sc., is a research officer at The Economic and Social Research Institute, Dublin. She has studied many aspects of marriage in Ireland and has published on such subjects as desertion and homogamy. She was involved in a Council of Europe study of marriage guidance and family counselling services. Her present work includes looking at some determinants of marital choice in Ireland.

LISBETH SHORE PALUDAN, Ph.D., psychology, is a research fellow at the Institute of Social Medicine, University of Copenhagen. She is currently conducting a study of sex education in the public schools, with specific focus on adolescents' attitudes on puberty development and needs regarding sex education, with the aim of developing teaching materials and methods. She is also on the editorial board of the Danish Committee for Health Education.

SENTA RADVANOVA, Ju.Dr., CSc., is associate professor and on the teaching staff of the Faculty of Laws at Charles University in Prague. She is specialized in Family Law and has published extensively on family protection and on rights of children and adolescents. Several publications of which she is author or co-author appeared in other European countries.

HYMAN RODMAN is Director of the Family Research Center at the University of North Carolina at Greensboro and Excellence Fund Professor in the Department of Child Development and Family Relations. He received his B.A. (First Class Honours in Sociology) and M.A. at McGill University, where he was a McGill University Scholar from 1948 to 1953. He received his Ph.D. in Sociology at Harvard University in 1957. Earlier research and teaching positions were held at Boston University, the Brookings Institution, and the Merrill-Palmer Institute. He has served as consulting or associate editor for Journal of Marriage and the Family, Merrill-Palmer Quarterly, Journal of Applied Developmental Psychology, and Social Problems; and as editor of Social Problems. Among other professional activities, he has served as a consultant to two presidential commissions in the USA, as chair of the International Section of the National Council on Family Relations (NCFR), and on the Board of Directors of the NCFR. He has published widely.

JAN TROST is Director of the Family Research Center at Uppsala University. He received his Ph.D. at Uppsala University in 1962 and is affiliated with the Department of Sociology there. He serves as associate editor for many national and international journals and has published widely. Among other professional activities, he has served as consultant to the Swedish Government's Commission for revision of the matrimonial and parental laws, as first vice president of the Committee on Family Research of the International Sociological Association, as chair of the International Section of the National Council on Family Relations (NCFR), and on the Board of Directors of the NCFR.

birth control pill (*see* oral contraceptive)
births, marital vs. nonmarital, 64-65
Bogue, D. J., 244
book banning, 115

Canada: abortion situation in, 29-31; common law regarding consent, 25-26; drinking age in, 22-23; family law jurisdiction, 21-22; population of, 21; rights of minors in, 21-33; venereal diseases, treatment of, 32-33
Canadian Abortion Rights League (Ontario), 31
Catholic church, contraceptive practices of, 189
Catholic Marriage Advisory Council (Ireland), 117-118
celibacy, Catholic church contribution, 108
censorship, of contraception information, 115-116
Center for Disease Control, 183
Charter of Rights (Canada), 31
child abuse, 2, 82
child advocates, U.S., 165
child-parent relationships, changes in, 98-99
Child Welfare Act (Ontario), 24
children (*see* adolescents; minors)
Children's Act (Ireland), 119
Children's Act (Ontario), 23-24
Children's Law Reform Act (Ontario), 23
Coalition for Reproductive Choice (Manitoba), 31
cohabitation, in Denmark, 59-60
coitus frequency, age-specific, 67-68
coitus interruptus, 148; adolescent choice of, 49
common law, regarding consent, 25-26
conception, age-specific outcome, 63
condoms: availability of, 214; popularity of, 12; rights of minors, 25; vending machines for, 162

Confederation Nationale des Associations Familiales (France), 84
Connell, K. H., 109
contraception: abortion as, 67; access to, 84-87; as behavior pattern, 15; Catholic views, 111; counseling, 73-79; effective vs. ineffective, 16; free access to, 63; knowledge and practice, 77-78; methods, 173; new legislation, difficulties in implementing, 131-136; parental involvement, 176-177; school studies, 77; value differences, 237-239
contraceptives: accessibility of, 12; advertisements for, 115, 127; attitude vs. behavior, 11; availability of, 213-214; definition, 114; effectiveness of, 7; at first intercourse, 8-9; importing of, 114-115; legal and social changes, 233-234; legalization of, 112-113, 146-147; limited use of, 242-243; medical regulation of, 12; minors use of, 172-178; parental approval for minors, 85; practices, 3-4; prescription and sale, 114; psychological studies, 9, 175; public attitudes, 147-148; regional legislation, 129-130; sexually active minors, 9; social class attitudes, 111; "squeal rule," 193 (*see also* oral contraceptives)
county clinics, clients by age and sex, 75-76
courting behavior, 200
cultural values, and adolescent dilemma, 1
Czechoslovakia: abortion committees, 50; abortions in, 50-52; adolescent dilemma in, 38-41; background information, 37-38; child labor laws, 44; contraceptive practices, 48-49; education and supervision of adolescents, 47; family planning in, 37-57; marriage of minors, 45-46, 52-53; minority and majority status, 42-43; parenthood educa-

tion in, 53-54; Population Commission, 38; rights of minors, 37-57; sex education programs, 233; sexual abuse in, 46-47

Danish Family Planning Association, 60-61
Denmark: abortion in, 59-70; age of majority, 74; background information, 59-60; contraceptive counseling, 73-79; contraceptives, access to, 234; family planning in, 59-70, 73-79; legal obstacles, 216; national health services, 73-74; rights of minors, 59-70, 73-79; sex education in, 73-79
delinquent girls, 92
diaphragm, availability of, 214
divorce, 186; age-specific rates, 41
doctors: abortions by, 183; common law rights of, 26; contraceptives prescribed by, 12-13; objections of, 131; venereal diseases reported by, 32-33
drug abuse, 39
druggists (*see* pharmacists)
Dublin, adolescents in, 106

Eastern Europe, fertility rates in, 242
East Germany, sex education in, 208
educators, on adolescent rights, 22-23
Eichler, M., 23
elementary schools: parenthood education in, 54; sex education in, 78
11 Million Teenagers (Guttmacher), 178
employment, of adolescents, 39-40
enforced marriage, fear of, 6
Europe: abortion access, 236; adolescents in, 1; birth control attitudes, 213; contraceptives, availability of, 213-214; courting behavior, 200; family planning in, 199-228; homosexuality, attitudes toward, 210; institutions offering family planning services, 217; pornography in, 210; ratings of selected projects, 219-223; recom-

mendations, 227-228; sex education in, 199-228; target groups for family planning, 215

family: conflicts, 92; legal position of minor, 44-45; stem system, 106-107
family law, 21, 47
family planning: acceptance by adolescents, 217; access to services, 243-244; adolescent dilemma, 1; for adolescents, 199-204, 213-219; availability of services, 213; brochures, 10-11; classification scheme, 225-226; clinics, 172; comparative perspective, 231-244; contraceptive attitudes and, 10; cost of services, 218; by country, 230; "curative," 7, 13; deficient use of, 5-14; definition, 203-204; enthusiasts, 225; free sterilization, 69-70; governmental measures, 15, 222; institutionalized projects, 226; laws and policies, 167-168; legal basis for, 39; legal and social changes, 232-235; liberalization trend, 232-235; male acceptance of, 214-215; national programs, 10-11; natural method, 117-118; obstacles to, 219-221; policy implications for minors, 14-15; and population policy, 239-240; prerequisites for success, 213; preventive, 7; professionals, 226; questions, 3; ratings of selected projects, 219-223; recommendations, 228; research, 55-56; rights of minors, 25; services, 117-119; and sex education, 199-228; subsidies, 218-219; target groups, 214-215; WHO study, 199-228; women's status and risks, 235-237 (*see also* sex education)
Family Planning (booklet), 113
Family Planning Act (Ireland), 113
Family Planning Legislation (Swartz), 207

venereal diseases, treatment of, 32-33
virgins, 147-148
voluntary abortions, regional differ-
    ences, 133

Walsh, B., 117
Washington Post, 189
Westoff, C. F., 189
Wilson-Davis, K., 111
women: problems of, 236; spacing of
    children, 235; status and risks,
    235-237
World Fertility Study (Hungary), 101
World Health Organization (WHO),
    199-228; European Region, 232;

Family Planning Unit, 199, 207;
study, purpose of, 205-206

Young, L., 174
Young Offenders Act (Canada), 24
young people (*see* adolescents;
    minors)
Yugoslavia: contraceptive advertising
    in, 216; family planning in, 213;
    legal obstacles, 216; sex education
    in, 208

Zelnik, M., 166, 170, 172
Zero Population Growth, 179